Colour in glazes

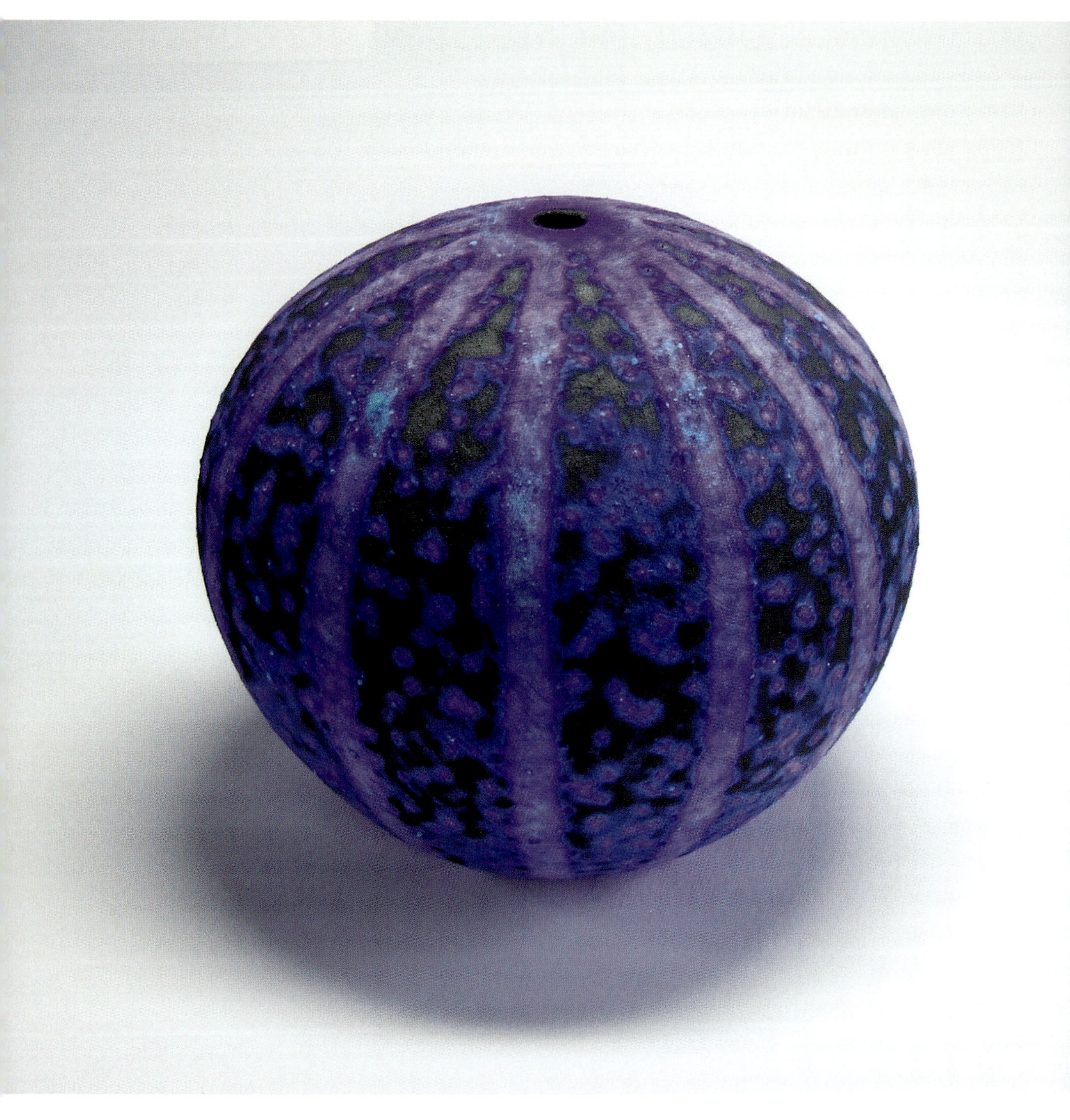

Colour in glazes

Linda Bloomfield

With photographs by Henry Bloomfield

HERBERT PRESS

LONDON • OXFORD • NEW YORK • NEW DELHI • SYDNEY

HERBERT PRESS
Bloomsbury Publishing Plc
50 Bedford Square, London, WC1B 3DP, UK
Bloomsbury Publishing Ireland Limited,
29 Earlsfort Terrace, Dublin 2, D02 AY28, Ireland

BLOOMSBURY, HERBERT PRESS and the Herbert Press logo are trademarks of Bloomsbury Publishing Plc

This edition published in Great Britain 2019
First Edition published 2012 and reprinted in 2015, 2016, 2017 and 2018

A catalogue record for this book is available from the British Library
Library of Congress Cataloguing-in-Publication data has been applied for

ISBN: PB: 978-1-9122-1782-3; ePub: 978-1-7899-4117-3

6 8 10 9 7 5

Edited and designed for Herbert Press by Plum5 Limited
Printed and bound in India by Thomson Press India Pvt Ltd

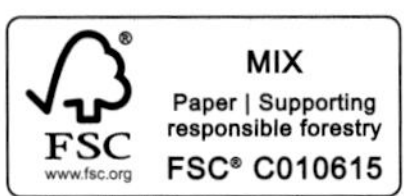

To find out more about our authors and books visit www.bloomsbury.com and sign up for our newsletters
For product safety related questions contact productsafety@bloomsbury.com

FRONT COVER: *Pink and mint bowls* and *photo by Katie Robbins. Grey-green bowl photo by Dorte Januszewski* @lewesmap

BACK COVER: *Vase* by Clara Castner, *photo by Yeshen Venema*

FRONTISPIECE: *Medium Urchin Form*, Emma Williams, 2009. Coiled stoneware, impressed and textured, inlaid copper oxide covered with dry barium glaze, fired in oxidation to 1054°C (1927°F), ht: 9cm (3½in).

Contents

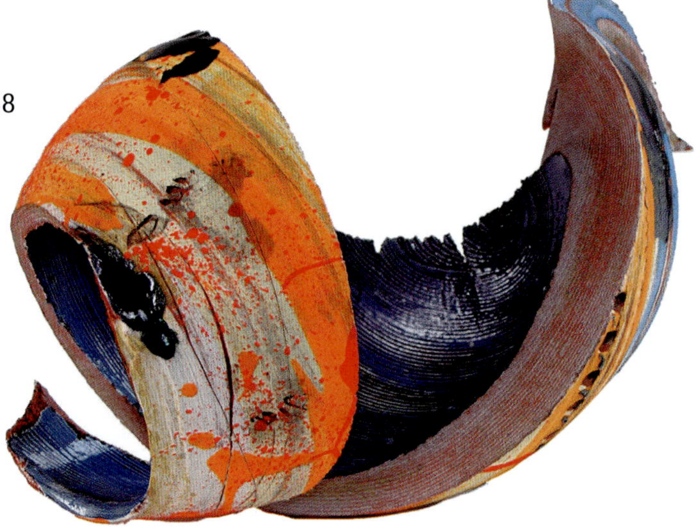

Freedom, Leyla Folwell, 2008. Thrown and cut grogged red earthenware, with white slip, glazes, oxides and underglaze colours. *Photo: James Folwell.*

Acknowledgements

I would like to thank Dr Sheila Cousens for passing on her enthusiasm for chemistry and Professor Keith Bowen for encouraging me to do research. Thanks to Alison Stace of A & C Black for giving me the opportunity to write this book.

Many thanks to Lok Ming Fung, Lucy Burley, Mirka Golden-Hann and Helen Brown of Wolverhampton University for contributing glaze tests. Thanks to Gerry Barnett of Potterycrafts for information on ceramic stains.

Thank you to Jeannine Vrins for her zinc orange glaze testing.

Thank you to the following for images of their work:
Chris Barnes, Richard Baxter, Heike Brachlow, Karen Bunting, Tom Butcher, Clara Castner, Amy Cooper, Carys Davies, Bridget Drakeford, Ken Eardley, Hollis Engley, Avril Farley, Stanley Field, Doug Fitch, Sara Flynn, Leyla Folwell, Tanya Gomez, Gwyn Hanssen Pigott, Adam Harvey, Kerry Hastings, Akiko Hirai, Joanna Howells, Jill Fanshawe Kato, Anne Marie Laureys, Leah Leitson, Roger Lewis, Hannah McAndrew, Emily Myers, Jeremy Nichols, Andrew Palin, Sue Paraskeva, Stephen Parry, Katie Robbins, Suleyman Saba, Barry Stedman, Chris Taylor, Louisa Taylor, Ruthanne Tudball, Sue Ure, Jeannine Vrins, Clementina van der Walt, James and Tilla Waters, Emma Williams, Rachel Wood and Pauline Zelinski.

Chun Liao images are courtesy of Marsden Woo Gallery.
Lucie Rie images are courtesy of a private collector.

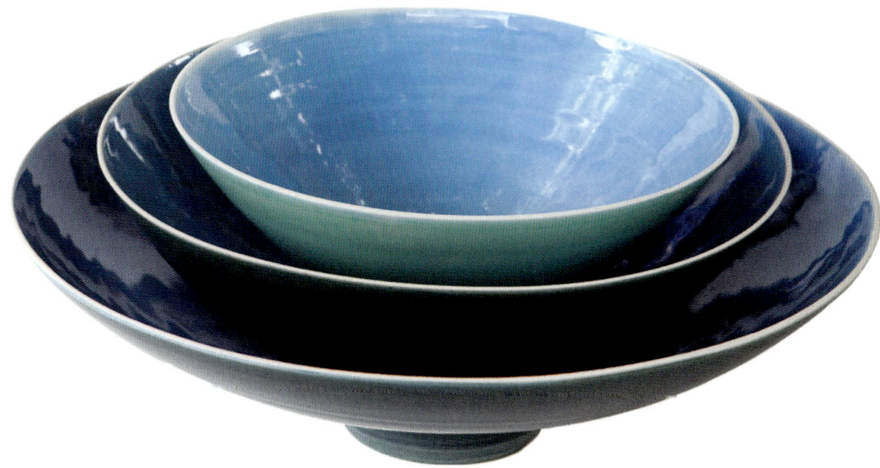

Thrown porcelain bowls,
Stanley Field, 2010.
Vanadium zircon blue stains.
Photo: Nadia Mackenzie.

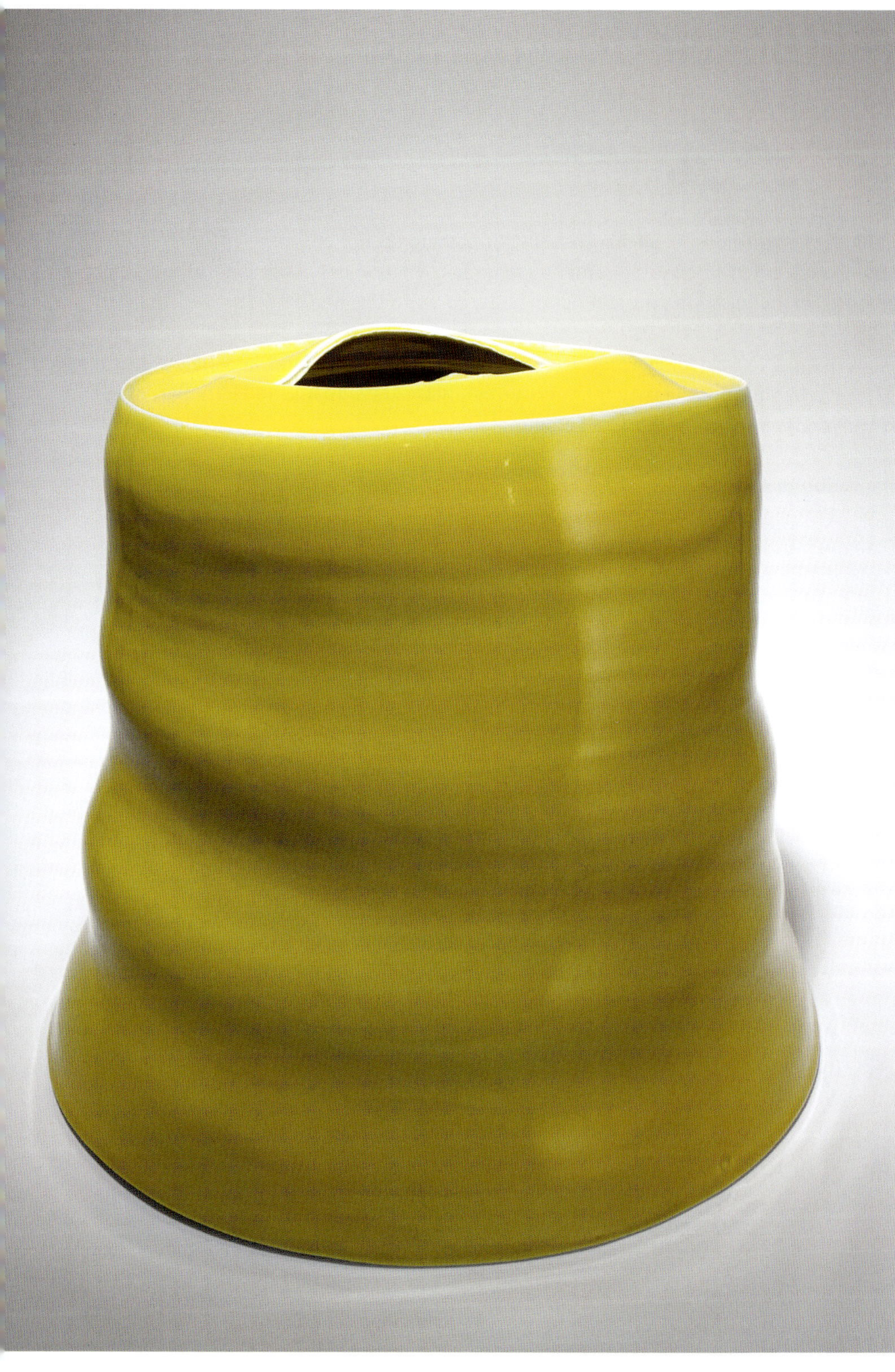

Bliss, Tanya Gomez, thrown porcelain, yellow stain, ht: 45cm (17¾in), 2010. *Photo: Dominic Tschudin*.

Introduction

Colour is often introduced into ceramic glazes by adding commercial stains, which have been manufactured by heating together colouring oxides and opacifiers. This book shows how to make coloured glazes directly from oxides, as well as showing what kinds of base glazes best bring out different colours. This knowledge is important when using commercial stains as well as colouring oxides. The book concentrates on colours used in oxidation (electric kiln) firings, where colours obtained are generally brighter, although glazes fired in reduction are included for comparison.

Much has changed since the first edition of *Colour in Glazes* was published in 2011. More elements have been discovered, so that the periodic table is now complete. The use of rare earth oxides in ceramics is spreading, including the more unusual elements such as holmium. Pottery is now more popular than ever, with many people taking pottery classes and wanting to learn about glazes. Potters' materials have changed, with old mines closing and new materials being sourced. In this second edition there are new glaze recipes, methods of testing glazes and information on how to make stable, dishwasher-safe glazes.

Linda Bloomfield, 2019

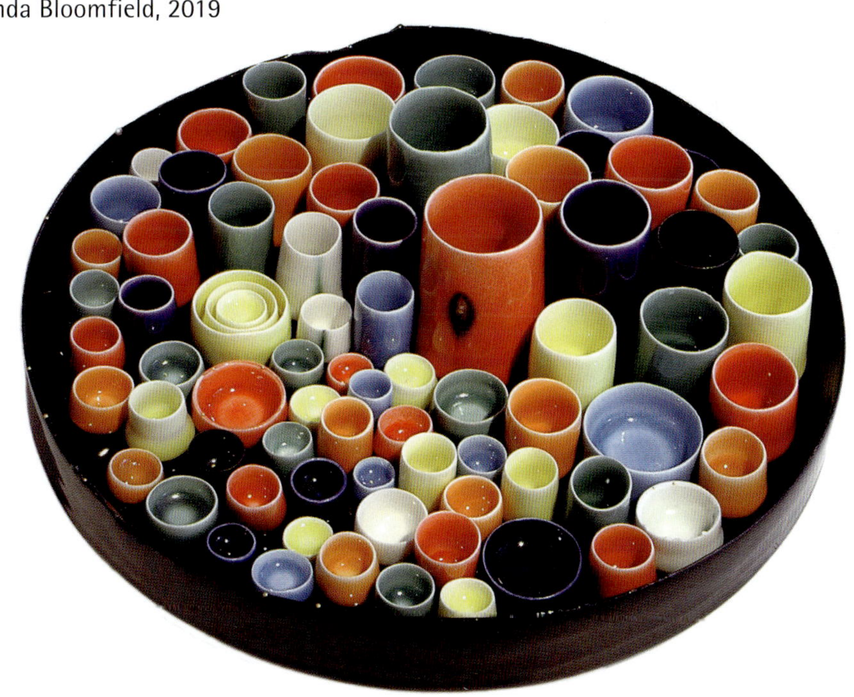

Installation, Chun Liao, 2009. Porcelain, gold, fired to 1255°C (2291°F). *Photo: courtesy of Marsden Woo Gallery.*

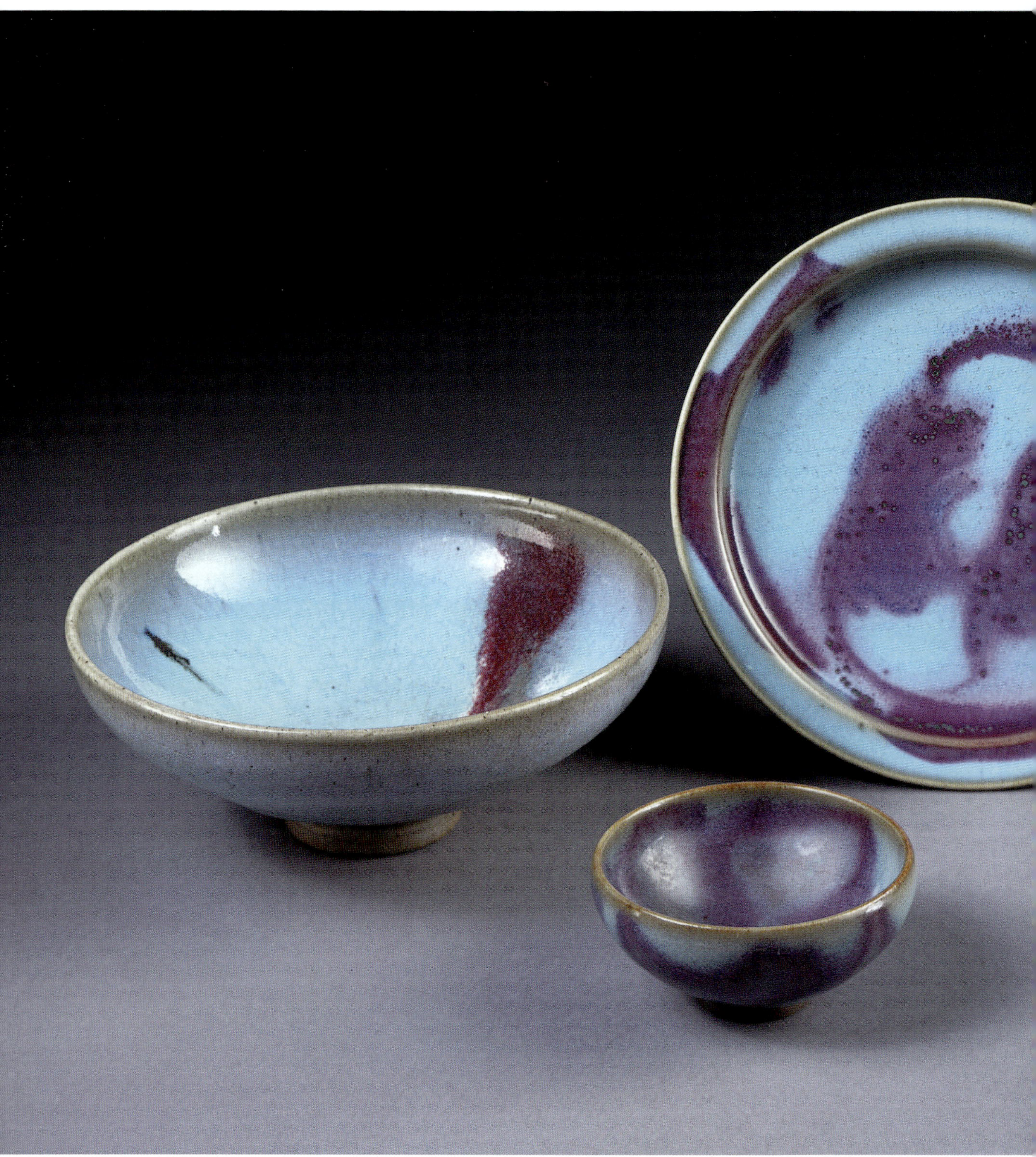

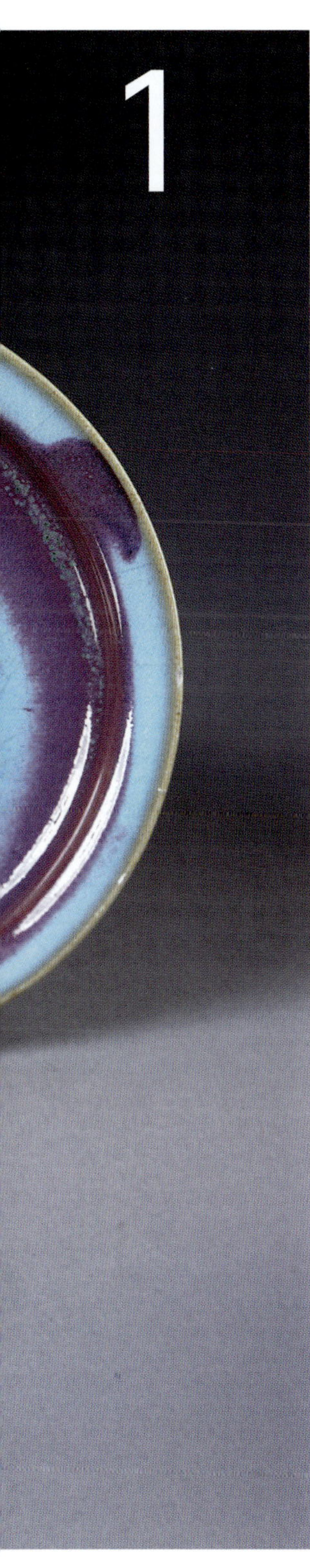

1 A brief history of colour in glazes

The first glaze was discovered by the Ancient Egyptians around 4000BC. They mixed sand with natron, a naturally occurring mixture of soluble sodium salts, which formed a substance called Egyptian paste. As the paste dried, the salts migrated to the surface. Upon firing, these salts melted to form a glaze. If copper oxide was added, brilliant turquoise beads and amulets could be made. This is now called Egyptian faience, although it did not contain clay and was not the same material as the tin-glazed earthenware made much later in Renaissance Italy.

During the first millennium BC, potters in Mesopotamia made moulded bricks glazed with bright alkaline glazes. These were used to make decorative friezes such as those on the Ishtar Gate in Babylon. Various oxides were used to colour the glazes, including copper, manganese, iron and cobalt. Lead and antimony were also used, although only in small quantities. By the end of the first millennium BC, lead glazes appeared in China and in the eastern Roman Empire. Lead glazes were less liable to craze and disintegrate than alkaline glazes. The potters of the Chinese Tang dynasty (AD618–907) used three colours (sancai): green from copper, white, and yellow-brown from iron. The use of lead glazes spread to the Middle East and Europe where the lead ore galena was dusted onto pots.

In China, kiln technology advanced so that higher temperatures (above 1200°C/2192°F) could be achieved. Climbing kilns with a fire at the lowest end were built and fired using wood. The kilns were sometimes multi-chambered so that the heat could be recycled from one chamber to the next. The Chinese potters noticed that where the wood ash settled on the pots it melted and formed a glassy deposit. They combined wood ash with clay and limestone to make a runny green ash glaze. During the Tang dynasty, the southern Yueh potters added China stone, a feldspar which melted to form green celadon glazes which resembled jade. Porcelain was also developed around this time, using China stone mixed with China clay. During the Song dynasty (AD960–1279) many beautiful glazes were developed, including the thick, unctuous Lung Chuan celadons, opalescent Chun blue and iron-rich, black tenmoku (named after a Chinese mountain temple where black-glazed tea bowls were used).

In the Ming dynasty (AD1368–1644), a pure form of cobalt was imported from Persia, and blue and white porcelain was developed. The Chinese created many other colours, including copper red and iron yellow, the latter a low-temperature lead enamel applied after the first, high-temperature firing.

Chun glazed bowls and dish with copper red splashes, stoneware, Henan province, Song dynasty. *Photo: © Victoria and Albert Museum, London.*

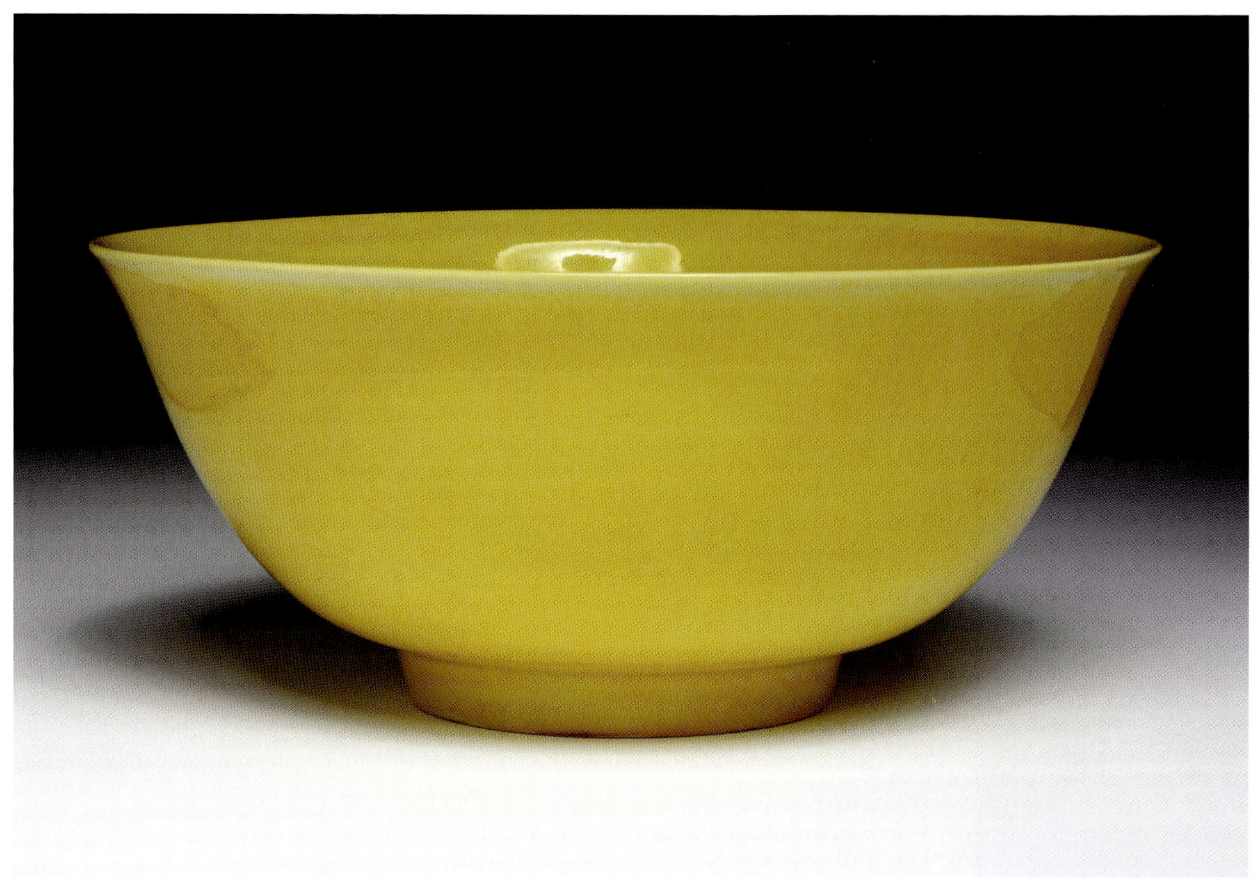

Yellow bowl, porcelain, fired with a transparent glaze, then covered with a yellow glaze and re-fired at a lower temperature, Jingdezhen, Ming dynasty. *Photo: © Victoria and Albert Museum, London.*

In the Middle East, Chinese porcelain was imitated by coating earthenware with a tin-opacified glaze that was decorated with cobalt, copper, manganese and iron. The ware was biscuit-fired before glazing, to help the tin glaze adhere. Lustreware was developed by firing silver and copper oxides in reducing conditions to produce a gold metallic sheen. These techniques spread when the Moors invaded Spain from the 8th to the 15th centuries. Maiolica ware, traded through the ports of Malaga or Majorca, soon spread to Italy and to France, where tin-glazed earthenware was called faience (named after the Italian city Faenza), and the Netherlands, where it became known as Delftware. Various colours could be made using oxides: cobalt blue, copper green, manganese purple and orange from iron oxide. A bright yellow called Naples yellow was made from lead antimonate. The colours were brushed onto the unfired tin glaze, sinking into the surface when fired.

In Rhineland Germany in the 15th century, salt-glazed stoneware was developed. It was glazed by throwing salt into the kiln at high temperature, where it vaporized and reacted with the silica in the clay surface to form a glaze. Salt-glazed pots were usually brown, from iron oxide in the clay, or blue from applied cobalt. The salt gave a pitted, orange-peel texture to the stoneware in places where it reacted with sand particles in the clay.

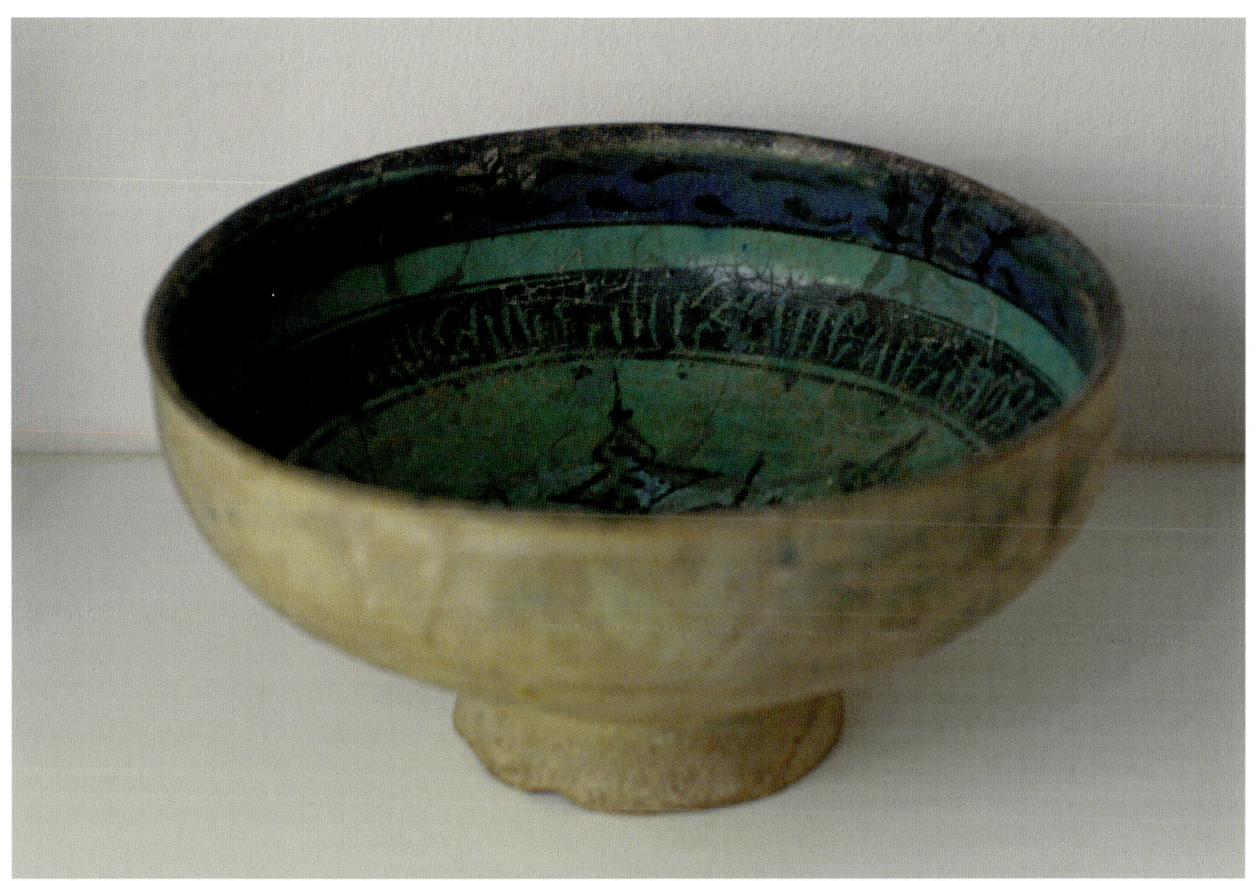

Persian bowl, turquoise alkaline glaze with calligraphic brushwork, earthenware, 14th century. Private collection. *Photo: Henry Bloomfield.*

Meanwhile, in the Far East the manufacture of porcelain had spread from China via Korea to Japan by the 17th century. Highly decorated wares, painted with underglaze blue and iron-red enamel, were made at Arita. In Europe the manufacture of porcelain began in the 18th century in Meissen, Germany. The wares, particularly those made at Sèvres, in France, were highly decorated with brightly coloured enamels, including rose pink (made from gold and tin chloride). In China during the Qing dynasty (AD1644–1911), many new enamel colours were developed, influenced by the new porcelain from Europe.

In the late 18th century in Sèvres, chromium oxide was used to make yellow and green glazes. It was discovered in Stoke-on-Trent, in England, that chromium oxide can also make pink when combined with tin oxide and calcium. In Bristol, zinc oxide was used as a flux to replace poisonous lead oxide in glazes. Zinc oxide enhances the colours from cobalt and copper, but destroys other colours such as chrome green or chrome-tin pink, which turn brown. Zinc oxide prevents crazing but in large quantities it can cause crawling and pinholes. Another flux with low thermal expansion is borax, sodium borate, which was introduced into glazes in fritted form to replace lead. Borates tend to produce cool colours rather than the warm colours obtained using lead.

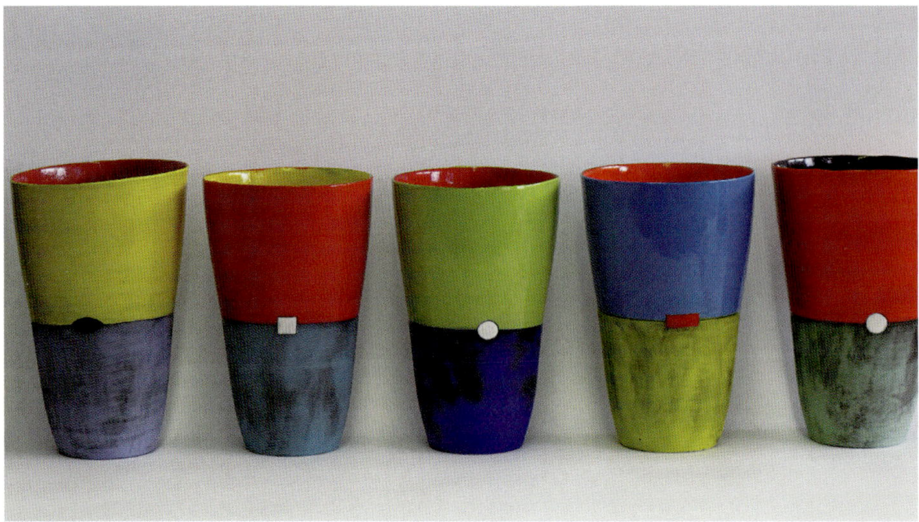

Slipcast beakers, Clementina van der Walt, 2010. Charcoal earthenware, underglaze colours, sgraffito, transparent earthenware glaze. Fired to 1120°C (2048°F), South Africa. *Photo: Clementina Van der Walt.*

During the late 19th century and early 20th century, uranium oxide (yellowcake) was used to make bright yellow glazes. Uranium is not now widely available; it is not considered safe because of its radioactivity.

Stains are now made by a few specialist companies, which do not widely publish their methods, although they reveal the materials and systems used to make the stains. For example, ZrVSi is a turquoise stain that includes vanadium and zirconium silicate, which was discovered in the USA in the 1940s. Vanadium is used to make several stains, including yellow, green and turquoise. The rare earth oxides are also used to make a range of colours for glass and ceramics, including praseodymium-zirconium yellow. Cadmium-selenium stains were developed to provide reliable reds, oranges and yellows. A cadmium-selenium stain can be fired to high temperatures when the stain is incorporated in a zirconium silicate matrix. It is now possible to print ceramic decals in any colour using combinations of yellow, red, turquoise and black stains.

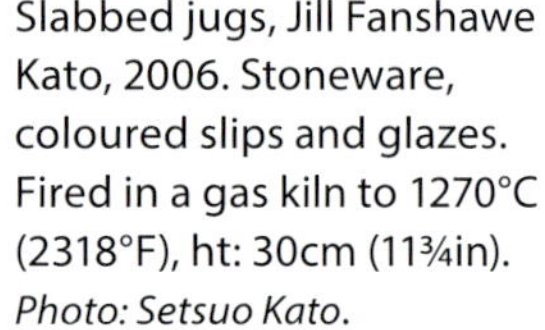

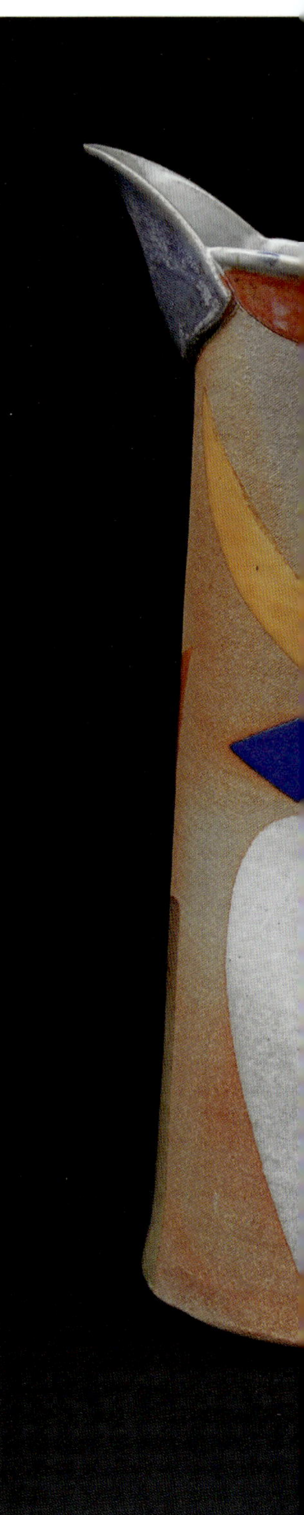

Slabbed jugs, Jill Fanshawe Kato, 2006. Stoneware, coloured slips and glazes. Fired in a gas kiln to 1270°C (2318°F), ht: 30cm (11¾in). *Photo: Setsuo Kato.*

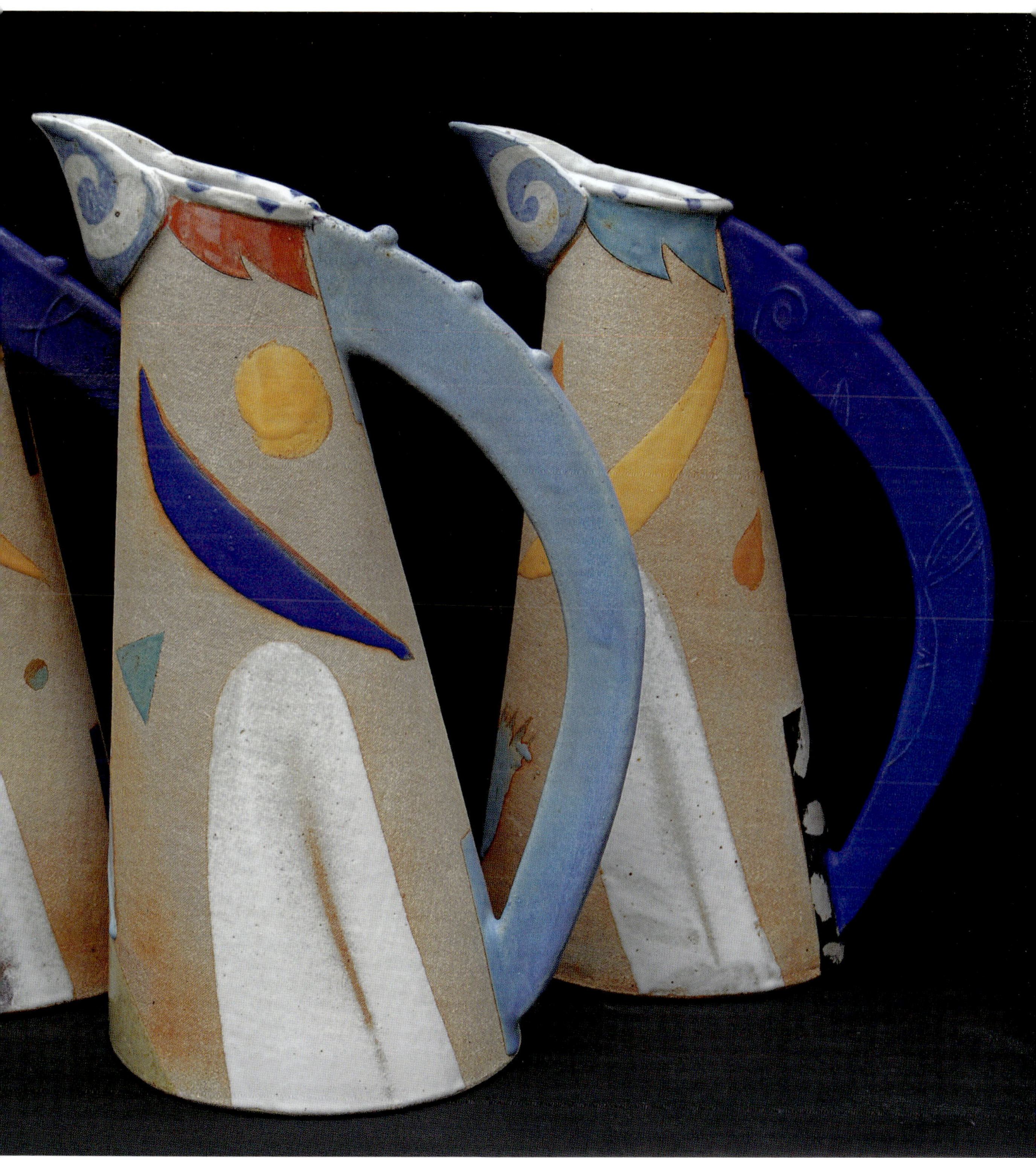

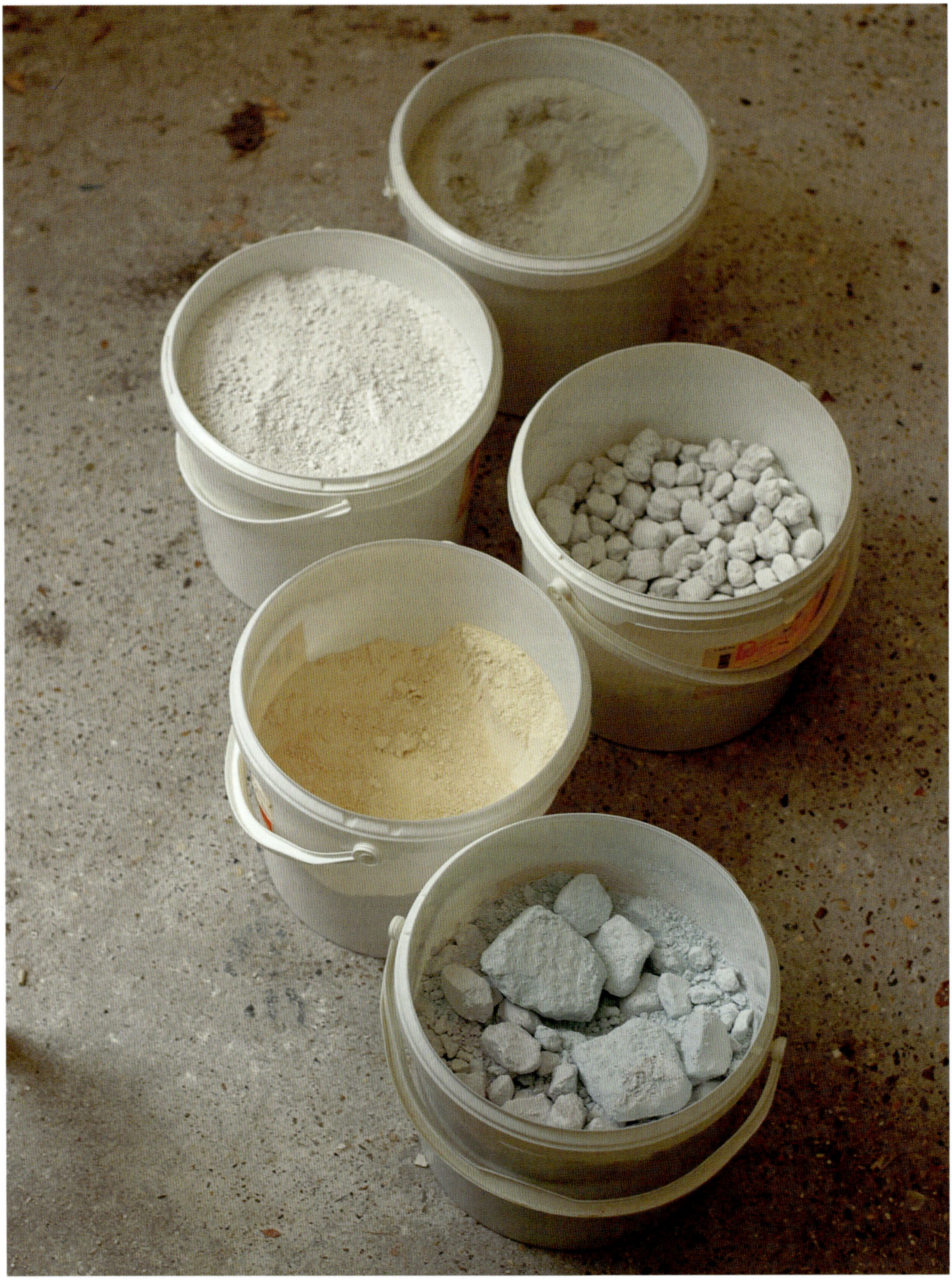

2 Principles of glaze chemistry

The three essential components of a glaze are: silica[1], a glass former (the basis of most glass); alumina, a stiffener (to make the glass more viscous); and feldspar, a flux, which melts the glaze. Secondary fluxes such as whiting, talc or zinc are usually added to help melt the glaze or to give particular surface qualities – glossy, matt or crystalline. In low-temperature glazes, fluxes such as lead or boron are used because they are active at lower temperatures.

Silica forms a three-dimensional network of linked silica chains, giving hardness and gloss to a glaze. Fluxes such as feldspar allow the glaze to melt at a temperature attainable in a kiln. The oxides of the alkali metals, sodium and potassium, which are present in feldspar, are very active fluxes and react with the silica, breaking the chains and making the glaze more runny. The alkaline earths, calcia[1], magnesia, baria and strontia are less active fluxes but they form part of the silica chain and make the glaze stronger and more durable. Alumina stiffens the glaze by cross-linking the silica chains, thus increasing viscosity. Glass is similar to glaze but contains very little alumina and often runs and crazes if used on pottery.

LEFT: Glaze materials. Clockwise from top: bentonite, bone ash, Cornish stone, dolomite, nepheline syenite.

Colouring oxides form bonds with various oxides in the glaze. They react preferentially with titanium and then tin oxide. If there is no tin or titanium present, they will react with boron, silica and other colouring oxides or fluxes. They do not usually react with alumina in a glaze, as silica is always present. The colour of oxides will depend on how many oxygen atoms they are bonded with and the colour may change

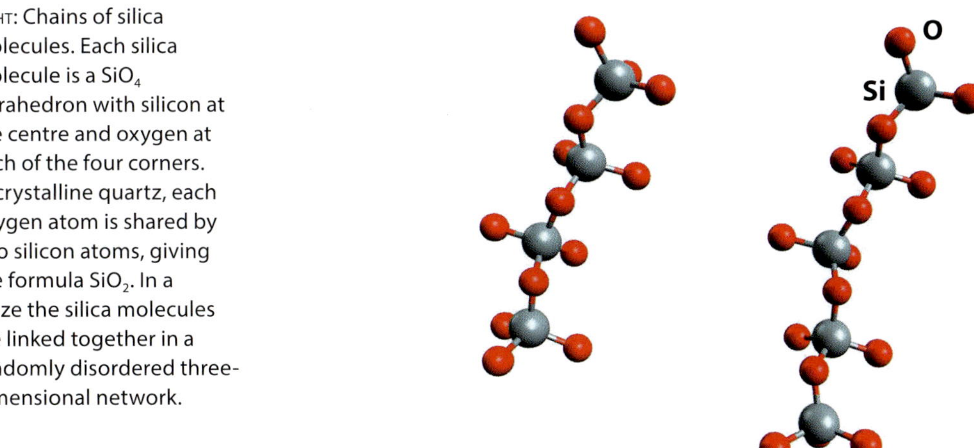

RIGHT: Chains of silica molecules. Each silica molecule is a SiO_4 tetrahedron with silicon at the centre and oxygen at each of the four corners. In crystalline quartz, each oxygen atom is shared by two silicon atoms, giving the formula SiO_2. In a glaze the silica molecules are linked together in a randomly disordered three-dimensional network.

[1] The 'a' at the end of silica denotes an oxide, i.e. silicon dioxide SiO_2. The ending 'ate', as in zirconium silicate, denotes an oxide combined with another material, e.g. $ZrSiO_4$.

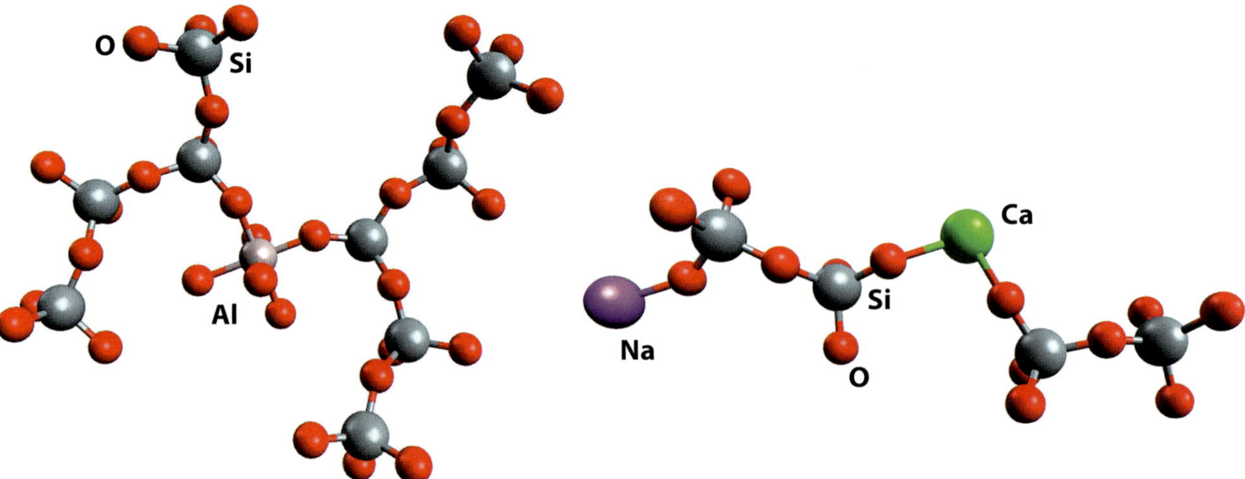

Alumina stiffens the glaze by cross-linking the silica chains.

Sodium oxide forms the ends of chains, causing them to break from other silica molecules. Calcium oxide forms part of the silica chain, linking silica molecules and strengthening the glaze.

with different fluxes in the glaze. The colour seen is the visible light that remains after some wavelengths of light are absorbed by the electrons around the metal atom. The shape of the electron cloud around the metal atom is influenced by the number of oxygen atoms bonded to the metal, and distorted by the presence of different fluxes in the glaze. Colours found in naturally occurring minerals, such as pink from manganese, do not always occur in glazes. To obtain pink from manganese, the colouring oxide must first be heated, together with alumina, to make a manganese alumina stain. This can be ground up and dispersed in the glaze, although this particular stain is only stable in high-alumina glazes and is generally used as a body stain. Cobalt can also be combined with alumina to make a cobalt alumina stain, which is a lighter blue than that obtained from cobalt silicate. The cobalt atoms are surrounded by alumina in a close-packed spinel crystal structure (see p. 48) and are protected from being dissolved in the glaze.

The behaviour of oxides in a molten glaze depends on the way they combine chemically. All glaze materials (oxides) are classified into three groups: acidic, alkaline or amphoteric. The acidic oxides are non-metals, and include silica (SiO_2) and phosphoric oxide (P_2O_5). They form a glass structure when melted. The alkaline oxides include oxides of the alkali metals sodium (Na_2O) and potassium (K_2O), as well as the alkaline earths baria (BaO), calcia (CaO) and magnesia (MgO) and many of the colouring oxides, including cobalt and copper. Zinc and lead also form alkaline oxides, used as fluxes at

Sodium and calcium form ionic bonds with oxygen, that are less stable than the silica network which is formed of covalently bonded silicon and oxygen.

lower temperatures. Amphoteric oxides include alumina (Al_2O_3), boric oxide (B_2O_3) and some of the colouring oxides, such as chromium oxide. Amphoterics usually stiffen the glaze and make it more refractory, although boric oxide is an exception and acts as a glass former and flux. It can be seen from the chemical formulae that acidic, alkaline and amphoteric oxides combine with different numbers of oxygen atoms. This governs how they react together in the molten glaze.

Glaze recipes are usually written as a list of materials, with percentages by weight, but they can also be represented in terms of relative numbers of molecules. In Seger's unity formula, the three groups of oxides – basic (alkaline), amphoteric and acidic – are written in three columns, with the basic oxides adding up to one. Representing the formula this way enables different glazes to be compared directly, or different materials to be substituted to obtain the same formula. For example, the glaze recipe below is a transparent alkaline glaze fired to 1260°C/2300°F (cone 8). The recipe by weight per cent is:

Transparent alkaline glaze fired to 1260°C /2300°F (cone 8)

Soda feldspar	47
Calcium borate frit	16
Whiting	14
Quartz	18
China clay	5

To convert to numbers of molecules, the weight of each material is divided by its molecular weight (see Appendix 1). The amount of each type of oxide present in each material is then calculated from the chemical formula, and the numbers adjusted so that the total basic fluxes are equal to one. This is the convention used so that different glaze formulae can be compared. There is glaze calculation software available which performs this calculation (see Appendix 3).

Basic		*Amphoteric*		*Acidic*	
Na_2O	0.19	Al_2O_3	0.38	SiO_2	3.10
K_2O	0.06	B_2O_3	0.38		
CaO	0.75				
Total	1.00				

In the glaze formula above, the ratio of alumina to silica is 1:8. It is a runny transparent glaze fired at 1260°C/2300°F (cone 8), which gives a bright colour response with colouring oxides, owing to its low alumina content. It contains sodium, potassium and calcium as fluxes. Boron also acts as a flux and a glass former, but it is included as amphoteric because of the number of oxygen atoms it bonds with. A ratio of 1:9 alumina to silica gives a shiny glaze, while around 1:5 will give a matt glaze. The amounts of each oxide present can be compared to limit formulae (see Appendix 3), which are guidelines within which the glaze is likely to be stable and durable. However, some interesting colour responses are found in glazes outside these limits, particularly those low in alumina (see also Appendix 3).

Stable glazes (those that are dishwasher safe and food safe) will generally have a ratio of alkali metal (potassium, sodium) to alkaline earth (calcium, magnesium) oxides of around 0.3:0.7. The amounts of silica and alumina will increase with firing temperature (see glaze limits, p.149). For glazes fired below cone 9 (1280°C), enough boron is needed to fully melt the glaze (0.1 boric oxide for cone 8 glazes to 0.5 B_2O_3 for cone 04 earthenware glazes).

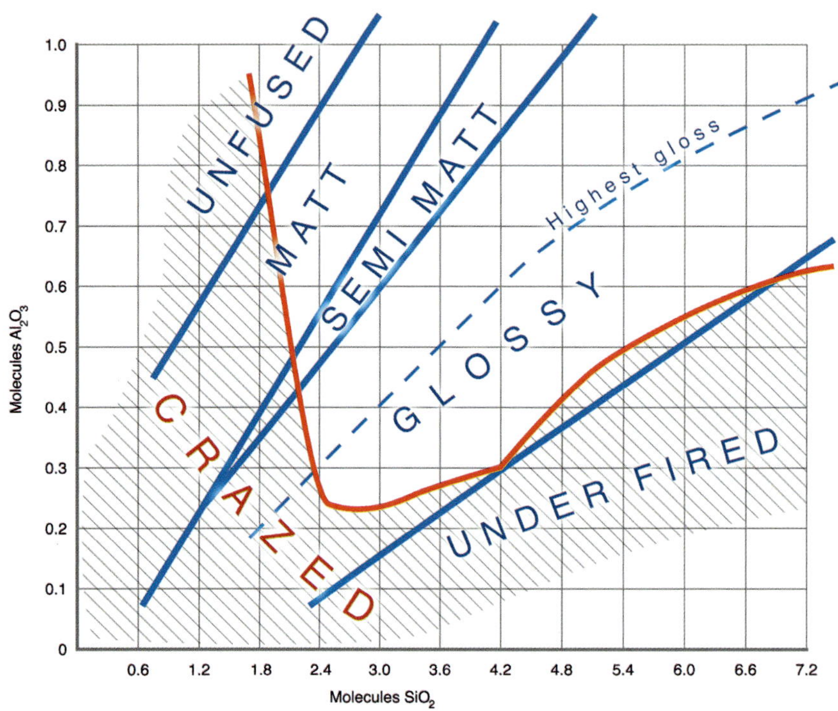

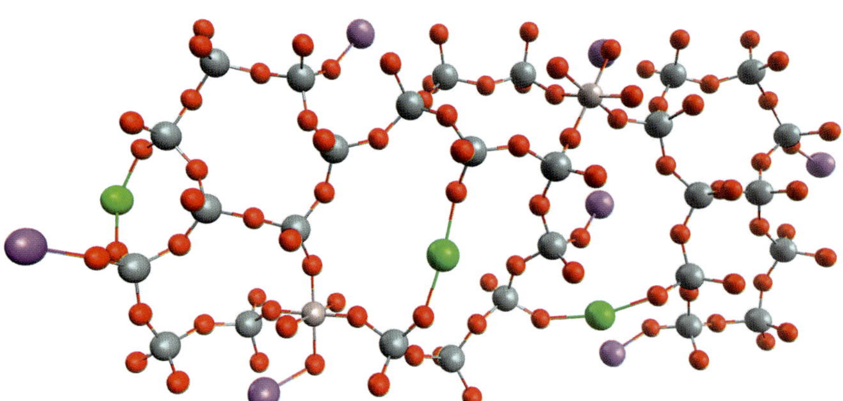

ABOVE LEFT: Graph of alumina against silica in porcelain glazes fired to cone 11 with constant flux 0.3 K_2O and 0.7 CaO. The ratio of 1:5 alumina to silica gives a semi-matt glaze, while 1:8 gives a shiny glaze. The straight lines on the chart represent alumina:silica ratios of 1:4 (matt) 1:5 (semi-matt) and 1:12 (glossy, crazed glaze). The dashed line is 1:8 Al_2O_3:SiO_2 (highest gloss glaze). The hatched area shows crazed glazes on porcelain. Data from R.T. Stull 1912.

BELOW LEFT: Diagram of glaze structure. The silica chains and alumina are joined by covalent bonds to oxygen and form the network structure. Sodium and calcium form ionic bonds with oxygen that are less stable than the covalent bonds in the silica network.

RIGHT: Clare Castner's porcelain vases. *Photo: Yeshen Venema.*

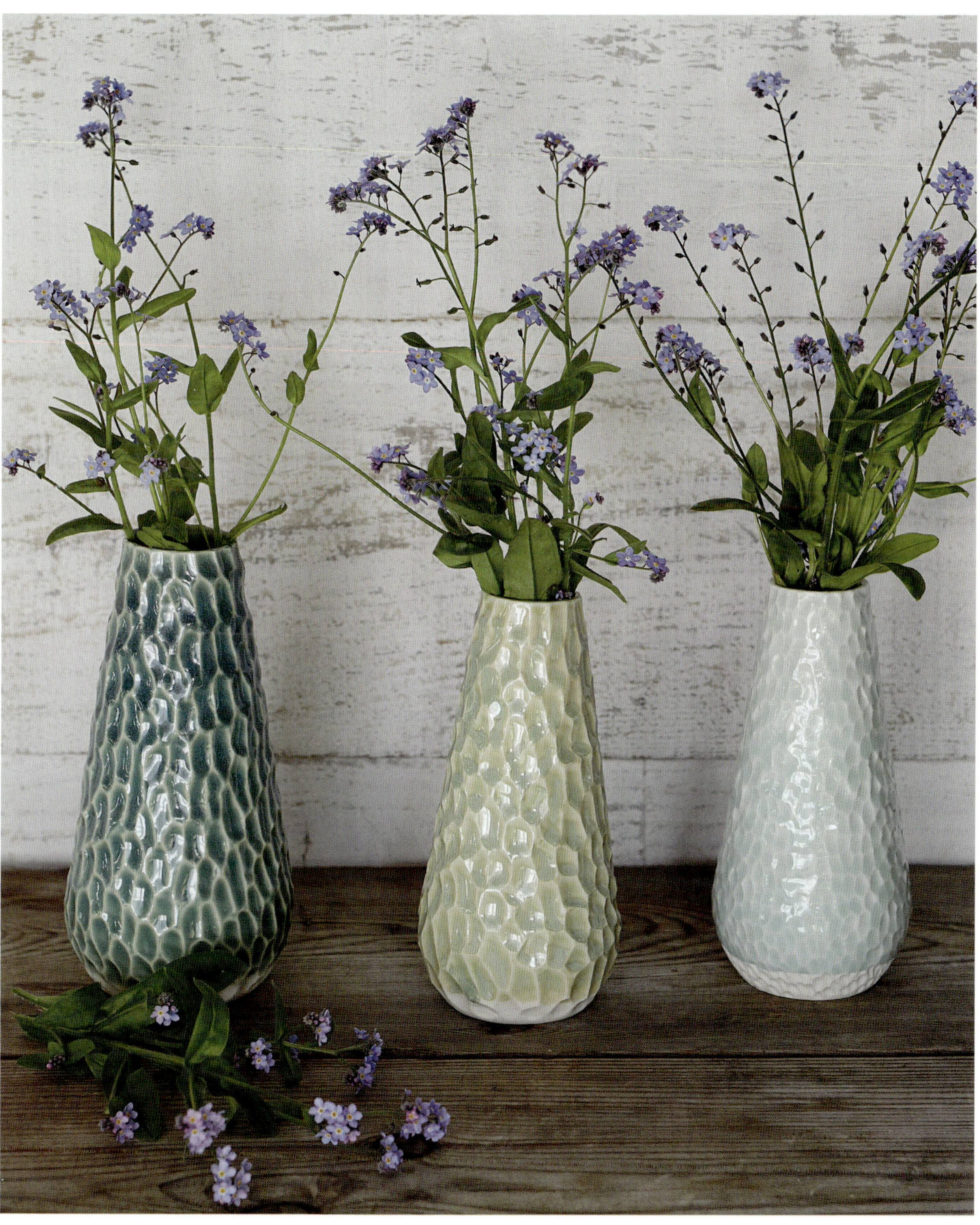

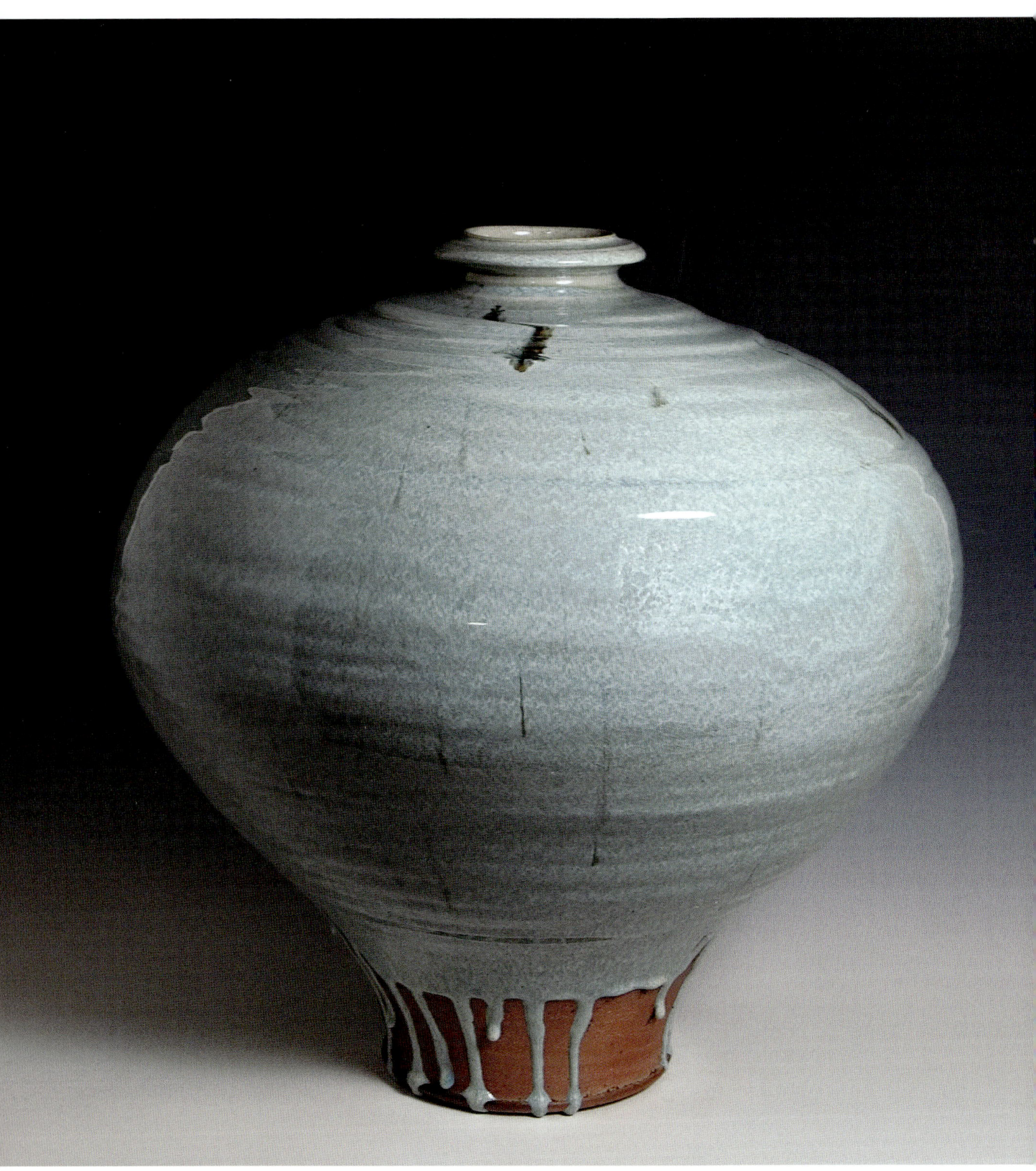

3 Glaze materials

Glaze materials used in the ceramics industry are available in finely powdered form, usually ground to 200s- or 300s-mesh size (the number of holes per linear inch of sieve). Quartz and flint are ground even more finely, to 300s- or 400s-mesh size, to aid melting. Some potters use locally found materials such as wood ash, locally occurring clay deposits and granite dust from quarries.

Silica

Silica is an essential component of a glaze, and forms a glass when fired at a high-enough temperature. To enable it to melt at temperatures attainable in a kiln, feldspar and other fluxes are added. Sources of silica include quartz and flint. Other materials that contain silica include feldspar, clay, talc and wollastonite. Care should be taken not to inhale the dust when handling silica sources.

Alumina

Alumina is used to stiffen the glaze and prevent it from running off of the pot. It also prevents crystallization in the glaze, although high levels of alumina can result in a matt glaze. Alumina (and silica) is found in clay, including China clay, ball clay and bentonite – a very plastic clay used to prevent glazes from settling and to increase the raw strength of the glaze. Alumina hydrate can also be added to glazes without adding silica. Many interesting colours are obtained from colouring oxides in very runny glazes low in alumina: turquoise from copper, chartreuse green from chromium and plum purple from manganese.

Feldspars

Feldspar is a mineral found in granite and it contains aluminosilicate, sodium, potassium and sometimes calcium. There are many types of feldspar available, including potash feldspar, soda feldspar, Cornish stone and nepheline syenite. Cornish stone has a high silica content, and therefore a higher melting point than other feldspars and is used in high-temperature, reduction-fired glazes. Most feldspars contain both potassium and sodium, but are named after whichever is dominant. FFF (Finnish floated feldspar) is higher in sodium than most other potash feldspars (see Appendix 4). Nepheline syenite

Large jar, Stephen Parry, 2008. Stoneware, ash glaze, wood-fired, ht: 55cm (22in). *Photo: Stephen Parry.*

is a feldspathic material high in sodium and potassium. It melts at a lower temperature than other feldspars, but sometimes gives a matt surface because of its high alumina and low silica content. Soda feldspars give a more fluid melt and brighter colour response than potash feldspars. However, they tend to craze, are slightly softer and scratch more easily.

Some feldspars contain lithium, a very active flux used in glazes to promote bright colours. Lithium feldspars include petalite, spodumene and lepidolite (a lithium mica containing fluorine). Lithium is useful for counteracting crazing but can cause shivering, a condition in which the glaze is too large for the body and flakes off. Lithium carbonate can be used in small quantities (up to 10%), although it is slightly soluble in water.

Feldspars sourced from different mines can vary in composition. When a particular feldspar source runs out, potters' suppliers can sometimes make up a feldspar of the same composition by combining an alternative feldspar with additional materials.

Secondary fluxes

The alkaline earth fluxes calcia, magnesia, baria, strontia and zinc oxide are the most important in influencing the colour response of a glaze.

The most widely used secondary flux is calcium oxide, found in whiting or limestone. Calcium carbonate breaks down to calcium oxide and carbon dioxide gas upon firing. Calcium strengthens and stabilises the glaze. It is used in shiny transparent glazes, but in large quantities it makes the glaze matt by the formation of small calcium silicate crystals (wollastonite or anorthite). It tends to bleach out colours, particularly in lime-matt glazes. It is an essential ingredient in chrome-tin pinks (including pink stains), where around 15% whiting is needed in the glaze. Wollastonite (calcium silicate) is a source of calcia, which is preferred by industry, as it does not give off carbon dioxide during firing, nor does it produce air bubbles in the glaze, owing to its needle-shaped particles which trap less air during glaze application.

Magnesia, found in dolomite (magnesium calcium carbonate) and talc (magnesium silicate), is a useful flux that counteracts crazing and, in large quantities, produces crystalline matt glazes. The matt surface forms when the excess magnesia crystallizes out of the molten glaze on cooling. If the glaze is cooled slowly, more crystals form. Magnesia turns cobalt a lavender-mauve colour, sometimes with pink crystals if the glaze is low in silica. Magnesium carbonate is sometimes introduced into special-effect glazes to promote shrinking and crawling for sculptural or decorative reasons (otherwise these traits are usually avoided).

Barium is another member of the alkaline earths that can produce matt glazes. It has a strong colour response with colouring oxides, producing brilliant blues with cobalt, turquoise from copper, chartreuse green from chrome, pink from manganese and purple from nickel. However, barium carbonate is toxic and should not be used in large quantities (above 15%) in glazes for use on functional ware. A non-toxic substitute is strontium carbonate, although it does not give such bright colours.

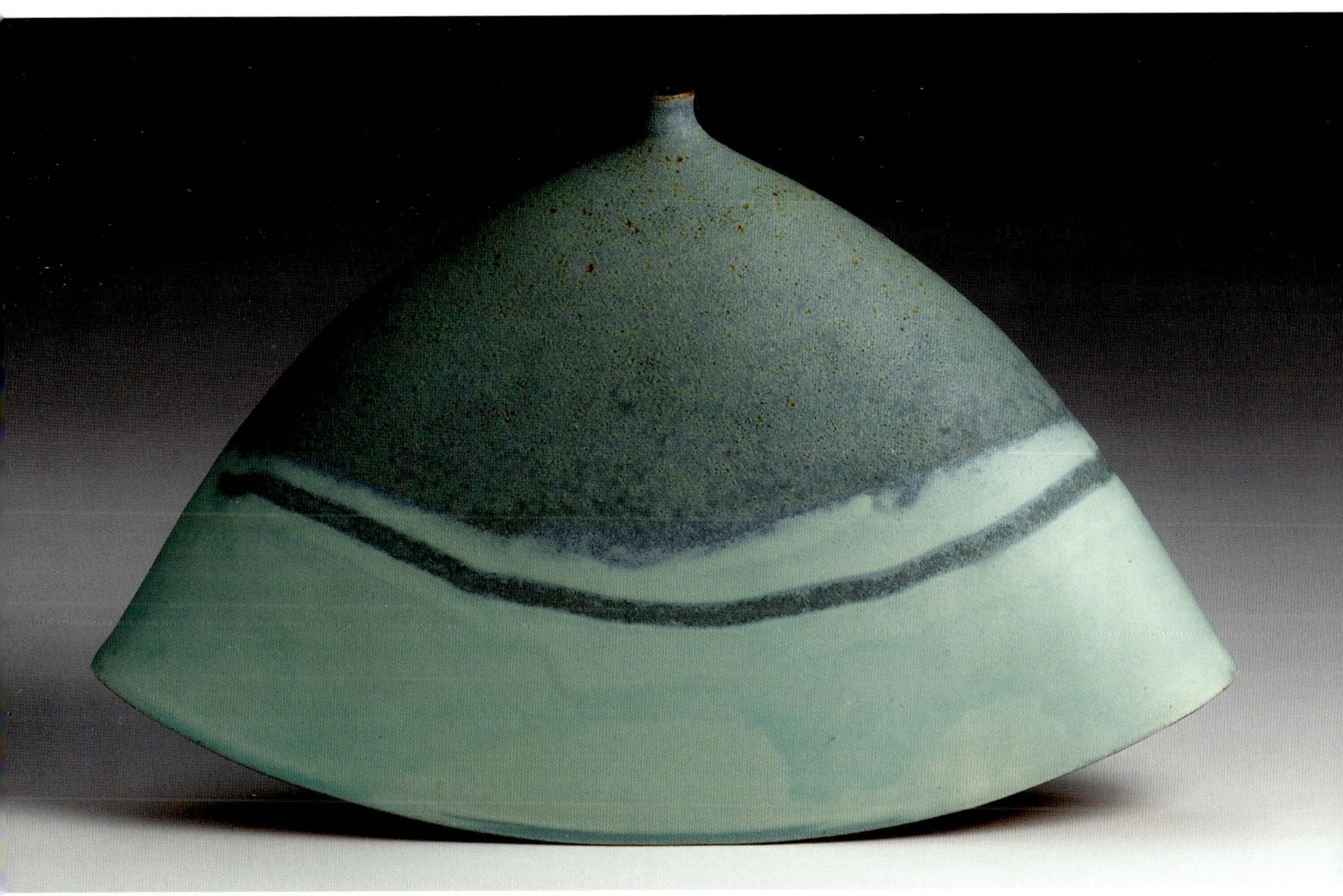

Green Rocking Pot, Emily Myers, 2009. Thrown red stoneware. Barium glaze, ht: 25cm (10in). *Photo: Mark Somerville.*

When a glaze is described as being 'alkaline', it is usually high in sodium, lithium, barium or strontium. These fluxes will promote bright colours such as turquoise from copper and chartreuse green from chromium. Fluxes such as magnesium and zinc tend to give a more muted colour response, such as pink-brown from chromium.

Bone ash contains calcium phosphate and is used in bone china, red-iron glazes and some Chun blue glazes. Glazes made with bone ash are often opaque and mottled or streaked. Although bone ash acts as a flux, phosphoric oxide is also a glass former and stays suspended in a silica glass, causing opacity. Phosphorus is also found in small amounts in wood and grass ash. Calcium borate, titanium or rutile can also cause a streaked, opalescent Chun effect in low-alumina glazes.

Wood ash

Wood ash has long been used as a glaze material, as it contains fluxes and silica. Different tree ashes contain varying proportions of sodium, potassium, calcium, magnesium, phosphorus and iron, and can be made into a glaze by adding clay and feldspar. Ash from

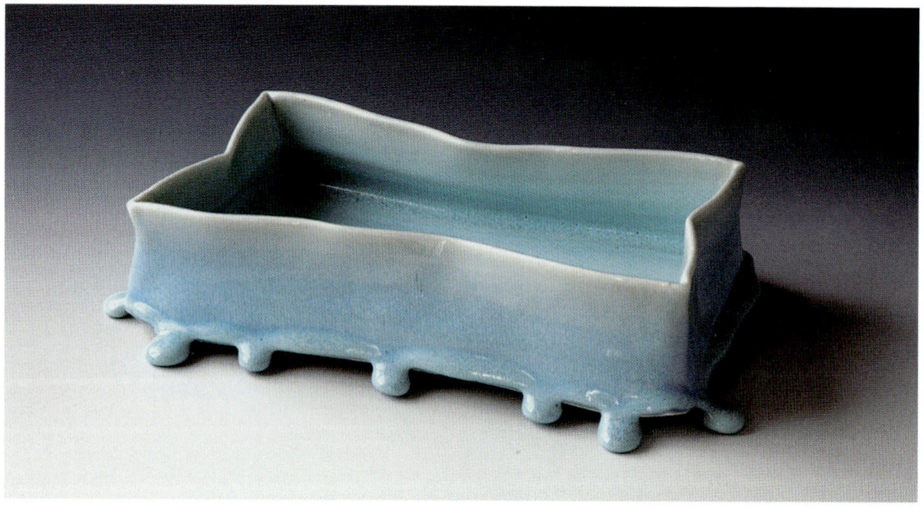

Dishipede, Joanna Howells, 2007. Opalescent Chun blue glaze with drips, reduction-fired porcelain, w: 25cm (9¾in). *Photo: Joanna Howells.*

grasses contains higher silica than wood ash. In Japan, straw and rice hull ash are used in Nuka glaze, a type of blue-white opaque Chun glaze. Before using in a glaze, ash is washed to remove the soluble alkalis, and then sieved to remove any unburned charcoal. The subtle colours of ash glazes are best brought out by reduction firing (see p.22).

Low-temperature fluxes

Boric oxide is used to promote glossy, bright glazes and counteract crazing. It acts as a glass former, like silica, as well as a flux, reducing the melting temperature of glazes over a wide firing range. It is used as a substitute and in combination with lead in earthenware glazes. It occurs in colemanite and Gerstley (or Gillespie) borate, which are slightly soluble and cause the glaze to thicken and gel, so frits are often used instead. Commonly available frits are borax (sodium borate) frit and calcium borate frit (or Ferro frit 3134). Boric oxide inhibits the growth of crystals in matt glazes, causing the glaze to become less matt. Calcium borate frit may cause the glaze to become cloudy, particularly if applied thickly. High levels of boron in a glaze may cause the glaze to blister.

Zinc oxide is a powerful flux originally used in the 19th century to replace lead in Bristol glazes. It is usually used in small amounts to encourage melting. Large quantities may cause crawling and pinholes in the glaze. Zinc reacts with chrome to form zinc chromate, a brown compound that makes it unsuitable for use in chromium green or chrome-tin pink glazes, although it is used to make reliable brown stains. However, in zinc-based glazes high in alumina, chromium will form chrome-zinc-alumina pink spinel (see p.48). Zinc oxide should not be used in reduction, as it reduces to the metal and evaporates.

Lead is used as the main flux, replacing feldspar in many low-temperature earthenware glazes. It is usually fritted to form the insoluble lead bisilicate or slightly lower-melting lead sesquisilicate. Lead sulphide (galena) and lead oxide (litharge) are soluble in water and highly toxic. Lead promotes warm, bright colours and can be used to make low-temperature reds, yellows and oranges with chromium oxide, although these are not food-safe. Owing to concerns about lead leaching from glazes, many commercial earthenware glazes now contain borosilicate frits, which have replaced some or all of the lead. Low-solubility glazes are those which include lead frit combined with borosilicate frit, ensuring the solubility of the lead in the unfired glaze is less than 5%. Leadless glazes contain alkaline and borosilicate frits.

Frits

Frits are made by melting flux materials with silica and some alumina in a furnace, then cooling and grinding to a powder. Because they have already been fired together, they melt again more readily than unfritted materials. They are used when the material would otherwise be soluble in water, causing problems in the glaze. Sodium, potassium, boron and lead are all available in fritted form for use in low- and mid-temperature glazes. Some frits (e.g. Ferro frit 3195) are almost a complete glaze on their own, but most require the addition of clay and some silica to make a glaze. Frits high in sodium and potassium are called high-alkaline frits (e.g. Ferro Frit 3110). They have a high coefficient of expansion and often cause crazing. Low-expansion frits containing calcium borate or magnesia are also available (see Appendices 4 and 5 for frit analysis). Calcium borate frit (similar in composition to colemanite) can be used at slightly higher temperatures than borax frit, which is used to replace lead frits in earthenware glazes. Many commercially available low- to mid-temperature glazes contain frits.

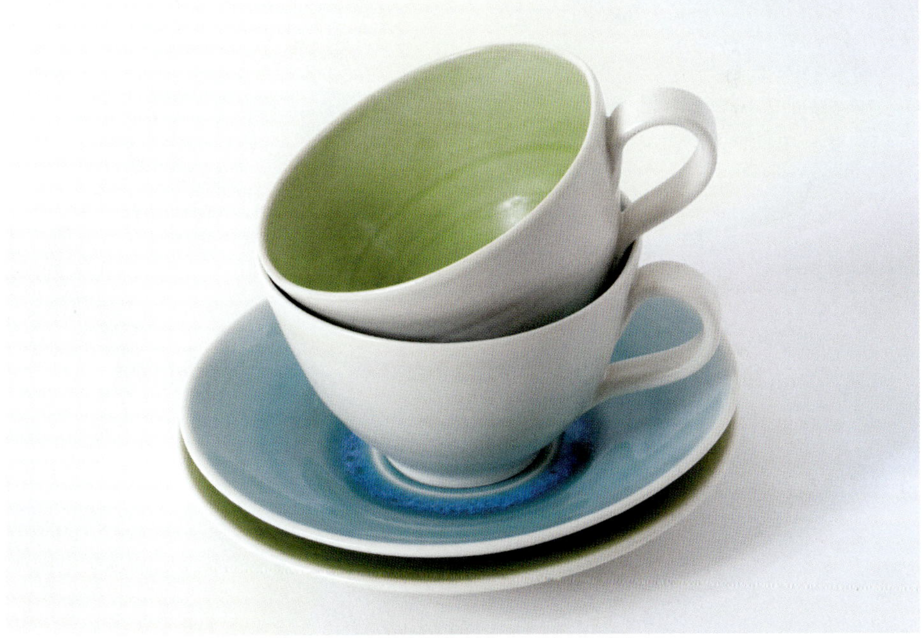

Porcelain cups and saucers, Linda Bloomfield. Copper-turquoise and chrome-green glaze containing calcium borate frit. *Photo: Jacqui Hurst.*

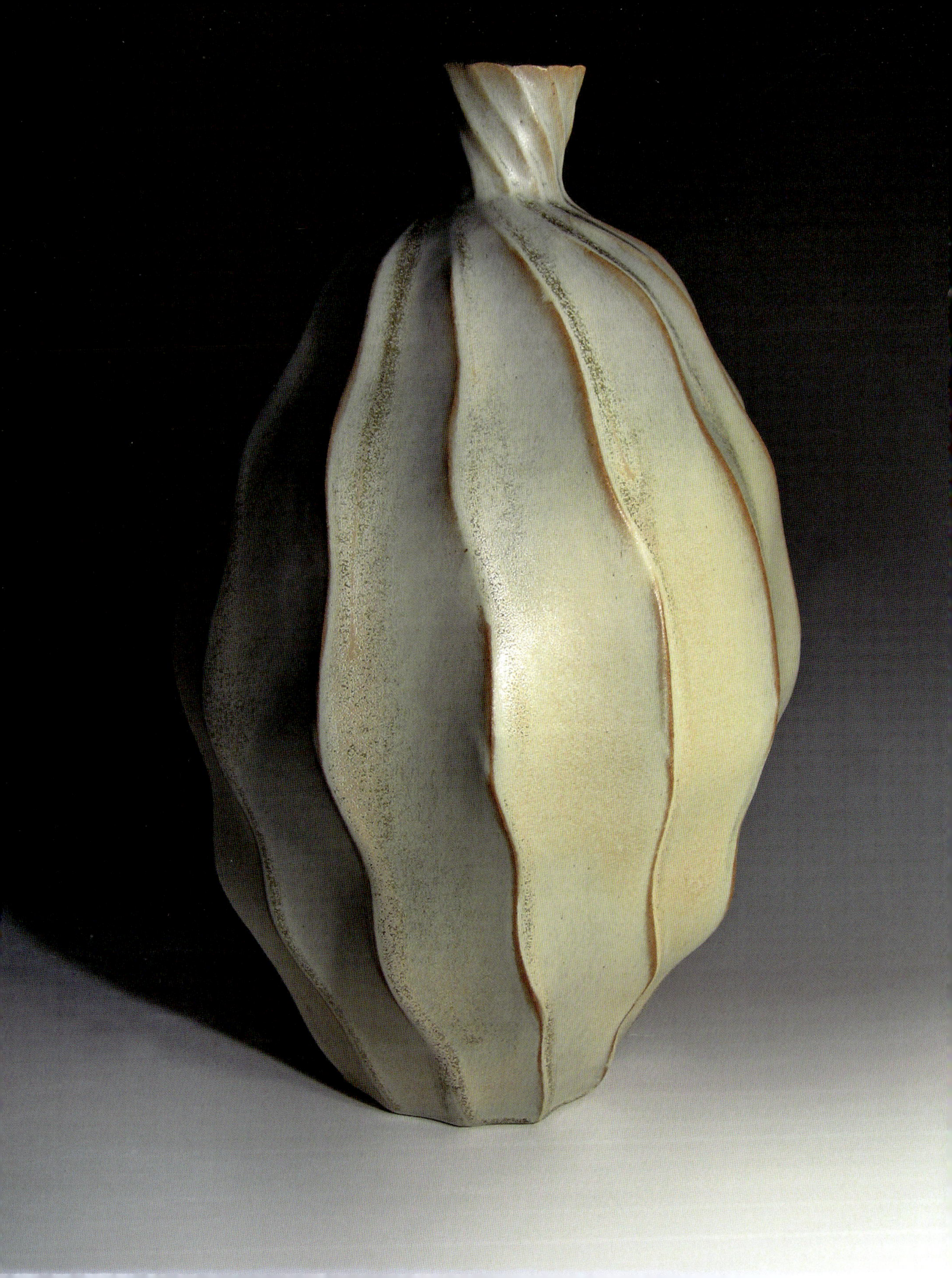

4

Base glazes

Glossy and matt glazes

When silica, fluxes and alumina are combined in a eutectic mixture and fired to a high-enough temperature, a glossy transparent glaze results. In a eutectic, the melting temperature is lower than that of either of the component materials (silica or alumina) alone. A combination of several different fluxes also helps to melt the glaze. In glossy glazes, the alumina to silica ratio should be around 1:9. A stiff, stable glaze with a ratio of around 1:7 is preferable for painting with oxides or underglazes. To make the glaze matt, excess alumina can be added so that the alumina to silica ratio is around 1:5 (see diagram on p. 20). This is known as a true matt as it will be matt however high the firing temperature. The addition of any of the alkaline earths (calcia, magnesia, baria or strontia) can also cause the glaze to become matt. Any excess material not involved in the melt remains suspended in the glass or crystallizes out on cooling. Crystals form in fluid glazes with low alumina. More crystals grow if the glaze is cooled very slowly. These crystals are often calcium or magnesium silicate and can cover the surface forming a smooth, matt texture. When there are only a few crystals in an otherwise glossy glaze, they are called 'floating crystals' and are often a different colour from the glaze in which they are growing.

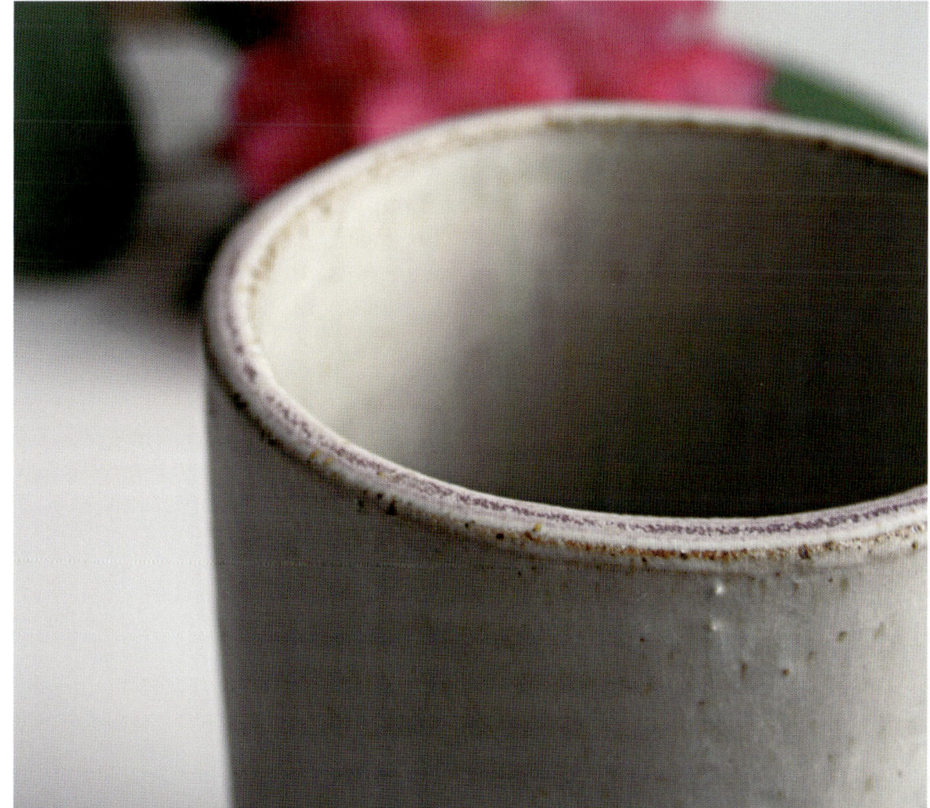

LEFT: *Wavy spiral*, Roger Lewis, 2006. Slab-built stoneware, layered dolomite glazes with rutile and zirconium, nickel and chromium oxides, ht: 50cm (19¾in). *Photo: Roger Lewis*.

RIGHT: Extruded stoneware vase, Tom Butcher, 2009. Reduction-fired with matt glaze, showing crystals on the rim. *Photo: Rosie Brown*.

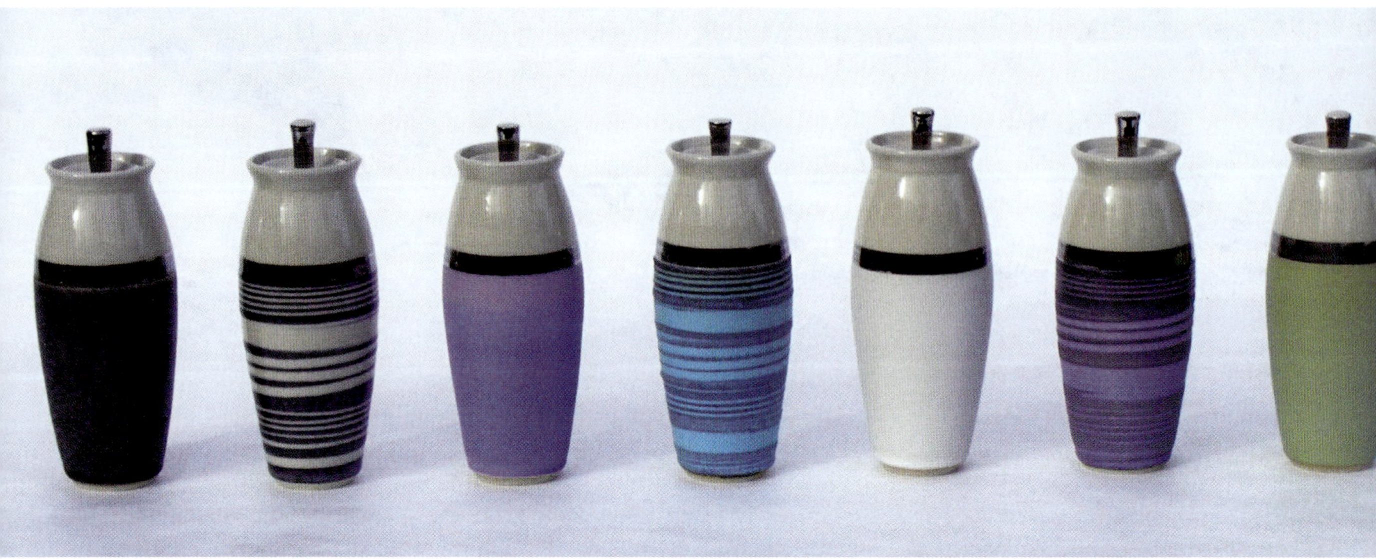

Lidded jars, Sue Ure, 2009. Thrown jars with glossy and matt glazes and lustre, ht: 17cm (6¾in), fired to 1260°C (2300°F). *Photo: Evan Brett.*

Adding rutile to a runny glaze can encourage streaking and mottling. The rutile acts as an opacifier and appears blue, particularly on stoneware fired in reduction. Phosphorus, found in bone ash and wood ash, and calcium borate can also cause opalescence.

Crystalline glazes

In glazes containing excess zinc oxide and very low alumina, large zinc silicate crystals can be grown on cooling by holding the glaze at 1100°C/2012°F for several hours. These glazes are very runny and often contain titanium to help seed the crystals. The crystals are coloured with oxides, and usually take up certain oxides in preference to others. For example, cobalt and copper will give blue crystals on a green background. Nickel oxide colours the crystals steel blue, and manganese colours the crystals pink in the absence of cobalt or nickel. Chromium oxide is not used in zinc silicate glazes, as it turns brown in the presence of zinc silicate. Crystalline glazes are fired on specially made dishes to catch the runny glaze. These are removed after firing and the foot ring ground until smooth.

Crystalline glaze, 1260°C/2300°F (cone 8) oxidation (Avril Farley)

Ferro frit 3110	47
Calcined zinc oxide	23
Calcined china clay	3
Flint	23
Titanium dioxide	4

RIGHT: Crystalline glaze detail, Avril Farley, 2004. Zinc silicate glaze with cobalt and erbium oxide, fired to 1255°C (2291°F), then re-fired to 800°C (1472°F) to change the background colour from lavender to orange. *Photo: Martin Avery.*

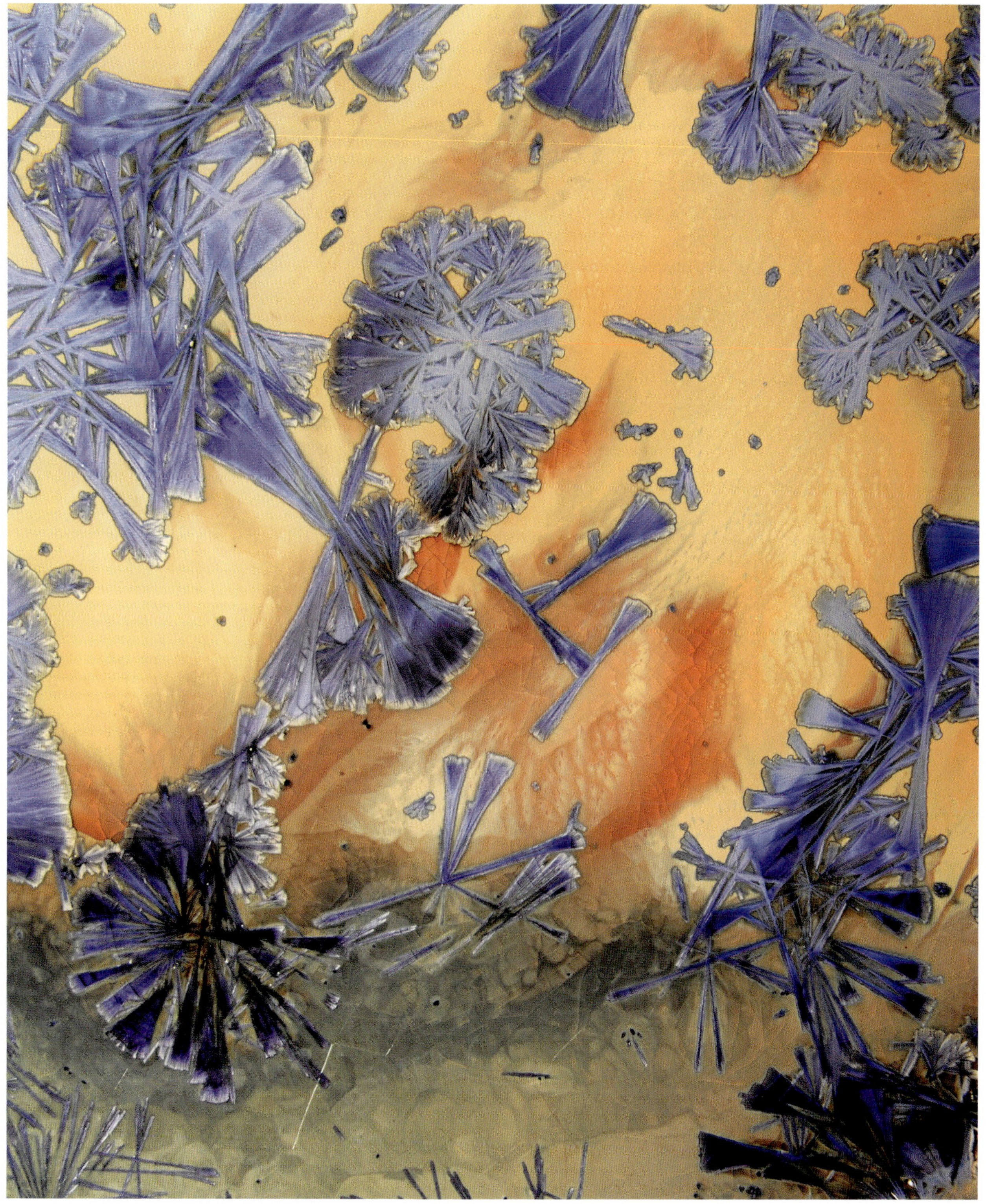

Slip glazes

Colourants are sometimes added to slips, which can be applied to unfired ware. This is less expensive than colouring the entire clay body. The colouring oxide in the slip causes the overlying glaze to become coloured. The amount of colouring oxide or stain required to colour slips is relatively high, around 10%. Slip glazes, sometimes called engobes, are vitreous slips that contain some feldspar and can be applied to biscuit ware.

Potters can make other types of 'special effects' glazes by enhancing various types of glaze faults, such as crazing, crawling or pinholes. Crazing occurs in glazes high in sodium and potassium where the glaze shrinks more than the clay body on cooling. This forms a network of fine cracks called crackle glaze. Crawling occurs in glazes high in alumina, zinc oxide or magnesium carbonate, and is often a feature of wood-fired Shino glazes. Pinholes are caused when bubbles of gas escape from the molten glaze without healing over. They can occur in thickly applied matt glazes, or those containing zinc oxide.

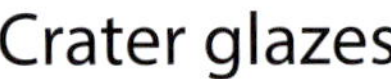

Crater glazes

If silicon carbide is added to a viscous matt glaze, craters form when carbon dioxide is given off during firing. Silicon carbide also causes local reduction in the glaze, causing copper to turn red owing to the lack of oxygen available.

Crater glaze 1260°C/2300°F, (cone 8) oxidation (Akiko Hirai)

Nepheline syenite 60
Barium carbonate 18
China clay 11
Flint 10
+
Titanium dioxide 2
Silicon carbide 2

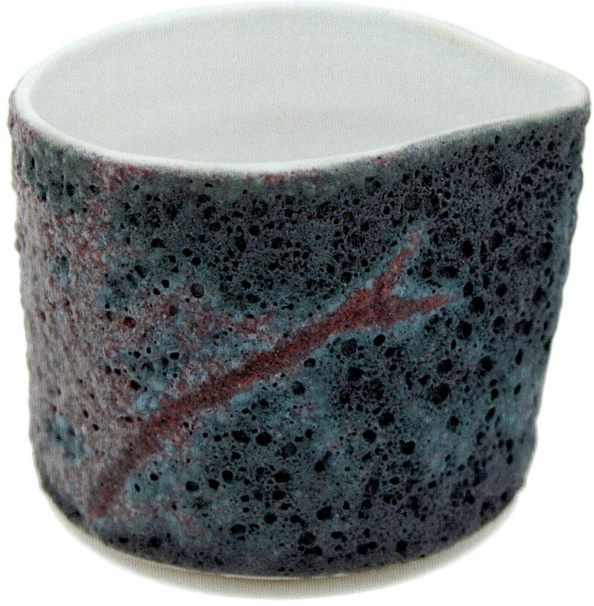

Moss jug, Carys Davies, 2010. Copper carbonate slip under crater glaze on porcelain, ht: 5cm (2in). The copper turns red where reduced by the silicon carbide in the glaze. *Photo: Carys Davie.*

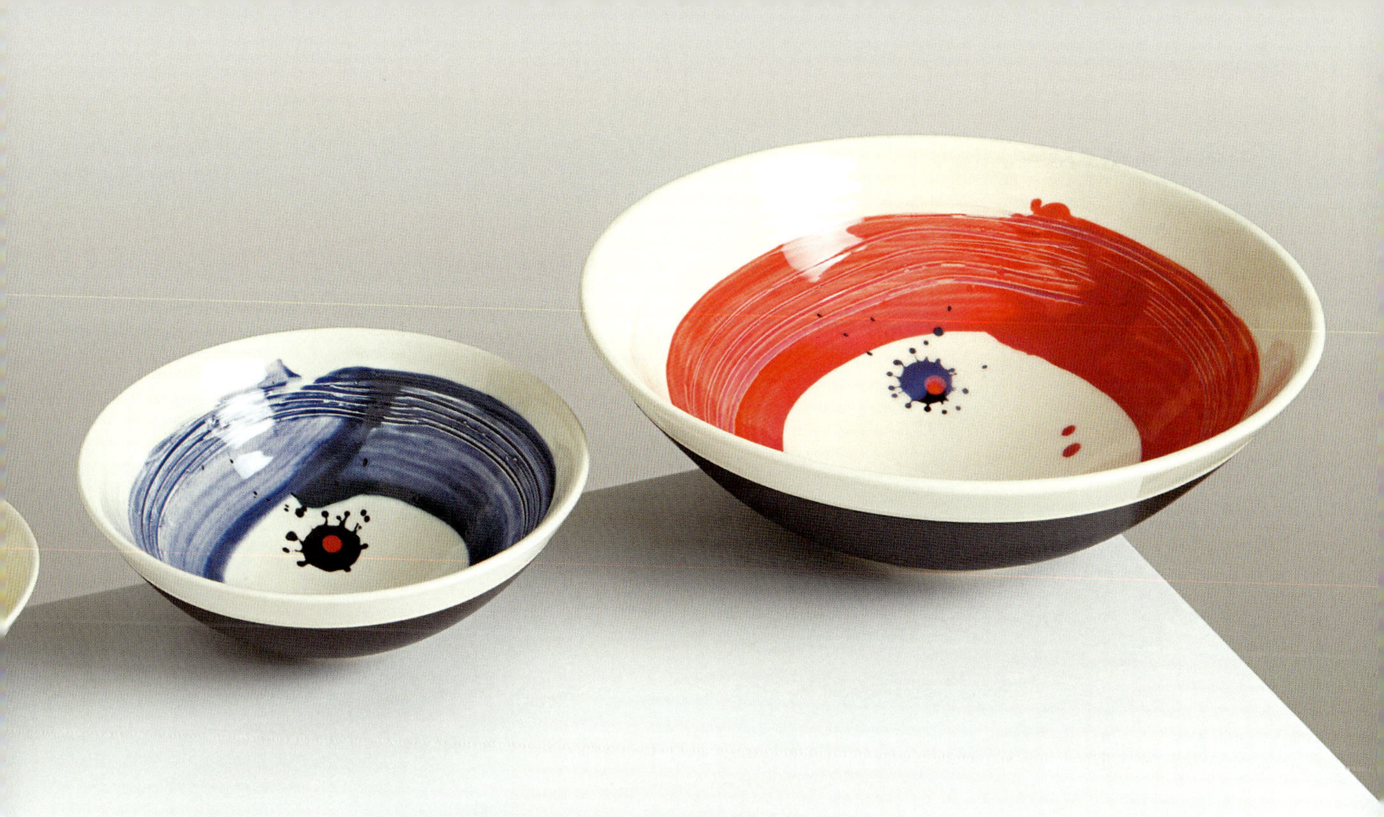

Three bowls, Chris Taylor, 2009. Thrown earthenware, coloured slip glazes, black slip, red underglaze, clear leadless glaze, bisque-fired to 1115°C (2039°F), then glaze-fired to 1055°C (1931°F), with a two-and-a-half-hour soak and slow cool. *Photo: Nick Clark*.

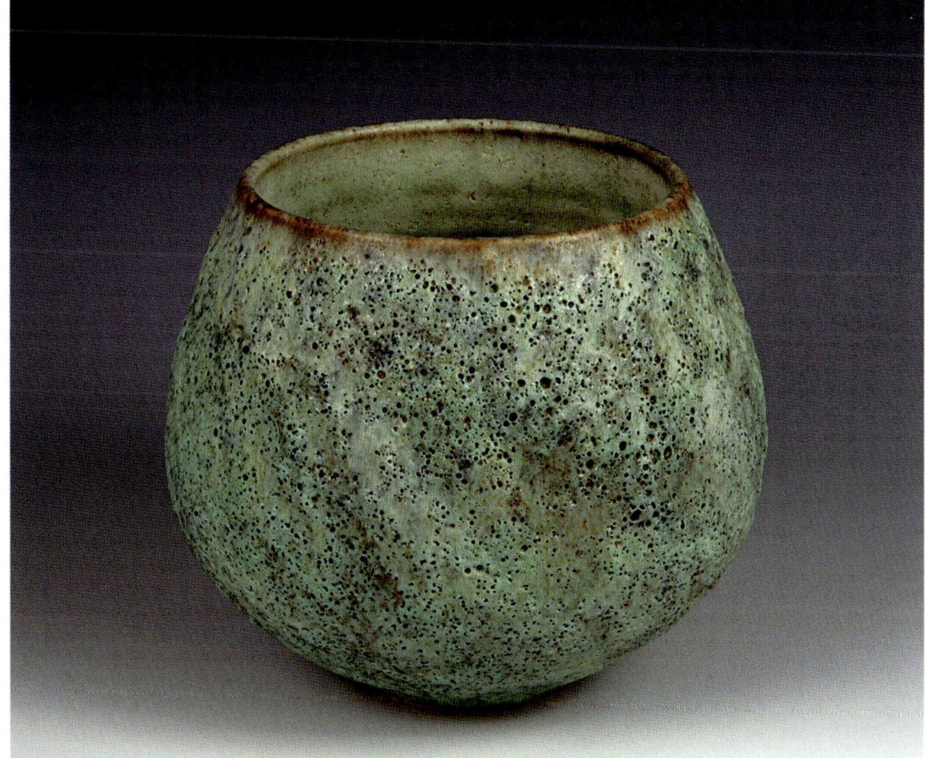

Volcanic vessel, Andrew Palin, 2008. Stoneware with copper, manganese, iron oxide and silicon carbide slip and matt glaze, fired to 1260°C (2300°F), ht: 14cm (5 1/2in). *Photo: Andrew Palin*.

Shrink and crawl glazes

Shrink and crawl, or lichen, glazes are those that contain a high proportion of materials that shrink on drying. These include clay, zinc oxide and light magnesium carbonate.

Shrink and crawl glaze 1260°C/2300°F (cone 8) oxidation

Light magnesium carbonate 31
Soda feldspar 30
China clay 19
Talc 8
Borax frit 6
Zinc oxide 6

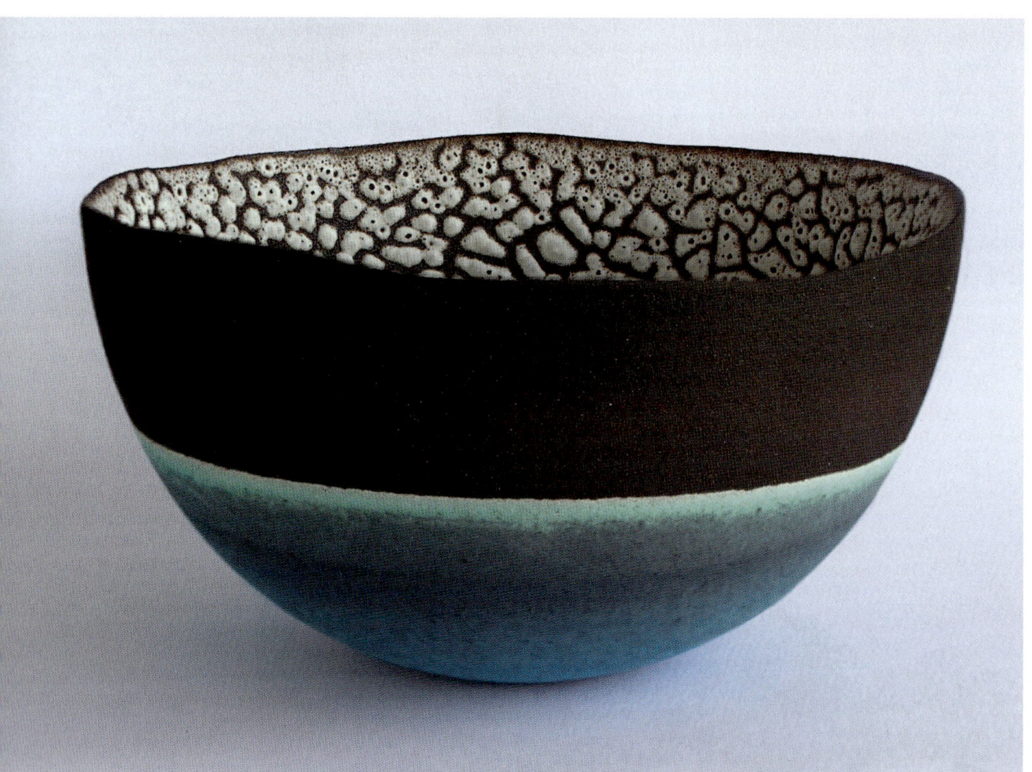

LEFT: Emma Williams, Pressmoulded bowl, black clay with barium matt and crawl glazes, earthenware, fired to 1055°C/1931°F, ht: 11cm (4.5in), dia: 18cm (7in), 2013. *Photo: courtesy of the artist.*

RIGHT: Emma Williams, Fingerprint resist bowl, crawl glaze, red earthenware, fired to 1055°C/1931°F, *Photo: courtesy of the artist.*

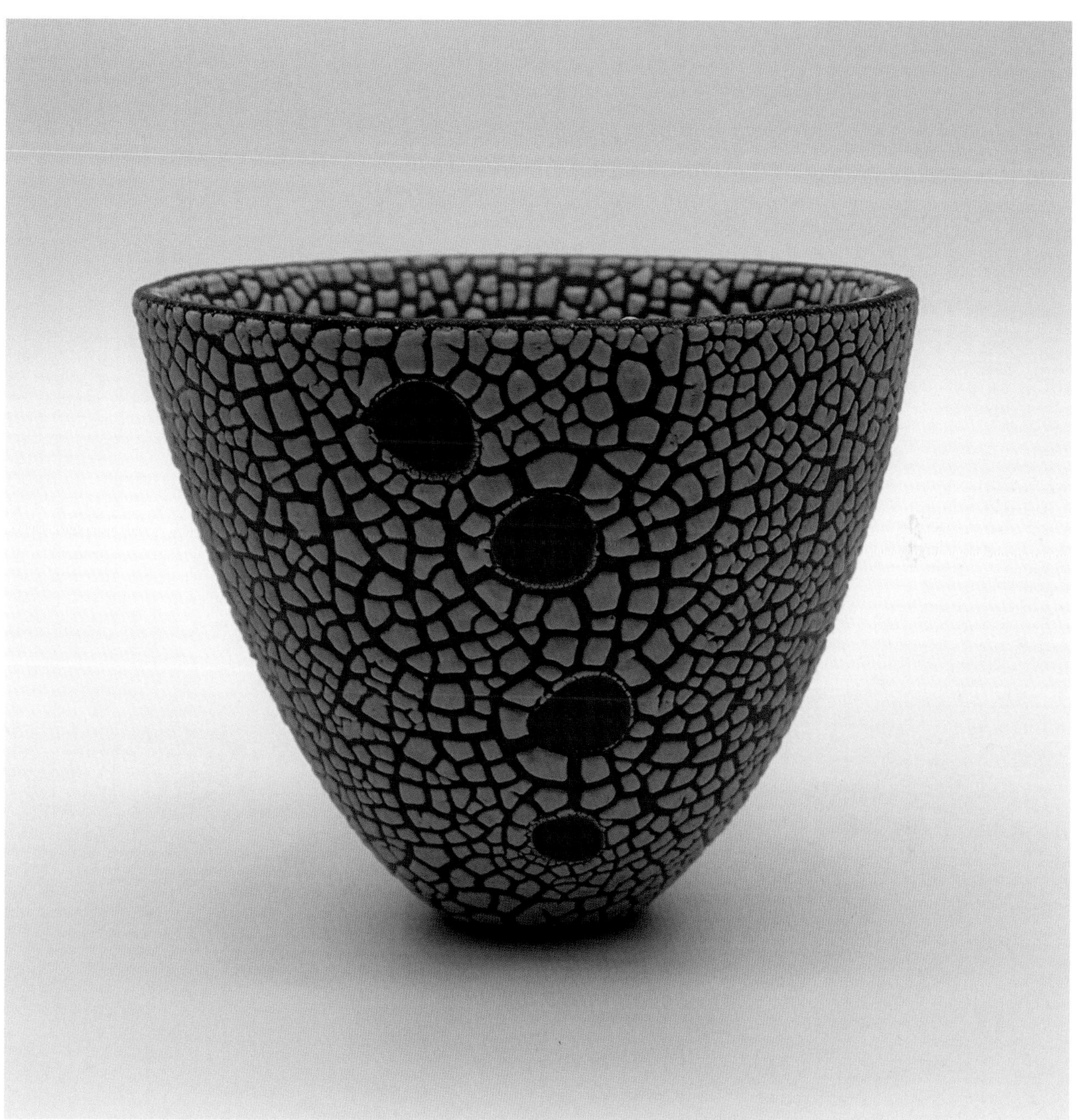

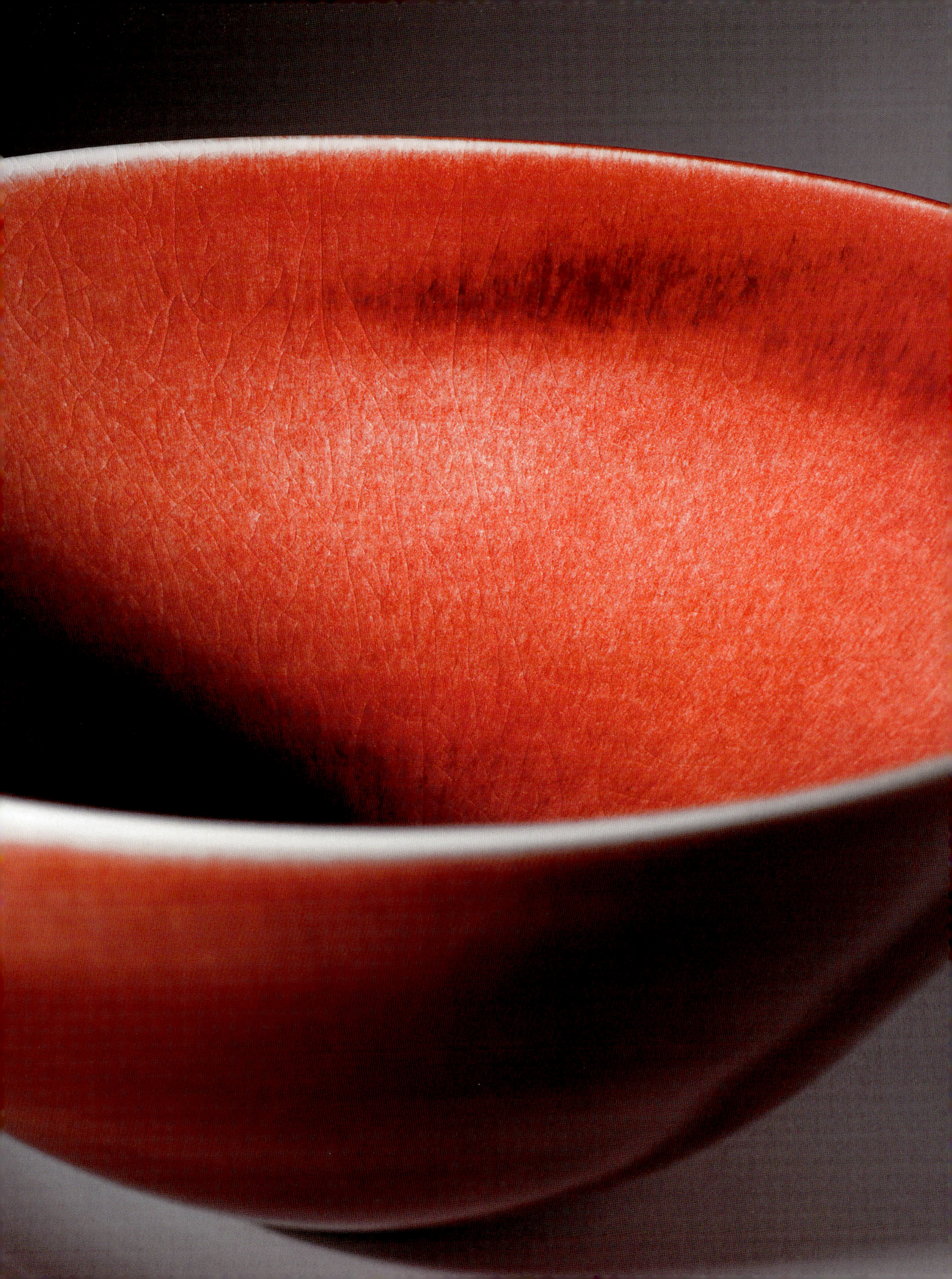

5 Colouring oxides and colour development

COLOURING OXIDES

LEFT: *Sang de Boeuf Bowl*, Sara Flynn, 2009. Thrown porcelain, reduction-fired. *Photo: Roland Paschhoff.*

The colouring oxides are the transition metal oxides of vanadium, chromium, manganese, iron, cobalt, nickel and copper. Transition metals can combine with different numbers of oxygen atoms to give different colours. They often change colour after firing, and the colour depends on the type of base glaze and whether it is fired in oxidation or reduction. In oxidation in electric kilns, there is sufficient oxygen for the metals to form their highest oxidation states, so iron will form ferric oxide (Fe_2O_3), which is rust brown. In reduction in fuel-burning kilns, the fuel is starved of oxygen and draws it from the clay and glaze, reducing iron to ferrous oxide (FeO), which is black and acts as a flux. Iron oxide (FeO or Fe_2O_3) in very small quantities in glazes (1–2%) is yellow in oxidation and blue-green in reduction. Colouring oxides are present in trace amounts in coloured gemstones, such as chromium in ruby, or iron and titanium in sapphire. (Both are coloured corundum, a crystalline form of alumina (Al_2O_3)).

Colouring oxides may not be 100% pure, and the composition may vary depending on where they are sourced, particularly rutile, which contains impurities including iron, chromium and vanadium. The mesh size may vary, so speckles can occur in the fired glaze, particularly with cobalt. Always test a new batch of glaze before using on a pot.

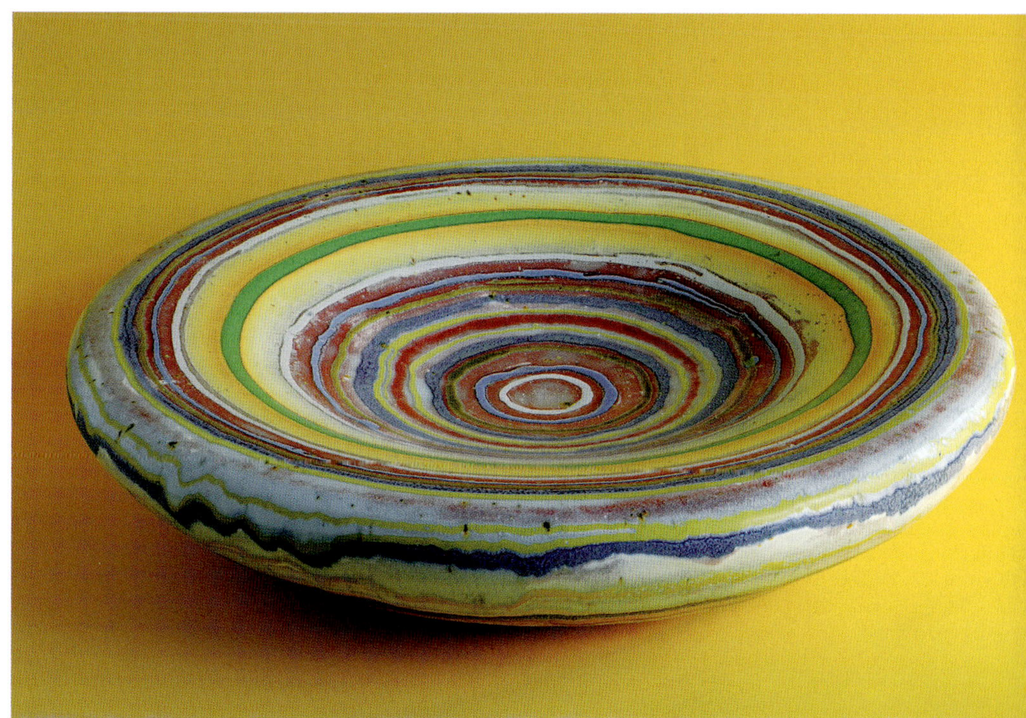

RIGHT: *Cushion bowl*, Chris Barnes, 2010. Stoneware with white slip, white base glaze, transparent reactive glaze, bands of coloured glazes. Blue: cobalt in dolomite glaze. Yellow: iron in barium/zirconium glaze. Red: copper in borax glaze. Green: chromium in potassium glaze. Pale duck egg blue/white: copper in barium/zirconium glaze. Mid-blue: cobalt and copper in barium/zirconium glaze, fired in reduction to cone 9. The wide band of yellow is titanium in a borax-based glaze that has been affected by the overlying band of green glaze, giving a bright yellow fading to pale yellow at the edges. *Photo: Val Corbett.*

Colouring oxides are usually added to glazes in small quantities (less than 5%), although iron and manganese can be added in larger amounts (up to 25%). Carbonates can also be used, but they are slightly weaker colourants and break down to form oxides, giving off carbon dioxide during firing. Soluble salts (chlorides, nitrates) can be used, but they are highly toxic. Some oxides, such as copper and cobalt, dissolve fully in the molten glaze to produce transparent glazes. Glazes can become saturated with over 5% of these colouring oxides, and the excess remains on the surface, often as a matt, metallic black. Other oxides, such as chromium and nickel, remain undissolved in quantities greater than about 1%, and may produce opaque glazes. Solubility of colourants in glazes increases with firing temperature, and is aided by active fluxes such as alkalis (sodium, lithium or barium) and boron. Certain colours require the presence or absence of particular ingredients in the glaze, such as tin oxide and calcium, required to obtain a pink colour from chromium. Some colouring oxides (cobalt, copper and manganese) act as fluxes in the glaze and in large quantities will cause it to become runnier. Many of the metal oxides are toxic and should be handled carefully, particularly nickel, chromium and manganese. Firing fumes should also be avoided and kilns should be well ventilated (see p.119, Health and safety).

Cobalt oxide, CoO

Cobalt oxide and carbonate are used to give a strong blue colour. Cobalt carbonate ($CoCO_3$) is a slightly weaker form in which the particles of cobalt are more finely ground. For example, 1.5g of carbonate contains the same amount of cobalt as 1g oxide. The carbonate is often preferred, as the cobalt will be more finely dispersed in the glaze, and less likely to leave blue specks. Cobalt forms cobalt silicate in glazes, which gives a bright blue colour, tending towards purple. Only a small amount of cobalt oxide (less than 1%) is required to give a strong blue. The colour can be modified using iron, manganese or nickel to make grey-blues. Magnesium glazes containing dolomite or talc will turn cobalt lavender blue. Cobalt acts as a flux.

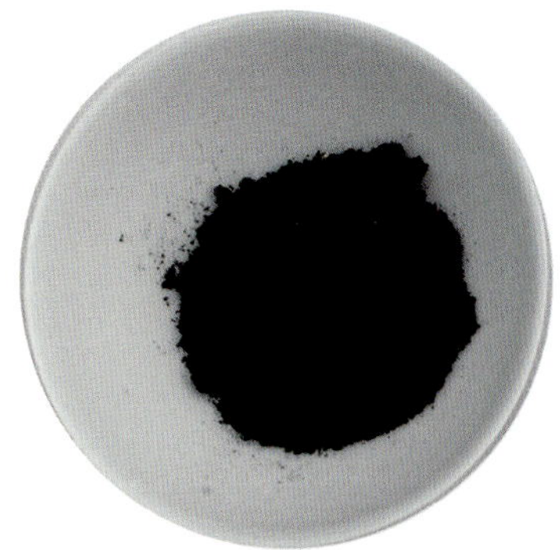

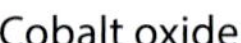

Cobalt oxide

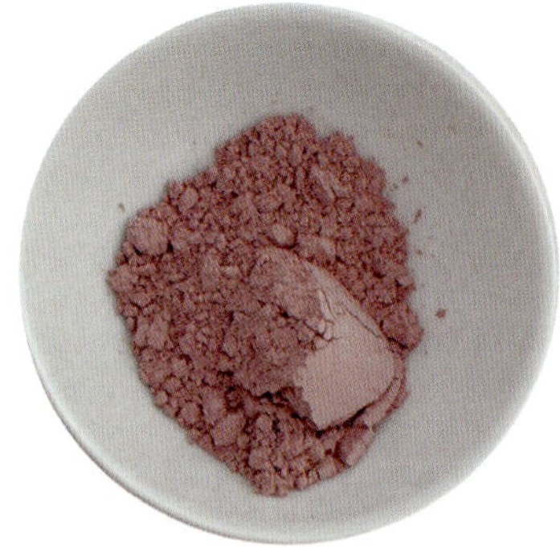

Cobalt carbonate

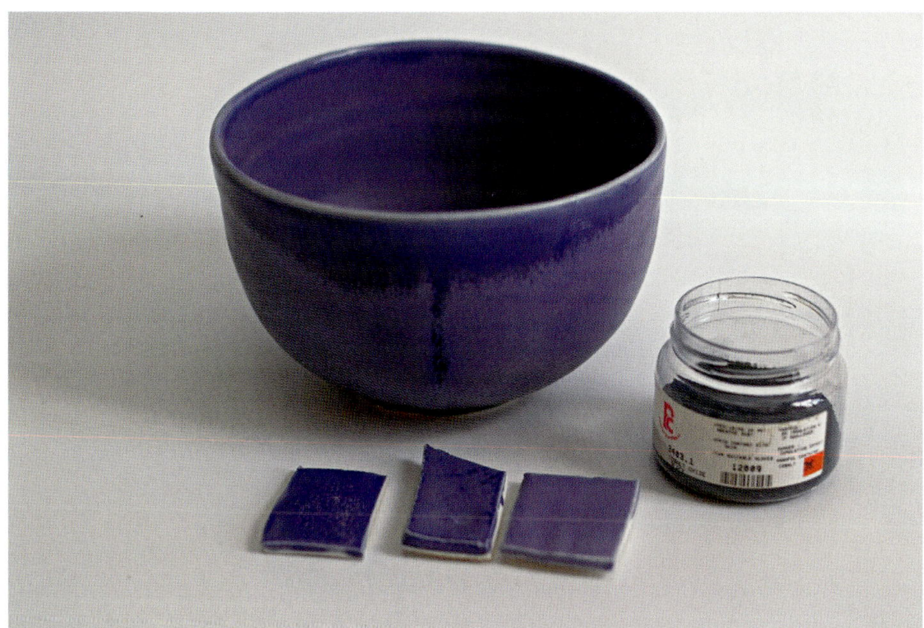

RIGHT ABOVE: Magnesium matt glazes containing cobalt oxide on porcelain.

Copper oxide, CuO

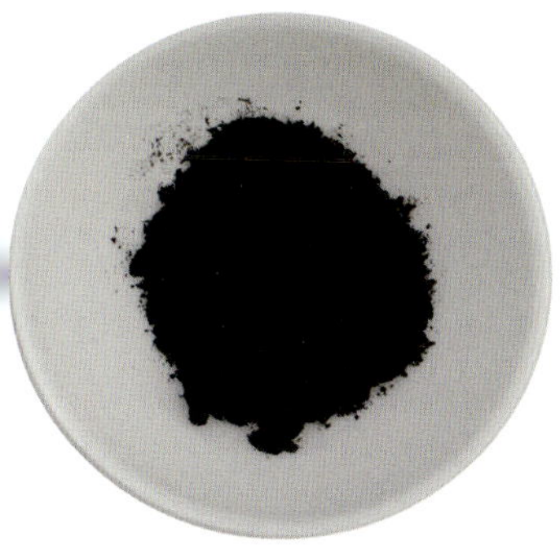

Copper oxide

Copper oxide and carbonate ($CoCO_3$) are used to give green in oxidation and ox-blood red in reduction. Copper oxide is volatile, and will cause a pink blush on surrounding pots in reduction. High in sodium, lithium, or barium, alkaline glazes with low alumina, may produce a bright turquoise in oxidation from 1–2% copper oxide. If a glaze becomes oversaturated with copper oxide (more than 5%), it turns a matt, metallic black.

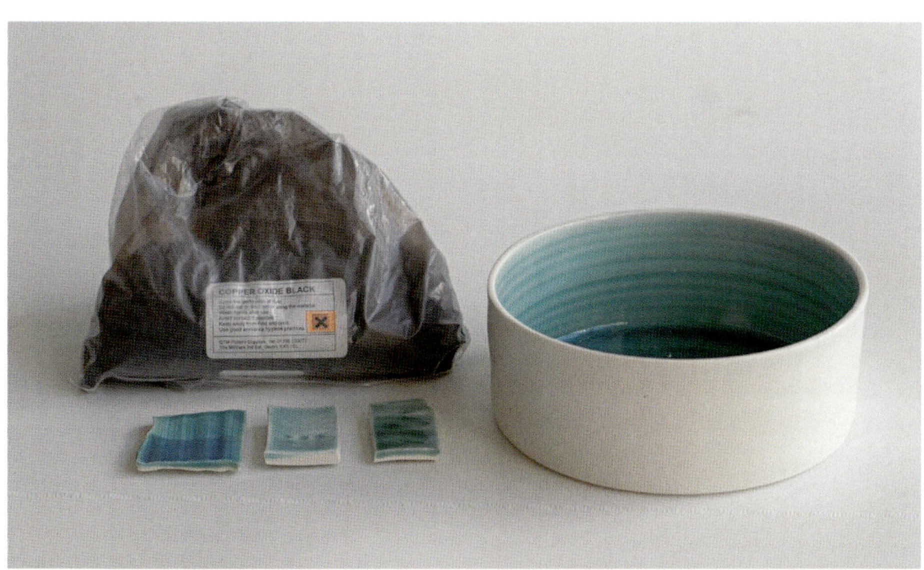

RIGHT BELOW: Turquoise glazes using copper oxide on porcelain fired in oxidation.

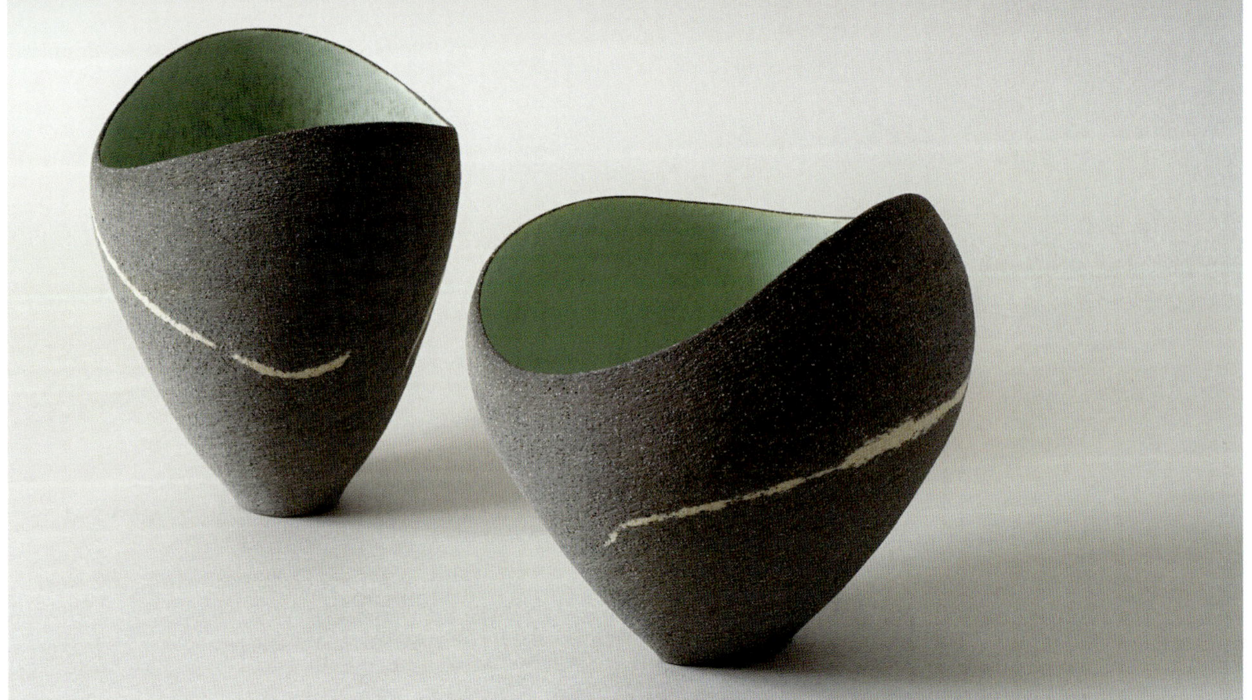

Bowls, Kerry Hastings, 2008. Coiled grogged stoneware coloured with chromium oxide, which has also coloured the matt glaze, fired to 1140°C (2084°F) with a two-hour soak. *Photo: Sussie Ahlburg*.

Chromium oxide, Cr_2O_3

Chromium oxide (also known as chrome oxide) gives a reliable green and is used, together with varying amounts of cobalt, in commercial green stains. Chromium oxide is not very soluble in glazes, except in sodium, lithium, or barium glazes, where it turns bright yellow-green. In the presence of tin oxide in calcium glazes, chromium turns pink. Only a very small amount of chromium is needed for this (0.1–0.5% to 5% tin). In glazes containing zinc, chromium forms brown zinc chromate except in high-zinc, high-alumina glazes where pink chrome-zinc-alumina spinel is formed. Iron chromate can also be used as a grey or brown colourant. In lead glazes with low alumina, chromium can give red, orange and yellow. Chromium oxide is refractory and toxic. It is volatile at

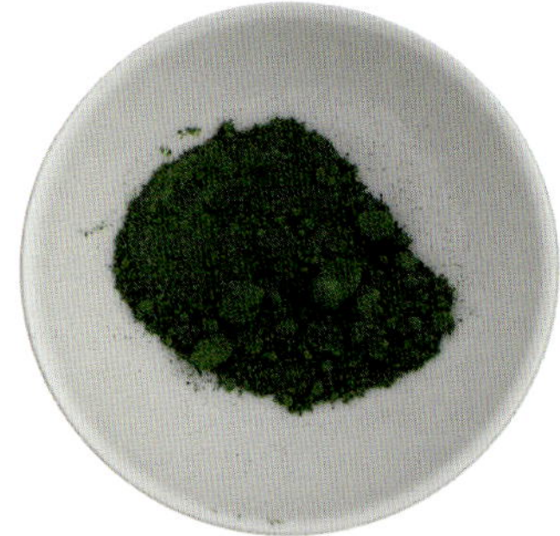

Chromium oxide

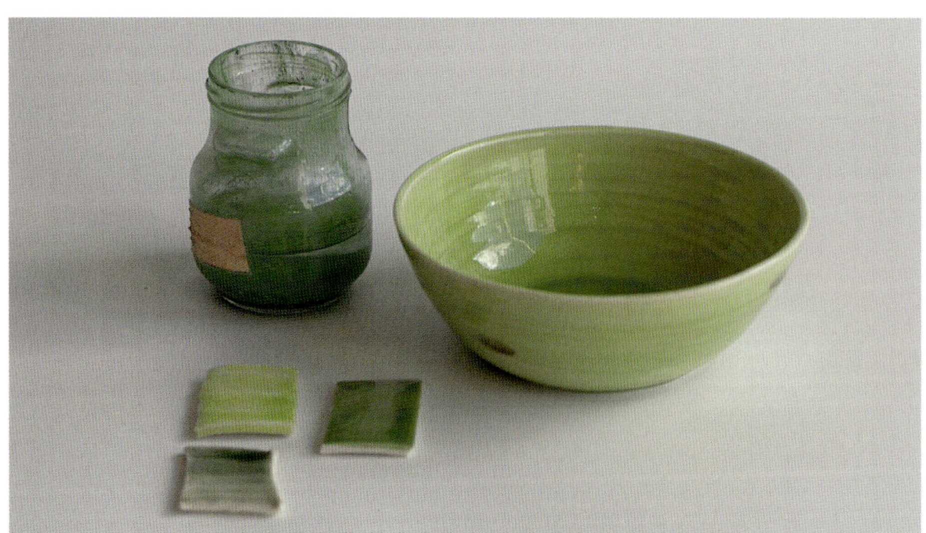

LEFT: Chromium oxide in alkaline glazes.
Top left: chromium 0.3%.
Top right: chromium 0.5%.
Bottom: copper and nickel, fired in oxidation.

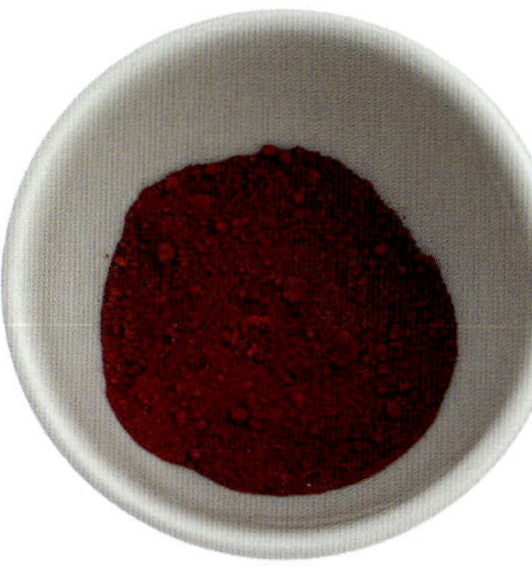
Red iron oxide

high temperatures.

Iron oxide, Fe_2O_3, FeO

There are many forms of iron oxide, but the most commonly used is red iron oxide (Fe_2O_3). Iron oxide is found in red earthenware clay, yellow ochre and umber. Yellow ochre is a type of clay containing hydrated iron oxide, while umber is a clay pigment containing iron and manganese. Black iron oxide (FeO) and magnetite (Fe_3O_4), used coarsely-ground to introduce speckling, are also available. Crocus martis is calcined iron sulphate and is soluble in water. In small amounts (0.5–2%), iron gives a honey-yellow colour in oxidation and celadon or blue-green in reduction. Iron oxide in moderate quantities (2–6%) turns yellow-brown in oxidation in lime matt and barium glazes. With larger quantities of iron oxide (6–12%), brown-black tenmoku and kaki glazes are obtained in reduction. In saturated iron glazes containing bone ash, an orange-red is produced. Iron oxide acts as a flux in reduction, and large amounts may cause the glaze to run. However, in oxidation, iron oxide acts as a refractory.

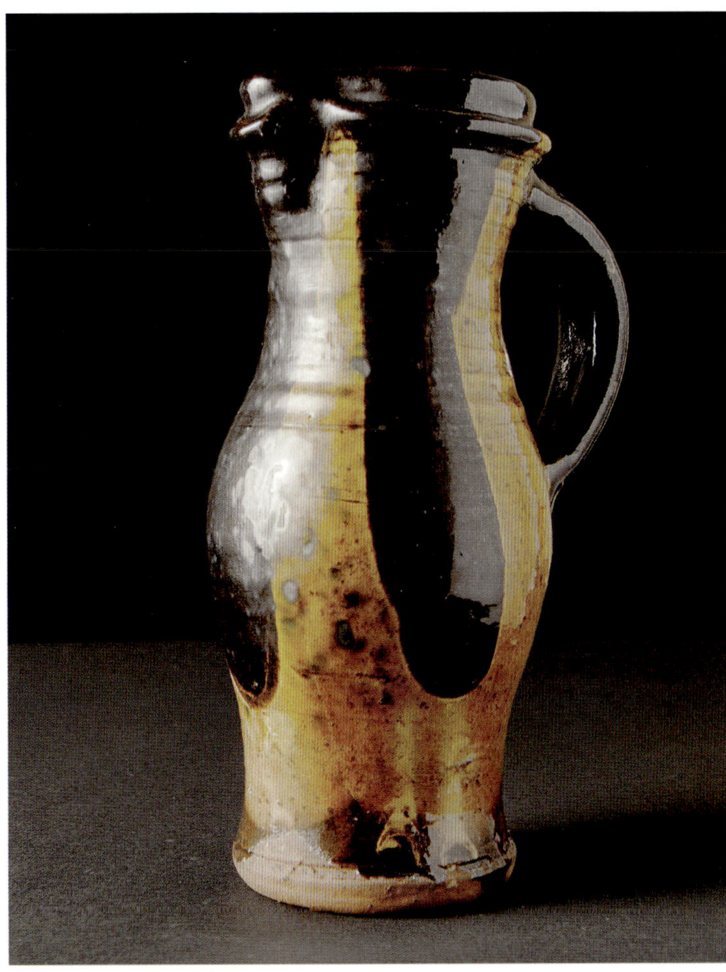
Baluster jug, Doug Fitch, 2008. Red earthenware, poured black slip (iron oxide 10%, manganese dioxide 10%), honey glaze (iron oxide 2%), wood-fired. *Photo: Jonny Thompson.*

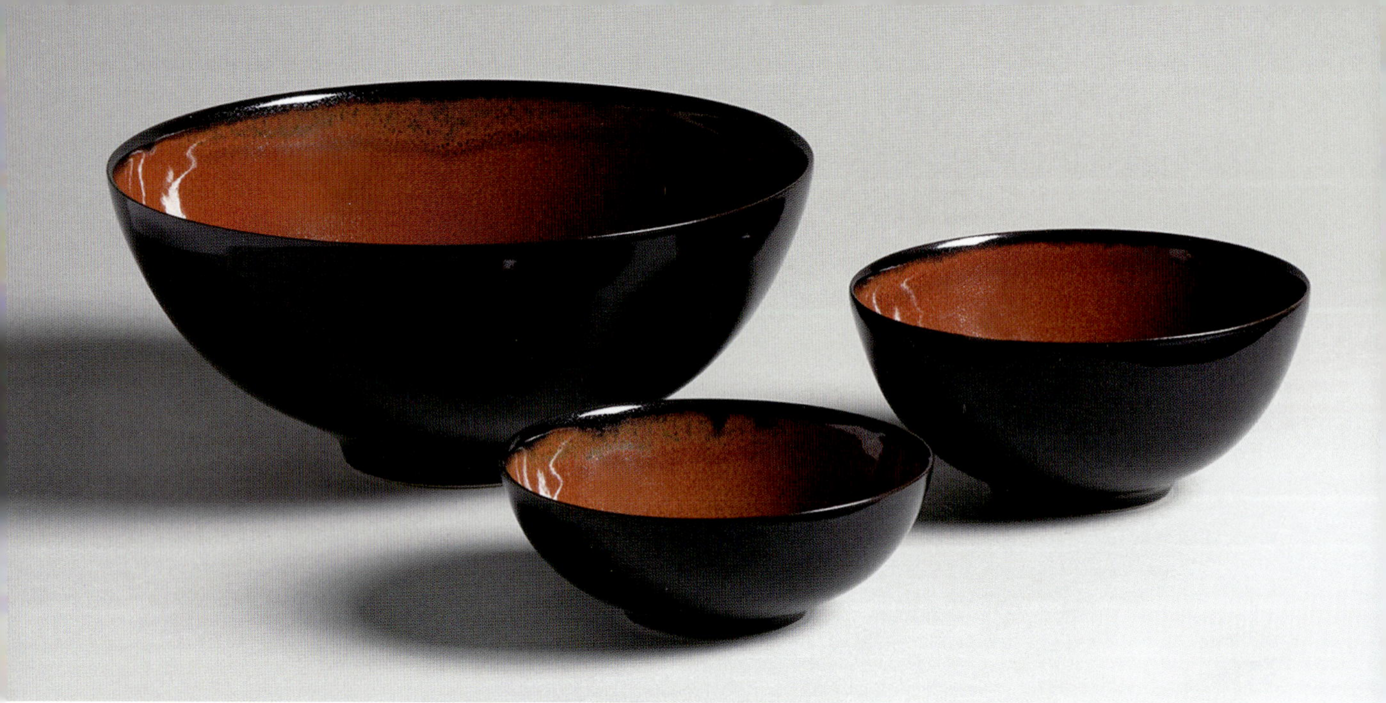

Two Tone Bowl Group, Suleyman Saba, 2009. Stoneware bowls, iron red glaze over black iron glaze with 8% red iron oxide, fired in oxidation to 1280°C (2336°F). *Photo: Stephen Brayne.*

Rutile and ilmenite, TiO_2 and $FeTiO_3$

Rutile and ilmenite both contain iron and titanium dioxide. Rutile contains up to 15% iron oxide and ilmenite has 50% iron oxide and 50% titanium dioxide. They are good additions to encourage break-up of glazes and introduce a pleasing, mottled texture. Rutile produces tan yellows in high alumina and high calcium glazes in oxidation. In low alumina glazes, opalescent blues can be obtained in reduction. Rutile sometimes contains contaminants, including vanadium and chromium oxide, which may produce a pink colour in tin-opacified glazes. Rutile also contains trace amounts of niobium, which causes opalescence.

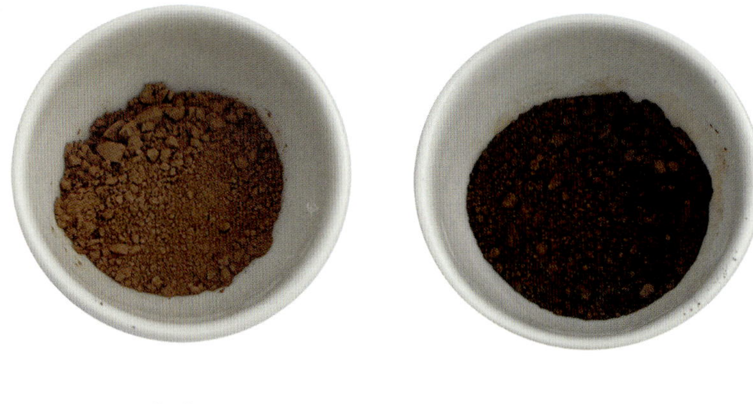

Rutile Ilmenite

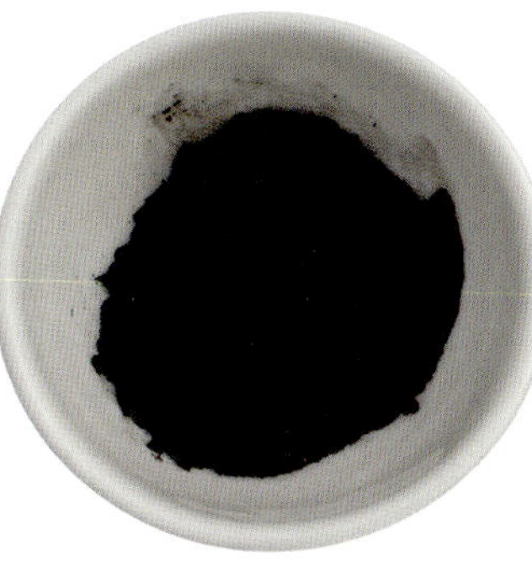

Manganese dioxide

Vanadium pentoxide

Manganese dioxide, MnO_2

Manganese dioxide (or carbonate) acts as a flux and produces a dark brown colour in glazes. In alkaline glazes (high in sodium, lithium or barium) with low alumina, it can produce plum purples, particularly when a small amount of cobalt is added. It can be used on its own as a dark brown pigment, or mixed with copper oxide to produce a metallic bronze. Manganese, iron and cobalt are used together to make dark blue and black glazes. The firing fumes from manganese are toxic (see p.119 in Health and safety).

Nickel oxide, NiO

Nickel oxide produces brown or green in most glazes, and is used to moderate other colours. It will produce grey with cobalt. Nickel is used in barium zinc glazes to give steel blue, pink and purple. It can also be used with titanium oxide to make green and yellow. Nickel oxide is refractory and toxic.

Vanadium pentoxide, V_2O_5

Vanadium is combined with tin to make yellow stains and with zirconium to make turquoise stains. Vanadium pentoxide added directly to glazes can produce mottled green or yellow. It is often used in dry matt glazes to give mottled colour variation. Vanadium pentoxide is slightly water-soluble and very toxic.

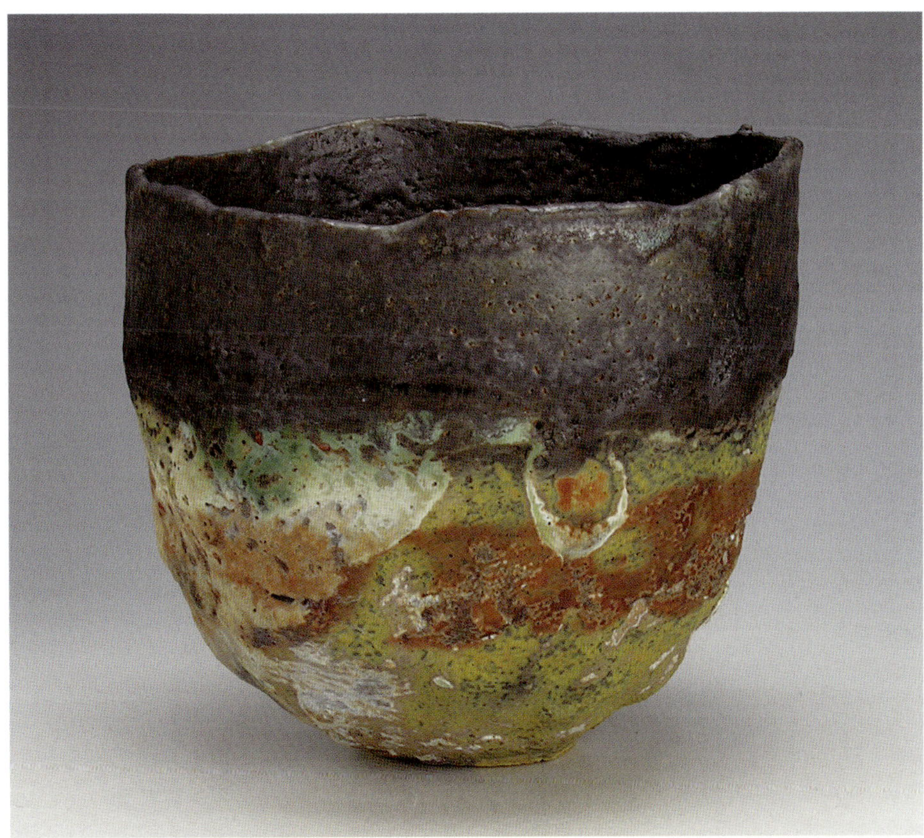

Conical Bowl, Rachel Wood, 2008. Thrown stoneware bowl. The top is copper slip and dolomite glaze, the lower part is vanadium slip and barium glaze, fired to 1260°C (2300°F), ht: 20cm (8in). *Photo: David Binch.*

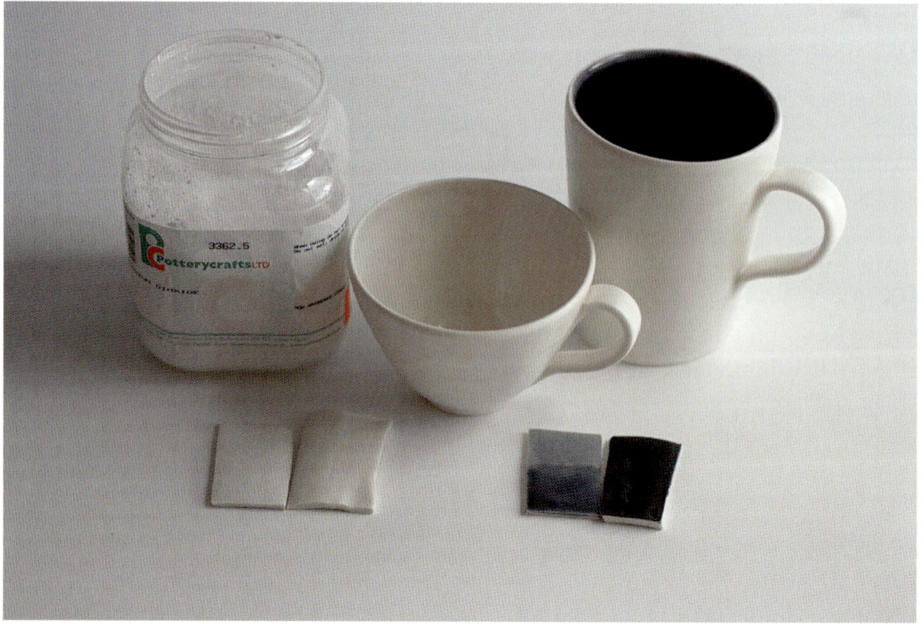

Test tiles. Left: opaque white glaze with 5% titanium oxide, transparent glaze. Right: transparent dark blue glaze, opaque black glaze. The opacity in the black glaze comes from the addition of 1% chromium oxide.

Opacifiers

Tin oxide (SnO_2), titanium oxide (TiO_2) and zirconium silicate (zircon) ($ZrSiO_4$) are used to make glazes opaque. They are refractory and remain suspended in the glaze, with only a small amount dissolving. Tin oxide is the most powerful, although it is also the most expensive. At least 5% tin oxide is required to opacify a glaze. Tin in a glaze may promote pink flashing if chromium (in oxidation) or copper (in reduction) is present in the kiln. Zirconium silicate is less expensive but 10–15% is needed to fully opacify a glaze. Zirconium silicate is used as a stabiliser in many stains, particularly high-temperature reds, oranges and yellows.

Titanium oxide can be used as an opacifier and promotes the formation of crystals, mottling and streaking. Titanium affects the colours of many oxides, turning iron oxide yellow (or green in reduction) and cobalt green. Rutile and titanium help to improve glaze stability.

Rare earth oxides

The rare earth oxides are not particularly rare, but they are expensive and have only recently become widely available. They are scandium, yttrium and the heavy metals found near the bottom of the periodic table, in the lanthanide series (following the element lanthanum) p.146. Of the fifteen metals in the lanthanide series, only four are widely used for colouring glass and glazes. These are cerium, praseodymium, neodymium and erbium. Cerium oxide can be used as an opacifier at low temperatures and gives a tan-yellow or orange colour in glazes, particularly when combined with titanium or rutile. Praseodymium oxide is black but gives pale green in glazes. It is combined with zirconium silicate to make a yellow stain. Neodymium oxide is pale lavender and gives a pale violet colour in glazes, although it looks blue under

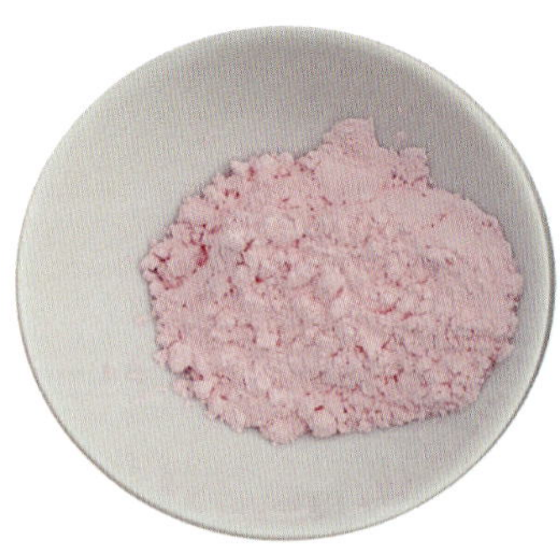

Erbium oxide

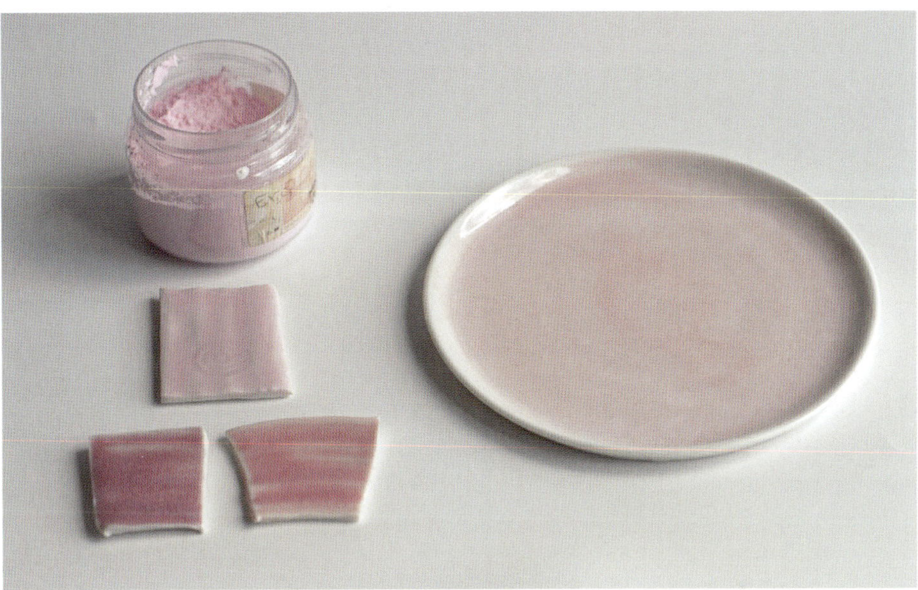

Test tiles. Top: erbium oxide. Bottom left: chrome-tin pink. Bottom right and plate: rutile-tin pink.

fluorescent light. Erbium oxide is the heaviest of the four and is pale pink. Holmium oxide is a less used rare earth, which causes glazes to change colour from yellow-green in daylight to pink in fluorescent light.

Other rare earth oxides – samarium, europium, terbium, dysprosium and thulium – can be used to make bright fluorescent glazes, although the colours (fluorescent orange, pink, green and blue) can only be seen under ultraviolet light and the glazes look colourless in daylight. The rare earth oxides settle quickly in the glaze bucket and require the use of bentonite or CMC gum in the glaze. They are refractory and are not toxic. They are quite weak colourants and 5–10% can be added to a glaze. They are best used in alkaline glazes (containing sodium, lithium, barium or strontium, which increase their solubility) on porcelain and are often used to colour glass.

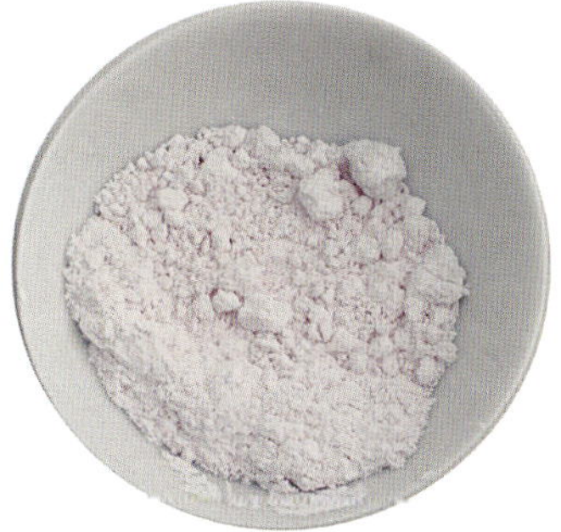

Neodymium oxide

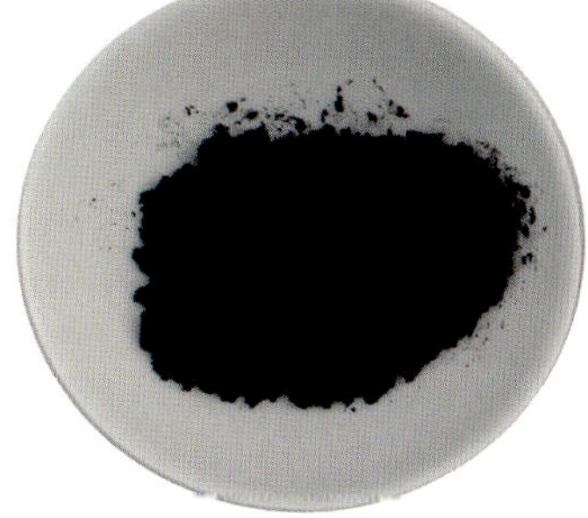

Praseodymium oxide

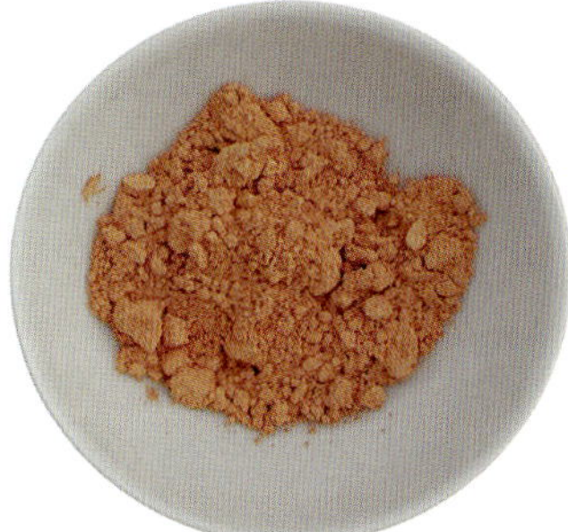

Cerium oxide

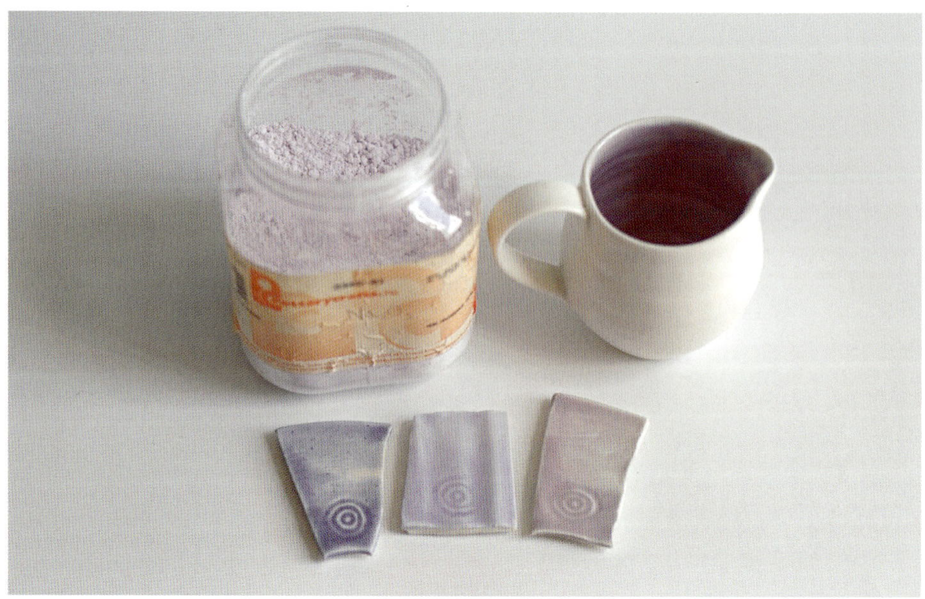

LEFT: Test tiles.
Left: manganese-cobalt.
Middle: neodymium oxide.
Right and jug: rutile-tin-cobalt.

RIGHT, TOP: Glass colour tests, Heike Brachlow, 2009. Soda-lime glass with neodymium, cerium, titanium, nickel, copper, chromium and iron oxides in stoneware crucibles, fired at 1260°C (2300°F). *Photo: courtesy of the Royal College of Art, London.*

RIGHT: *Theme and Variations I*, Heike Brachlow, 2009. Cast glass cubes, 6cm ($2\frac{3}{8}$in), neodymium, cerium and titanium line blend under fluorescent (top) and incandescent light (bottom). *Photo: Ester Segarra.*

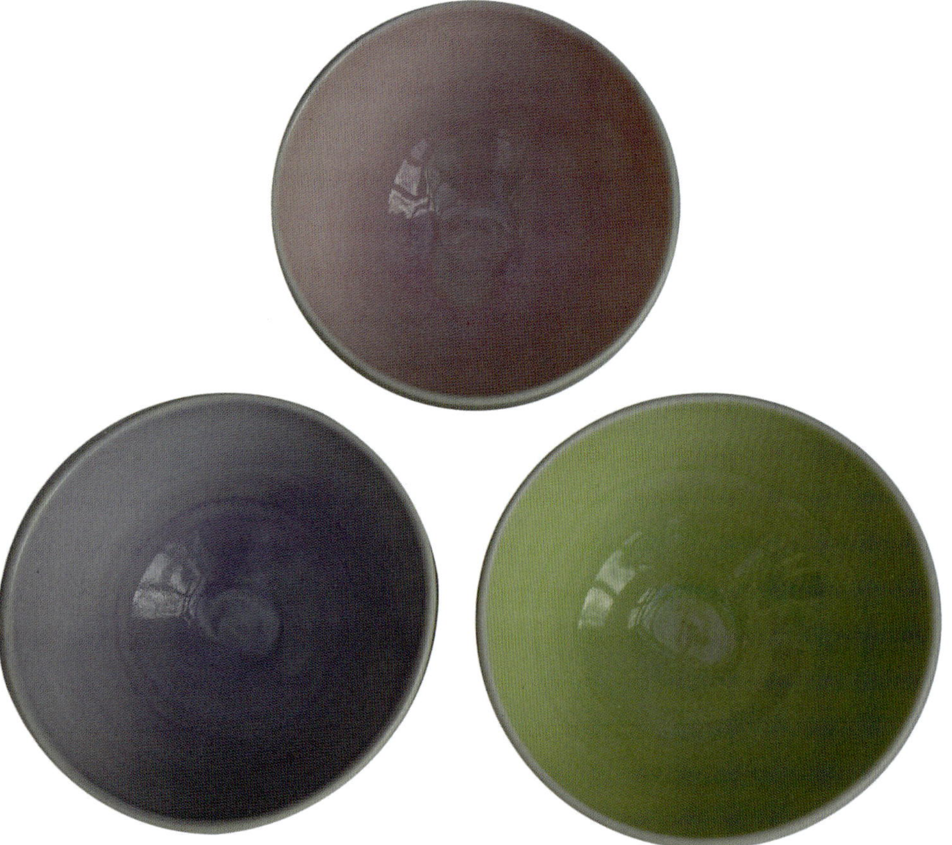

LEFT: Top: erbium.
Bottom left: neodymium.
Bottom right: praseodymium oxides, 6% in an alkaline glaze on porcelain, fired in oxidation.

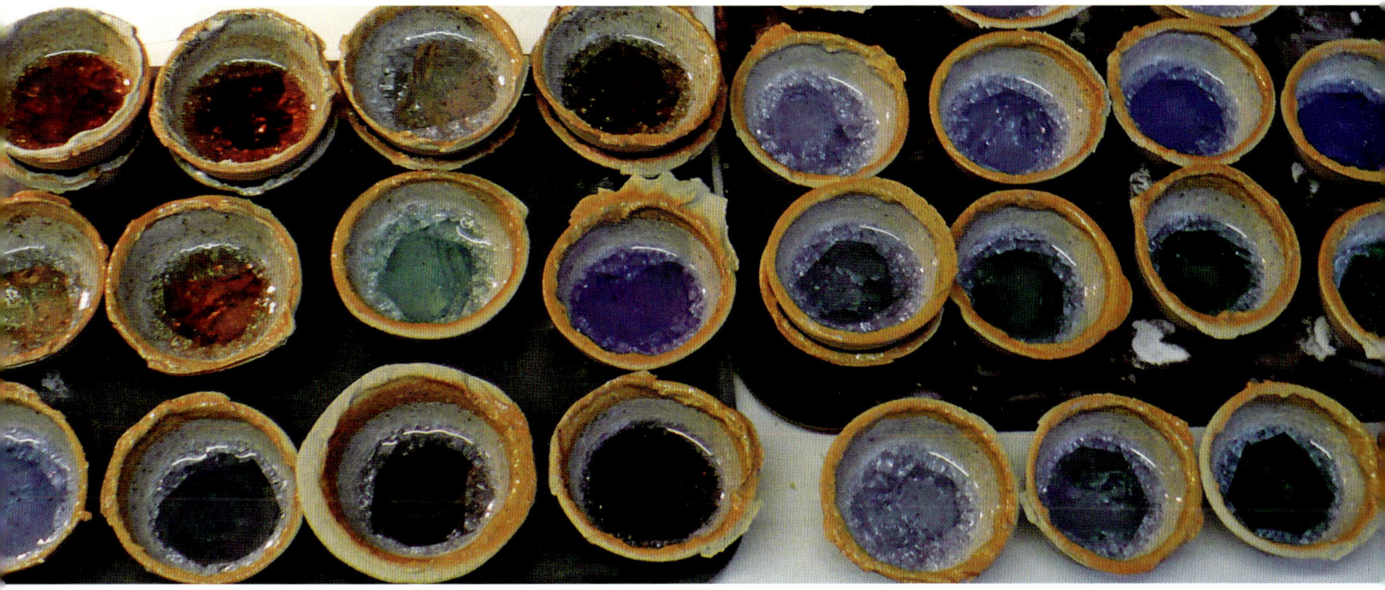

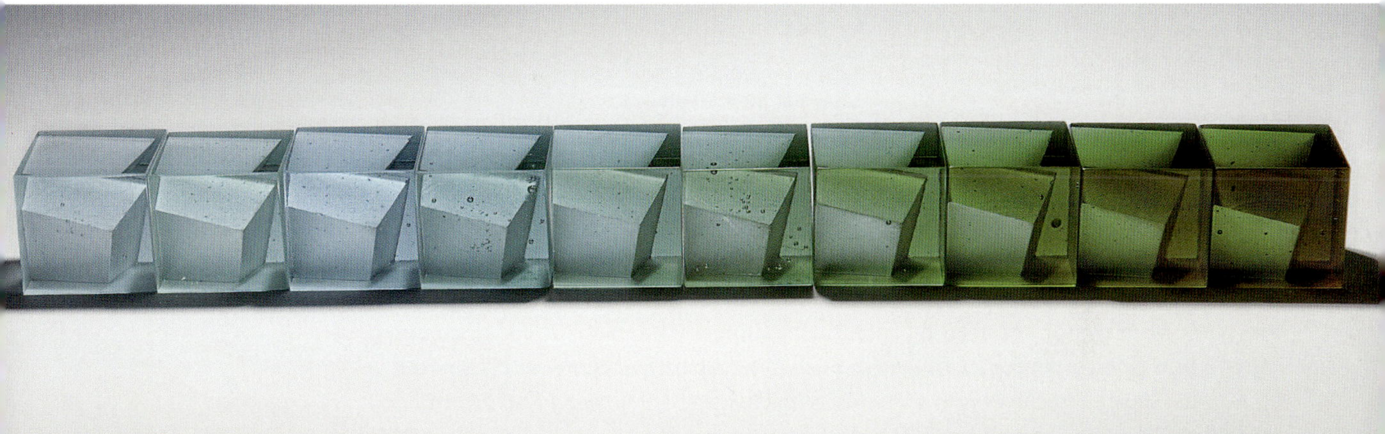

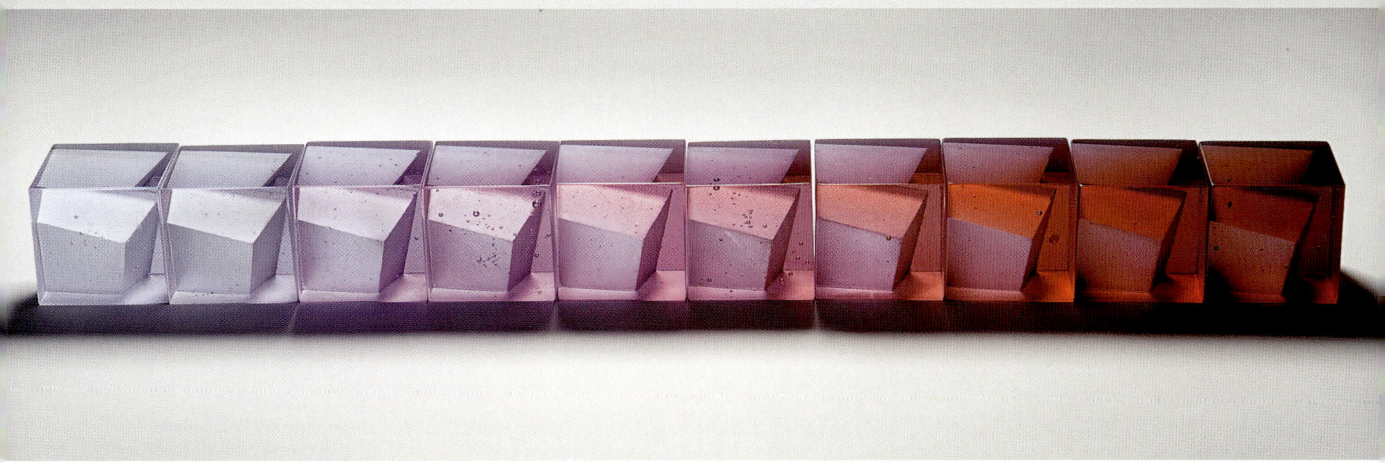

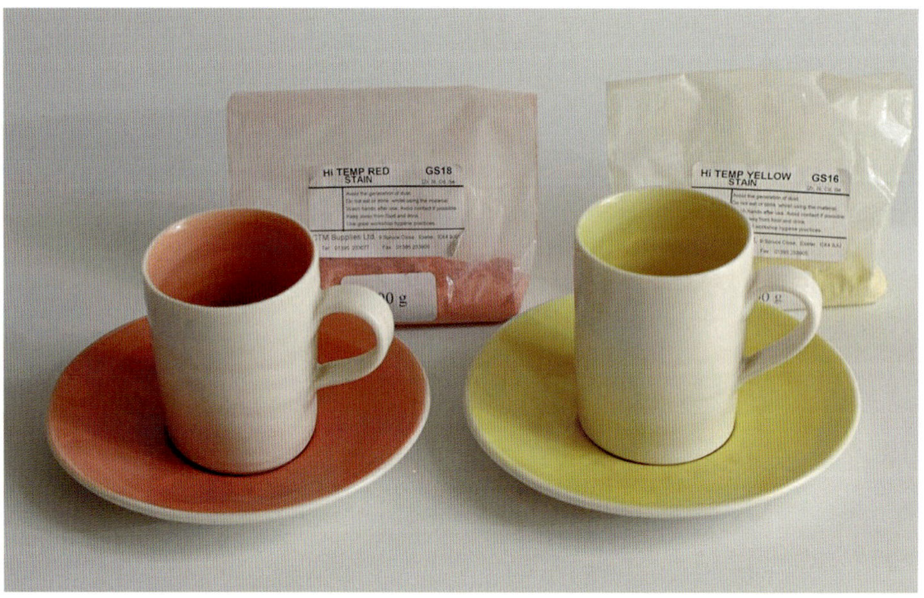

Red and yellow cadmium selenide stains on porcelain, fired to 1260°C (2300°F).

Stains

Stains are made by calcining (heating) colouring oxides together with silica, alumina and opacifiers in a kiln. They are heated, then cooled and ground to a powder, which can be dispersed in a glaze and remain suspended in the glaze during firing. Some stains have the spinel structure and are very stable and highly refractory, so they do not dissolve in the glaze. Spinel ($MgAl_2O_4$) is a mineral, with a cubic, close-packed crystal structure in which the atoms are packed as densely as possible. The magnesium and aluminium can be replaced by cobalt, zinc, iron or chromium to make coloured spinels. Iron zinc chromite is a brown spinel, while cobalt zinc alumina chromite is a blue-green spinel and cobalt iron chromite is black. These colours can also be obtained by adding the same oxides directly to a suitable base glaze.

Other stains are based on the zircon ($ZrSiO_4$) structure, with some of the zirconium replaced by colouring oxides. These include the vanadium turquoise stain[2], praseodymium yellow and iron zirconium coral. The oxides in these stains need to be heated together to produce the stain before adding to a glaze. Stains based on the same system are compatible and can be blended together to produce secondary colours, for example turquoise and yellow combine to make green. Red, orange and some yellow stains are made not from oxides but from cadmium sulphide, zinc sulphide and cadmium selenide. If these are encapsulated in a zirconium silicate crystal matrix, they can be fired to high temperatures. Manganese and alumina can be made into a pink stain, used as a body stain or added to glazes with a high clay content. Chrome and tin are combined with

[2] Stains based on ziconium silicate are written, for example, ZrVSi. The vanadium is substituted for some of the zirconium in the $ZrSiO_4$ crystal lattice, so the stain formula is actually $ZrVSiO_4$.

Stains and alternative oxides (for oxidation)

Stain		Alternative oxide
Dark blue	CoSi	Cobalt oxide, iron and manganese
Bright blue	CoZnAl	Cobalt carbonate
Blue green	CoCr	Cobalt oxide and chromium oxide
Green	Cr	Chromium oxide or copper oxide
Yellow green	ZrVSn	Chromium oxide in alkaline glaze
Turquoise	ZrVSi	Copper oxide in alkaline glaze
Pink	CrSn	Rutile and tin oxide
Maroon	CrSn	Chromium oxide and tin oxide
Purple	CoCrSn	Cobalt, chromium and tin oxide
Dark brown	FeZnCrMn	Iron oxide and manganese dioxide
Red brown	FeZnCr	Iron oxide and tin oxide
Yellow brown	FeZnCrAl	Iron oxide or ilmenite in calcium glaze
Yellow	ZrPrSi	Iron oxide and titanium or rutile
Bright yellow	ZrSiCdS	No alternative
Bright orange	ZrSiCdSe	Yellow and red stain
Rust red	ZrFeSi	Iron oxide and bone ash
Bright red	ZrSiCdSe	No alternative
Black	CoCrNiFe	Cobalt, iron, manganese and chromium
Grey	CoNiSn	Cobalt oxide and nickel oxide
White	ZrSi	Tin oxide or zirconium silicate

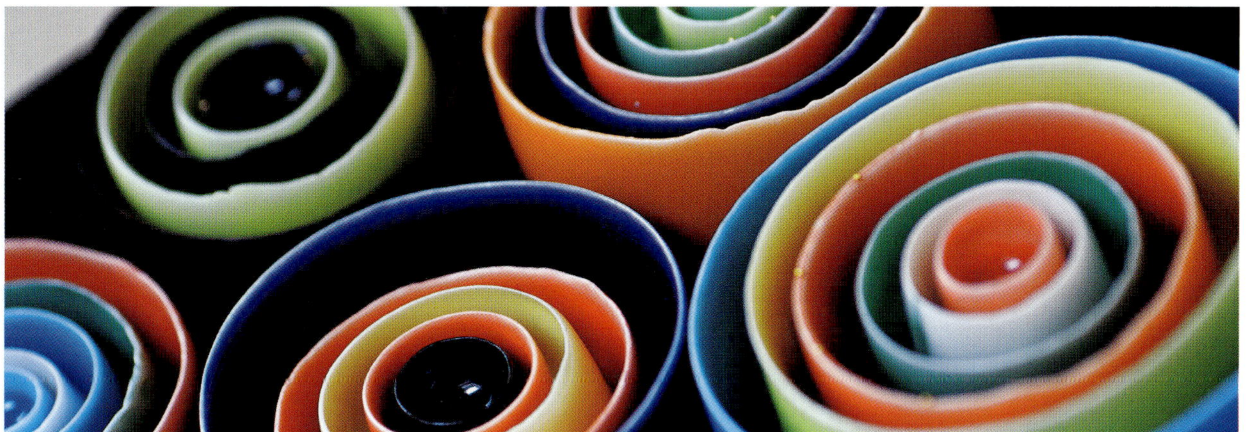

Installation, Chun Liao, 2009. Porcelain, gold, fired to 1255°C (2291°F). *Photo: Phil Sayer.*

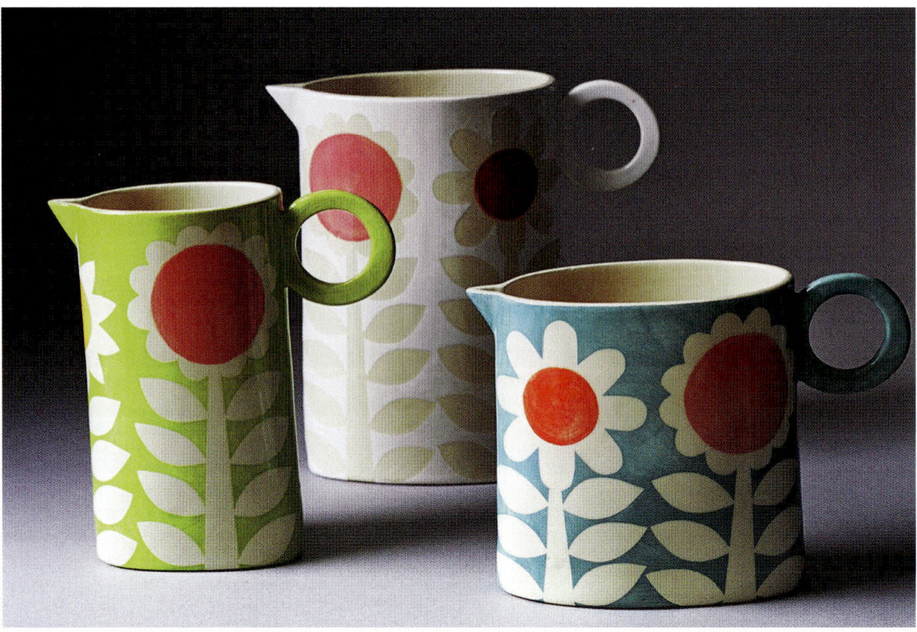

Flower jugs, Ken Eardley, 2002. Slab-built earthenware, paper resist, brushed on underglaze stains, ht: 17cm (6¾in). *Photo: Sussie Ahlburg.*

calcium and silica to make a chrome-tin pink stain widely used in glazes, although this is not as stable as zircon-based stains. Commercial stains are often stabilised with opacifiers such as tin or zirconium, and are refractory. They opacify glazes and increase viscosity, so glazes sometimes appear under-fired. If this occurs, the silica content in the glaze can be reduced. It is not necessary for studio potters to use stains for blues, greens or browns, as these colours can easily be obtained using cobalt, copper, chromium, manganese and iron oxides, which dissolve in the glaze, giving transparency and depth. However, stains are the only way to obtain bright yellow and red. Stains have some advantages over oxides, including stability and consistency, but they often look flat and opaque.

COLOUR DEVELOPMENT

In the following glaze recipes for earthenware, stoneware and porcelain, colours have been achieved using oxides wherever possible. Small amounts of oxides (0.1–2%) are generally used to give delicate transparent colours, and to avoid saturating the glaze. Earthenware glazes are based on borosilicate or alkaline frits, rather than lead. Alkaline glazes are transparent but often crazed, while calcium borate glazes are craze-free, but can sometimes be cloudy. Lead glazes are still used by some potters, but concerns with leaching of lead have resulted in the widespread use of lead-free glazes. Some of the glazes contain low alumina to encourage a good colour response, and may not be suitable for functional ware. Most of the following glazes have been fired in oxidation, but some reduction glazes for stoneware are included for comparison. The clays used are Valentines low-fire white earthenware, Scarva Earthstone Original white stoneware and Valentines Royale porcelain. Glaze recipes are written by weight per cent and should add up to 100, but where adjustments have been made this is not always the case. The feldspar and fluxes are listed first, then the clay, silica and, finally, the colouring oxide additions at the end of each recipe.

Blue glazes

Pure cobalt oxide gives a stark, bright blue, which can be toned down by adding iron and manganese oxides in this ratio: one part cobalt, one part iron and two parts manganese. In Imperial China and Japan, an unrefined cobalt ore (asbolite) was used, which gave a muted dark blue. The blue colour in a glaze is affected by the flux used: cobalt turns lavender in the presence of magnesia, and pink in magnesia glazes that are low in silica. Cobalt also tends towards purple-blue in high-boron glazes. A brilliant blue can be produced in barium glazes. A deep blue is produced with zinc, tending towards green with very large amounts of zinc oxide. Cobalt and titanium or rutile produces a crystalline pale green in high-alumina glazes or slips. If cobalt and chromium oxides are combined, a range of teal blue-greens may be obtained. Nickel and cobalt combine to make grey. Nickel oxide gives a steel blue in barium-zinc glazes and zinc crystalline glazes, but this is because it commonly contains a small amount of cobalt as an impurity.

Stoneware coffee pot, Jeremy Nichols, 2008. Sprayed cobalt-blue stain, salt-glazed. *Photo: Jeremy Nichols.*

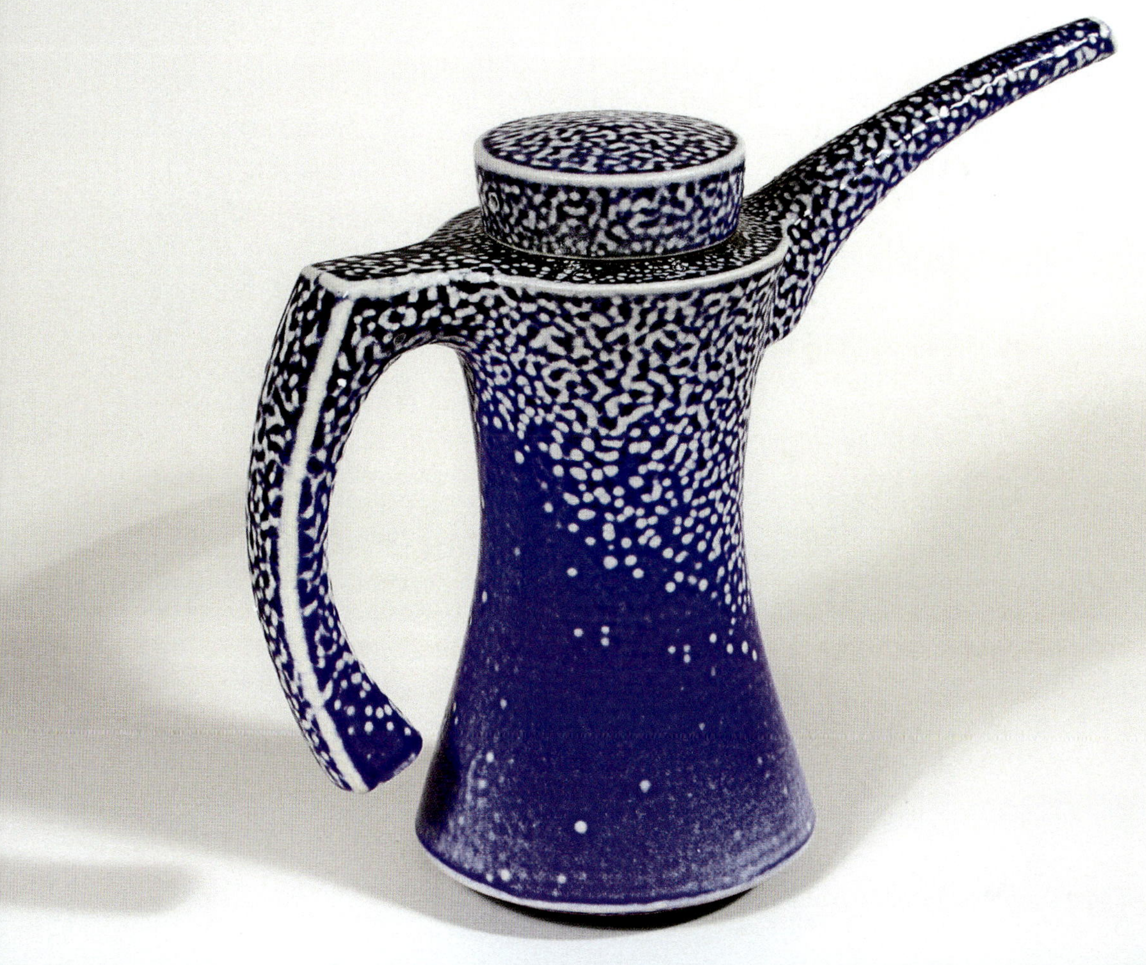

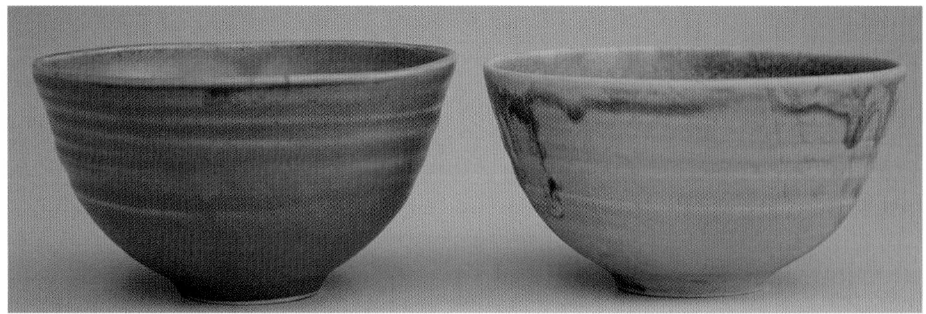

Cobalt blue magnesia glaze (left) (SiO_2: Al_2O_3 8.7, 22% quartz, 6% clay).
Cobalt pink magnesia glaze (right) (SiO_2: Al_2O_3 5.4 11% quartz, 20% clay).

Blue glazes for earthenware 1060–1100°C (1940–2012°F), (cone 04–02), oxidised

Transparent blue glaze, 1060°C/1940°F (cone 04) oxidised (John Solly)

Calcium borate frit	39
Soda feldspar	27
Whiting	5
China clay	6
Quartz	23
+	
Cobalt oxide	0.1

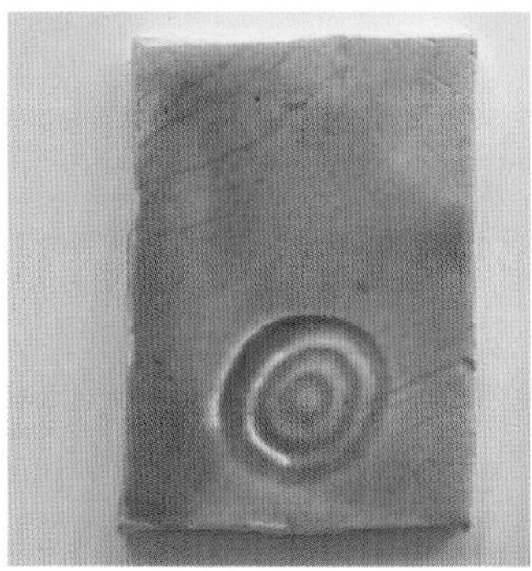

Mid-blue satin glaze, 1100°C/2012°F (cone 02) oxidised (Tony Hansen)

Calcium borate frit	44
Talc	8
Whiting	8
China clay	12
Quartz	28
+	
Cobalt oxide	0.5

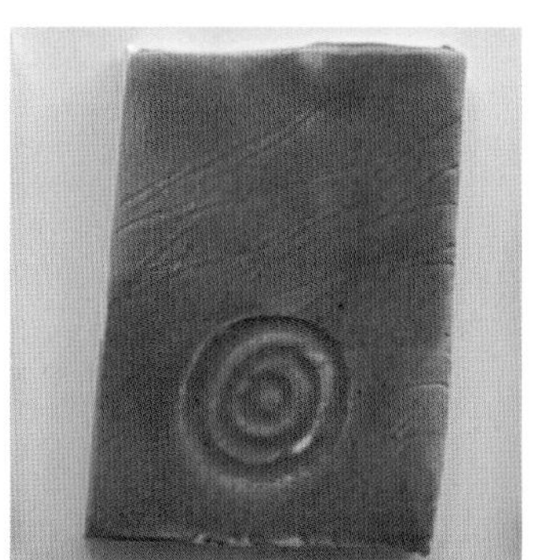

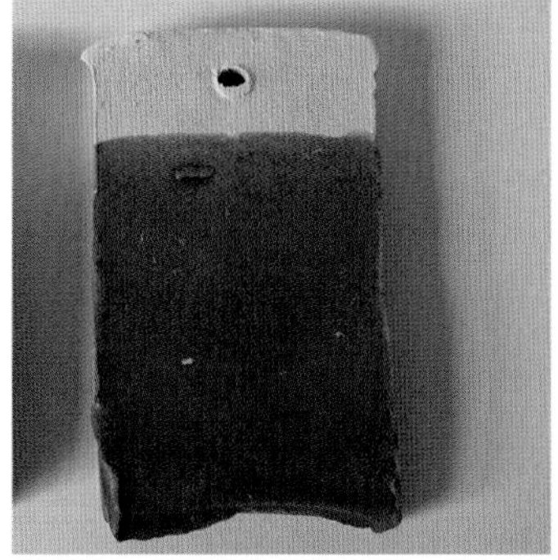

Grey-blue glaze, 1060°C/1940°F (cone 04) oxidised

Calcium borate frit	39
Soda feldspar	27
Whiting	5
China clay	6
Quartz	23
+	
Cobalt oxide	0.5
Rutile	2

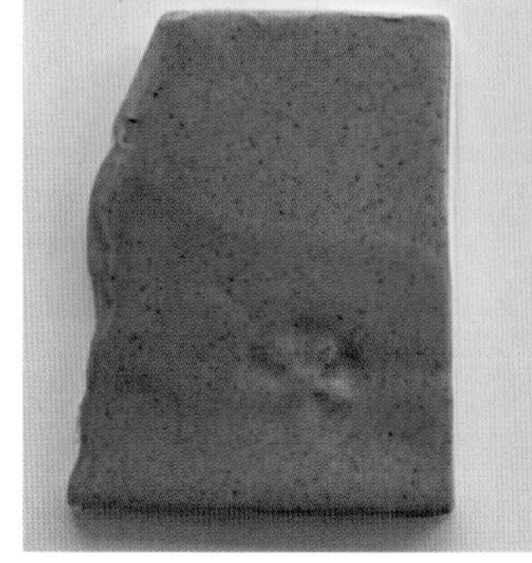

Matt cornflower blue, 1060°C/1940°F (cone 04) oxidised (Lucy Burley)

Borax frit	45
Potash feldspar	15
Barium carbonate	10
Ball clay	15
China clay	15
+	
Blue stain (CoZnSi)	2

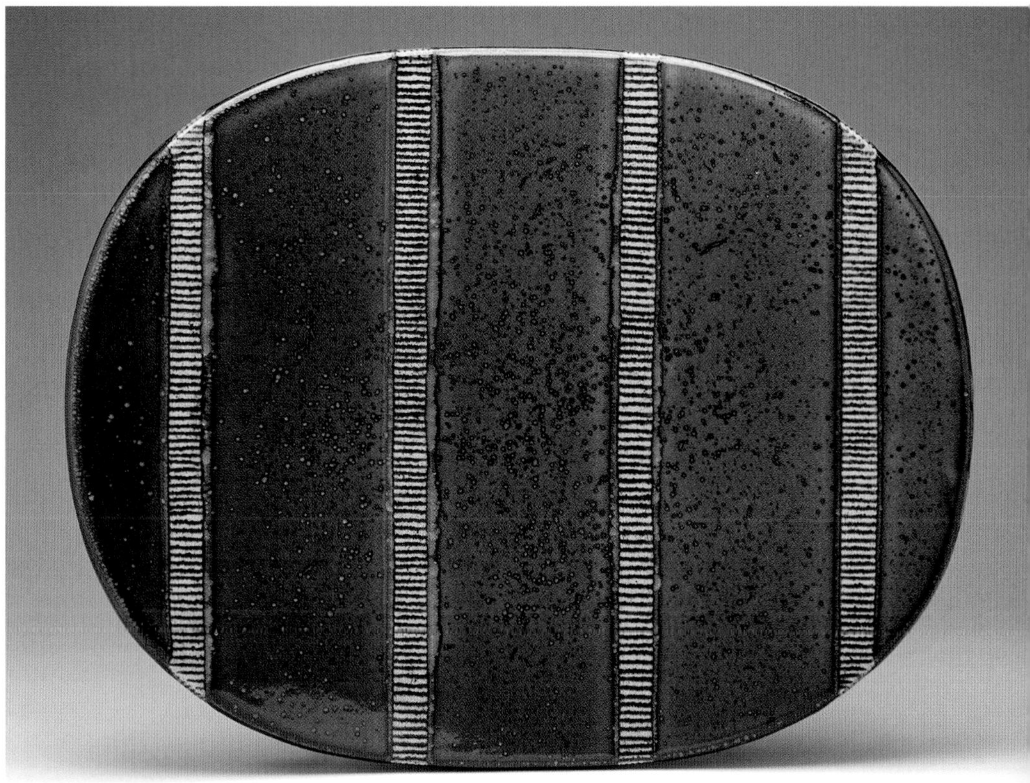

Dark striped platter, Karen Bunting, 2009. Stoneware, paper resist, inlaid oxide, cobalt, iron and manganese glaze, reduction-fired to 1280°C (2336°F). *Photo: Stephen Brayne*.

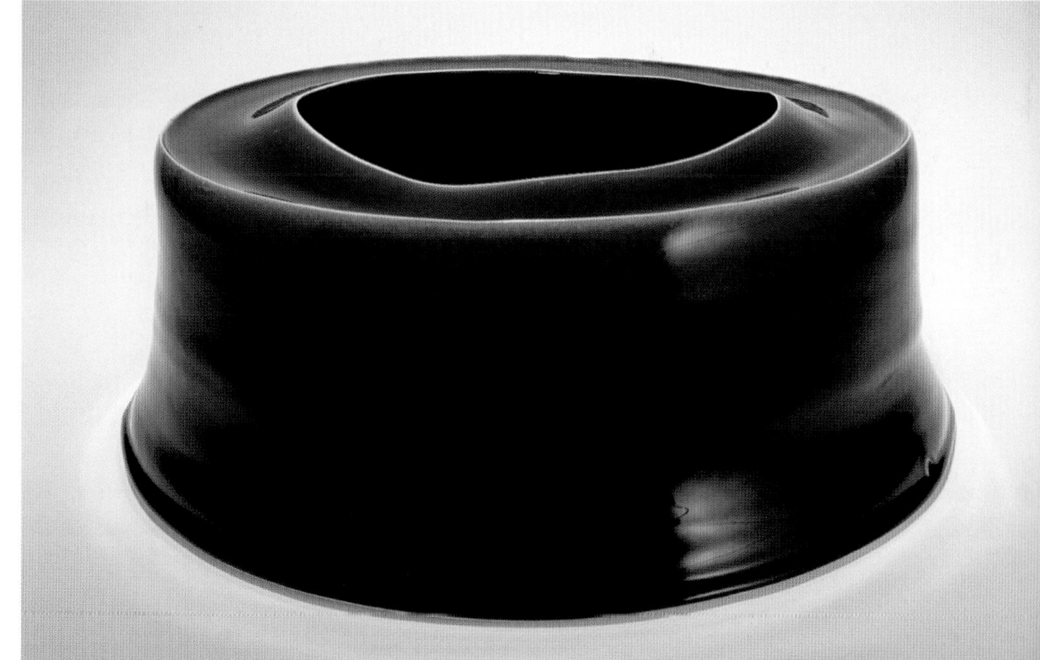

Large midnight, Tanya Gomez, 2010. Thrown porcelain, cobalt blue stain. dia: 45cm (17¾in), ht: 17cm (6¾in). *Photo: Dominic Tschudin*.

Blue glazes for stoneware 1240-1280°C/2300–2336°F (cone 6-9)

Cobalt blue runny transparent, 1260°C/2300°F (cone 8) oxidised (Stephen Murfitt)

Soda feldspar	47
Calcium borate frit	16
Whiting	14
China clay	5
Quartz	18
+	
Cobalt oxide	0.1

Blue runny transparent, 1260°C/2300°F (cone 8) oxidised

Soda feldspar	47
Calcium borate frit	16
Whiting	14
China clay	5
Quartz	18
+	
Cobalt oxide	0.1
Copper oxide	0.5

Barium blue matt, not food-safe, 1240–1260°C/2264–2300°F (cone 6–8) oxidised (Emmanuel Cooper)

Potash feldspar	38
Barium carbonate	38
Lithium carbonate	3
China clay	5
Quartz	16
+	
Cobalt oxide	0.1
Copper oxide	0.5

Blue stiff transparent, 1280°C/2336°F (cone 9) oxidised (Tony Hansen)

Potash feldspar	27
Whiting	21
China clay	20
Quartz	32
+	
Cobalt oxide	0.1
Copper oxide	0.5

Cobalt-chrome teal blue, 1280°C/2336°F (cone 9) oxidised (Tony Hansen)

Potash feldspar	27
Whiting	21
China clay	20
Quartz	32
+	
Cobalt oxide	0.2
Chrome oxide	0.5

Cobalt-chrome barium blue, not food-safe, 1240–1260°C/2264–2300°F (cone 6–8) oxidised (Emmanuel Cooper)

Potash feldspar	38
Barium carbonate	38
Lithium carbonate	3
China clay	5
Quartz	16
+	
Cobalt oxide	0.2
Chrome oxide	0.5

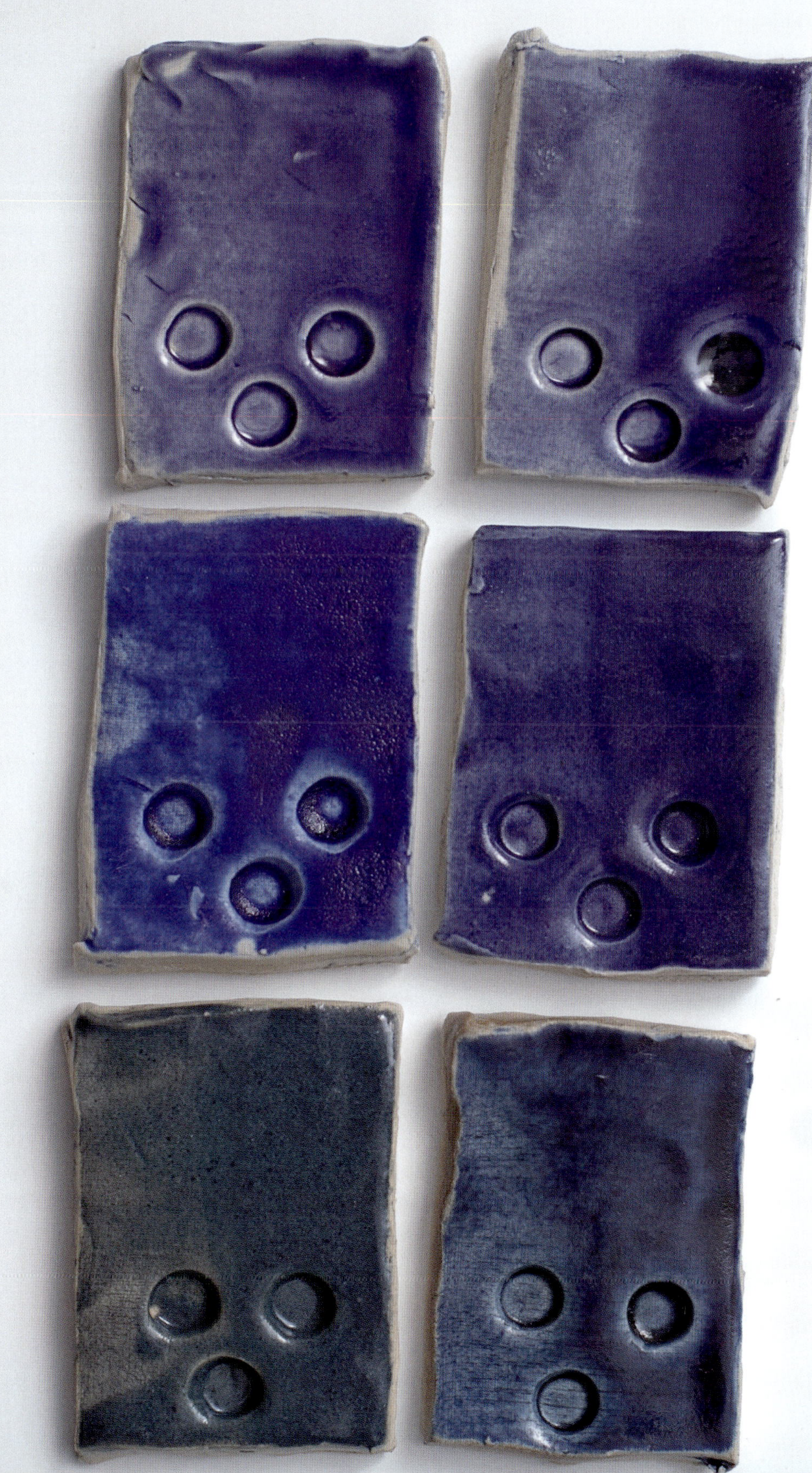

Blue glazes for porcelain 1240–1280°C/2264–2336°F (cone 7–9) oxidised

Blue-pink magnesium crystalline matt, 1260°C/2300°F (cone 8) oxidised

Soda feldspar	41
Dolomite	22
Whiting	3
Zinc oxide	5
China clay	18
Bentonite	2
Quartz	11
+	
Cobalt oxide	0.75
Tin oxide	4

Rutile-cobalt blue, 1260°C/2300°F (cone 8) oxidised (Stephen Murfitt)

Potash feldspar	34
Calcium borate frit	14
Whiting	11
Dolomite	5
China clay	13
Quartz	23
+	
Cobalt carbonate	0.4
Rutile	5

Blue magnesium crystalline matt, 1240–1260°C/2264–2300°F (cone 6-8) oxidised (Michael Bailey)

Soda feldspar	42
Dolomite	22
Whiting	3
Zinc oxide	5
China clay	4
Bentonite	2
Quartz	22
+	
Cobalt oxide	0.75

Grey-blue transparent, 1280°C/2336°F (cone 9) oxidised

Potash feldspar	26
Whiting	20
China clay	19
Quartz	30
Calcium borate frit	5
+	
Cobalt carbonate	1
Red iron oxide	1
Manganese dioxide	2

Blue crystalline glossy, 1260°C/2300°F (cone 8) oxidised

Soda feldspar	42
Dolomite	22
Whiting	3
Zinc oxide	5
China clay	4
Bentonite	2
Quartz	22
+	
Cobalt oxide	0.75
Tin oxide	2

Midnight blue-black, 1280°C/2336°F (cone 9) oxidised

Potash feldspar	27
Whiting	21
China clay	20
Quartz	32
+	
Cobalt oxide	2
Iron oxide	2
Manganese dioxide	2

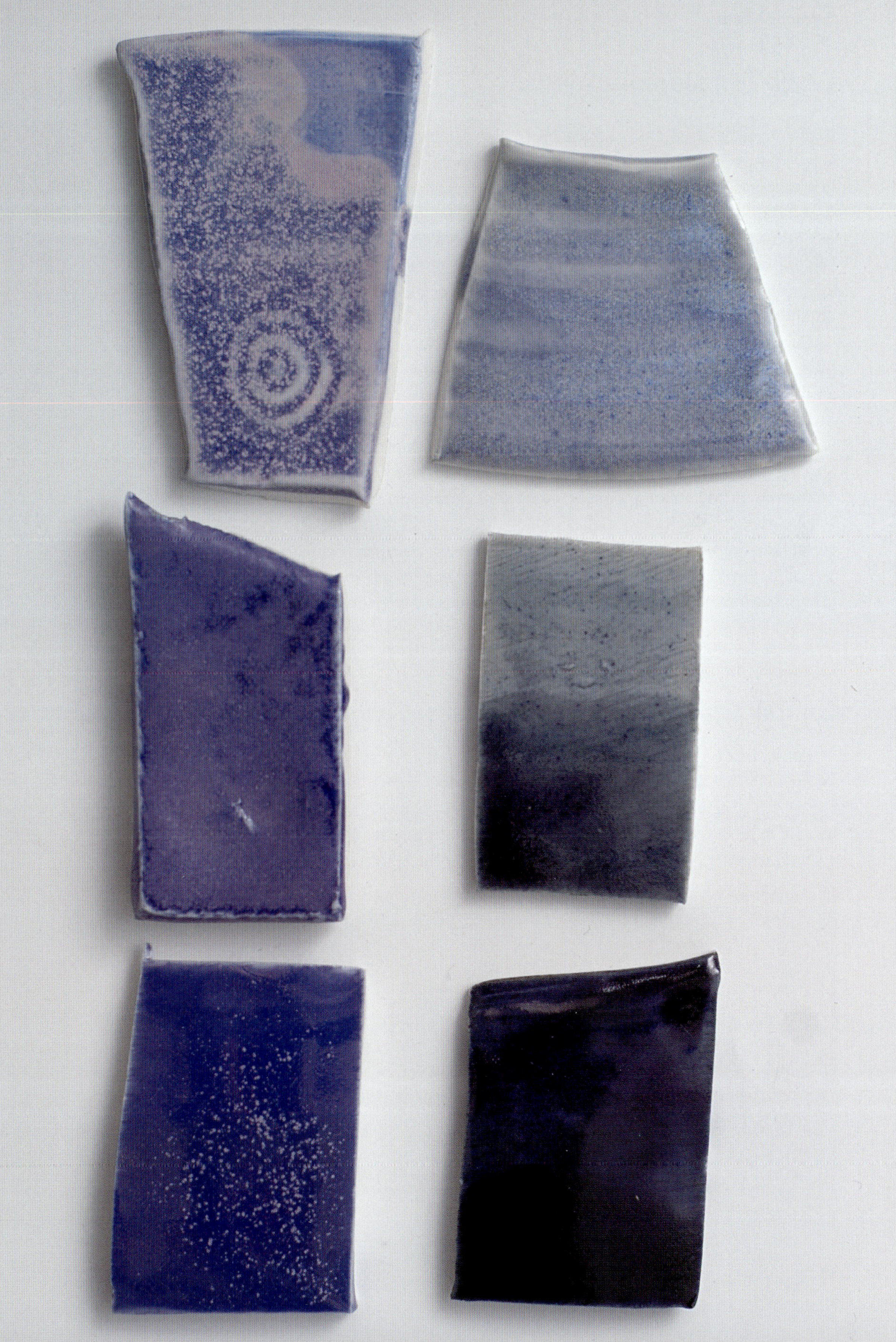

Green and turquoise glazes

Copper oxide is often used to make green glazes, although the colour is affected by the kiln atmosphere and flux used in the glaze. In reduction, copper reds can be achieved in alkaline glazes containing tin oxide (see p.90). Copper is volatile, and may cause pink flashing on surrounding pots. In oxidation, alkaline glazes with low alumina will give bright turquoise glazes with copper. Alkaline glazes are generally those high in sodium, lithium, barium or strontium. Other oxides can be added to change the colour: iron for yellow-green, nickel for olive green or ilmenite for blue-green. Turquoise can also be obtained using vanadium zircon stains, which are opaque.

Copper in lead glazes gives a deep green, but may cause lead to leach out if the glaze is in contact with acidic foods. Cobalt and iron can be used instead to make green in lead-based glazes.

Chromium oxide gives a reliable green, unaffected by kiln atmosphere, although it is volatile at high temperatures. Cobalt and chrome combine to make teal blue-greens. In alkaline glazes, a bright chartreuse green may be obtained using a small amount (0.2%) of chromium oxide. Zinc should be avoided in chrome glazes, as it turns the chromium brown, except in high-zinc, high-alumina glazes, which turn pink with the addition of chromium. Cobalt and titania or rutile can produce a pale green in high-alumina glazes and slips. Nickel and titania will give green in magnesium matt and zinc crystalline glazes. The rare earth praseodymium oxide provides a pale yellow-green in glazes.

Recipe for blue-green underglaze (19th century) (from *Pottery Gazette*, London, 1880s, Smith, Greenwood & Co)

Chrome oxide	30 lbs
Zinc oxide	20 lbs
Cobalt oxide	9.5 lbs
Flint	25 lbs

Calcine in glost oven (1050°C/1922°F/cone 04) in flinted saggars. This recipe produces a cobalt-chrome blue-green, which is stabilised by the addition of zinc oxide. The same

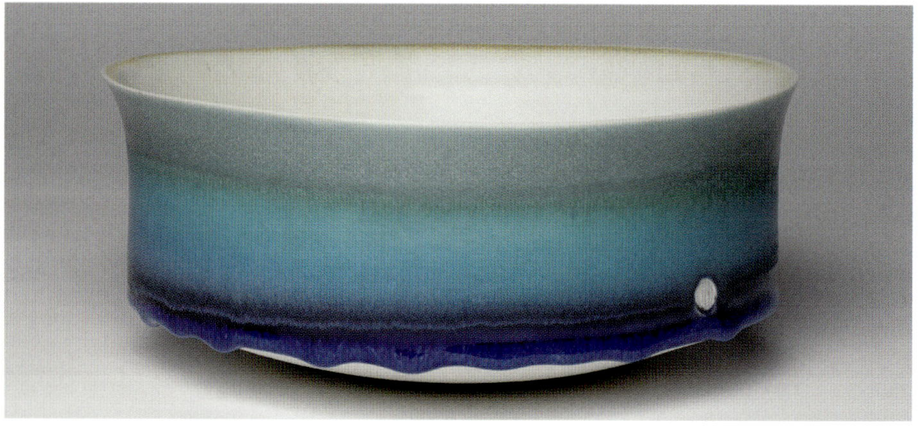

Storm brewing, Tanya Gomez, 2007. Thrown porcelain paper clay, turquoise and blue glazes, w: 25cm (9¾in). *Photo: Ray Fowler.*

Soda-fired bottle, Ruthanne Tudball, 2007. Cobalt and titanium slips. *Photo: Ruthanne Tudball.*

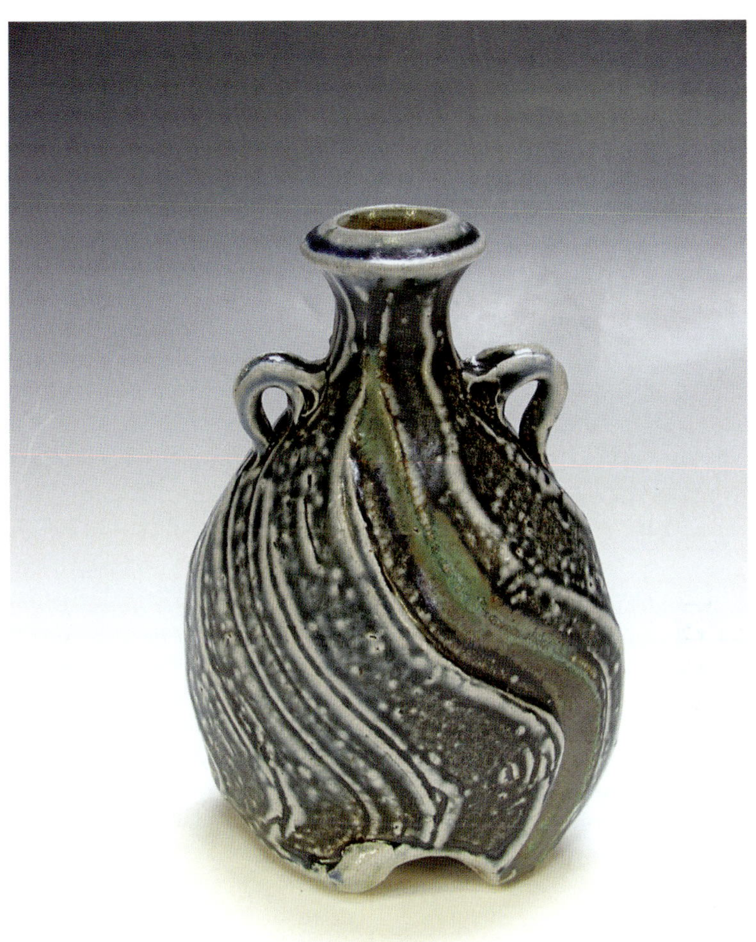

BELOW: *Oval bowl*, Leah Leitson, 2002. Thrown and altered porcelain, soda-glazed. *Photo: Tim Barnwell.*

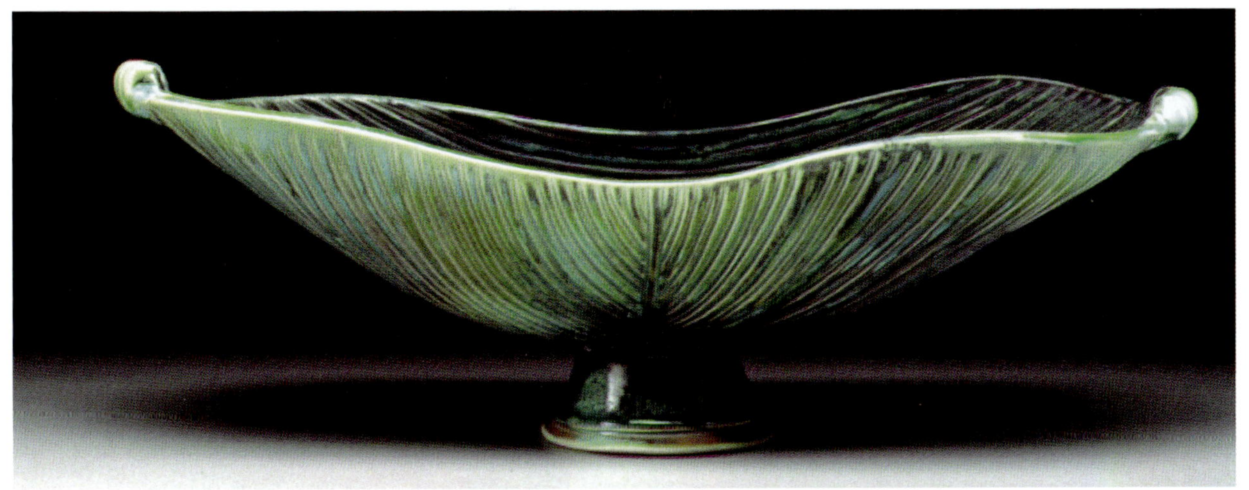

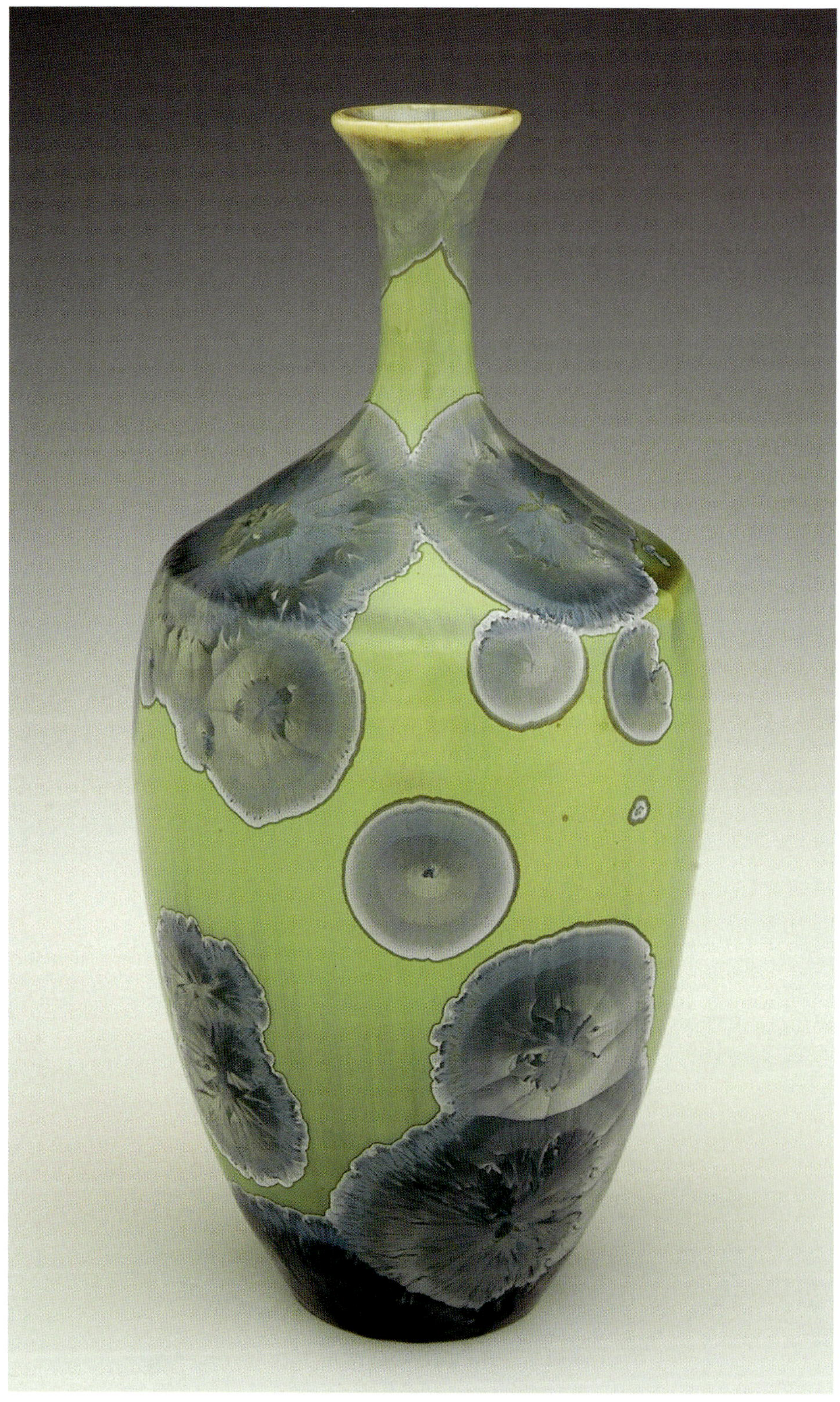

LEFT: *Porcelain bottle*, Avril Farley, 2007. Crystalline glaze with copper, cobalt and cerium oxide, ht: 18cm (7in). *Photo: William Campbell.*

RIGHT: *Two jars*, Stephen Parry, 2008. Ash glazes, wood-fired, ht: 9cm (3½in). The jar on the left shows cloudy opalescence from phosphorus in the ash. *Photo: Stephen Parry.*

colour can be obtained if cobalt and chrome are added to a suitable base glaze.
Ash glazes are often green, when fired in reducing conditions, the colour coming from iron oxide present in the ash. Ash from different trees contains varying proportions of minerals, which result in a range of colours in the glaze, from olive to apple green. Iron oxide is also used in celadon glazes, which are grey-green, or blue if there is no titanium present in the glaze or clay body. Low alumina and the addition of boron or barium carbonate also promote blue celadon colours.

Celadon 1280°C/2336°F (cone 9) reduction

Potash feldspar	37
Wollastonite	18
Talc	4
China clay	14
Quartz	27
+	
Red iron oxide	0.4

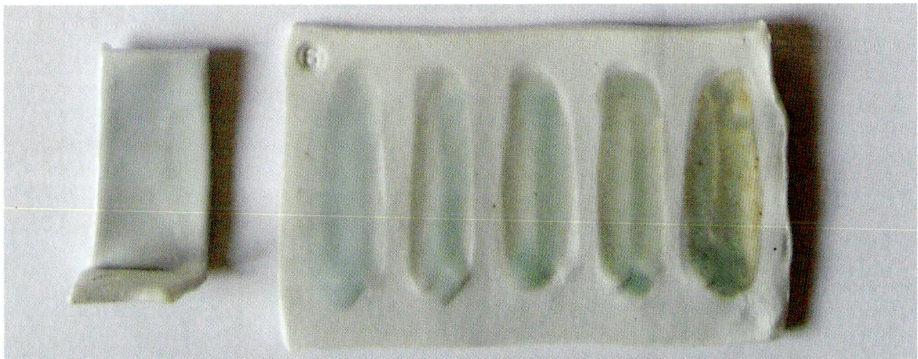

RIGHT: Mirka Golden-Hann, 2010. Celadon glaze with, from left, 0.4%, 0.7%, 1.0%, 1.4% and 1.8% iron oxide fired in reduction to cone 9. The L-shaped tile on the left is glazed with the base glaze containing no iron oxide. *Photo: Mirka Golden-Hann.*

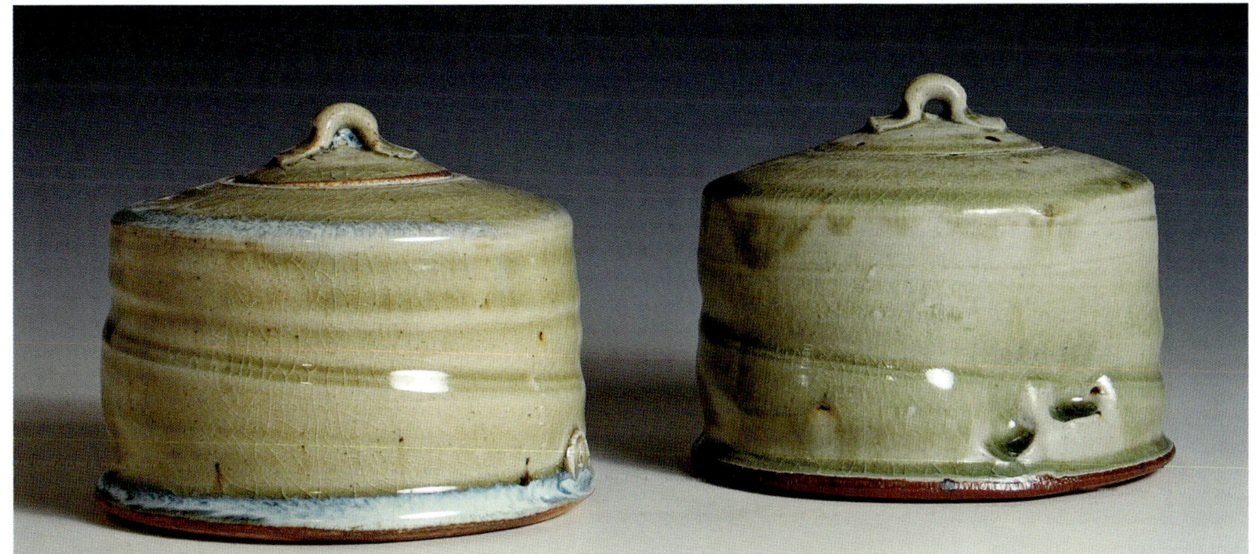

Green glazes for earthenware 1000-1100°C/1832–2012°F (cone 04) oxidised

(The discs show pooling of thickly applied glaze)

Not food safe. To avoid crazing, use borax frit instead of high-alkaline frit.

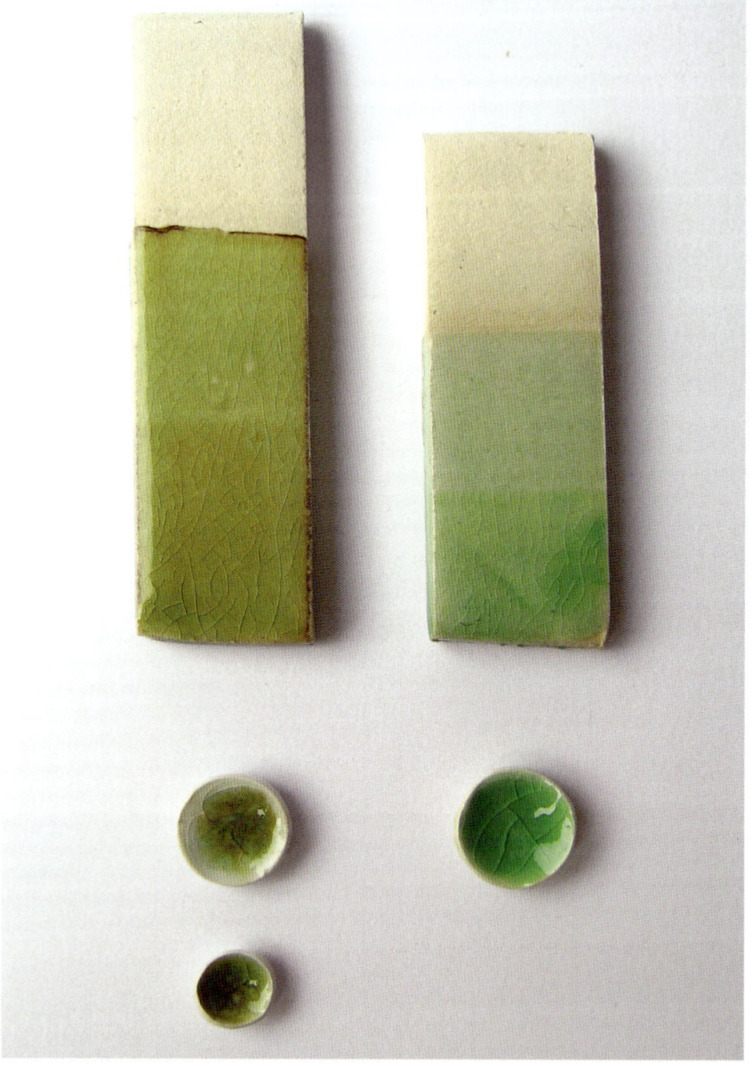

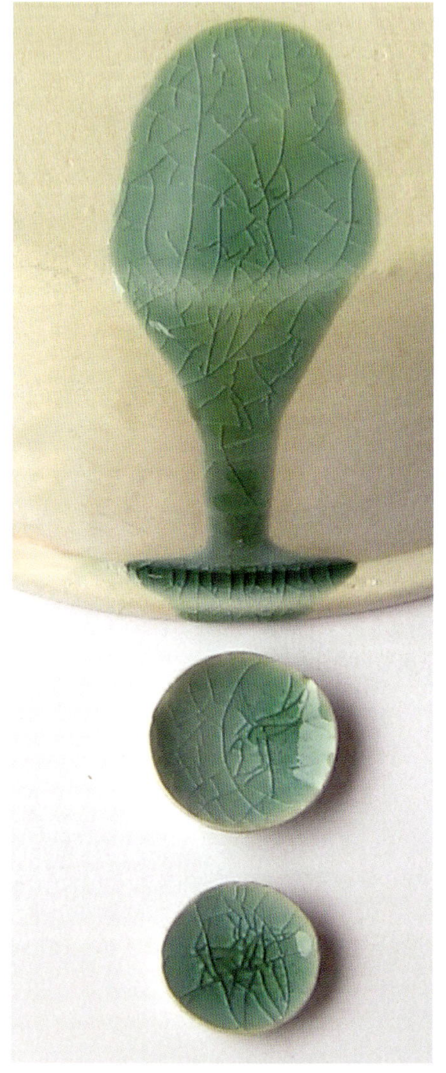

Copper-iron green, 1060°C/1940°F (cone 04) oxidised (Lok Ming Fung)

High-alkaline frit	75
China clay	15
Flint	10
+	
Copper oxide	0.75
Red iron oxide	8

Copper-chrome green, 1060°C/1940°F (cone 04) oxidised

High-alkaline frit	75
China clay	15
Flint	10
+	
Copper oxide	1.5
Chromium oxide	0.4

Copper-ilmenite green, 1060°C/1940°F (cone 04) oxidised

High-alkaline frit	75
China clay	15
Flint	10
+	
Copper oxide	1.5
Ilmenite	6

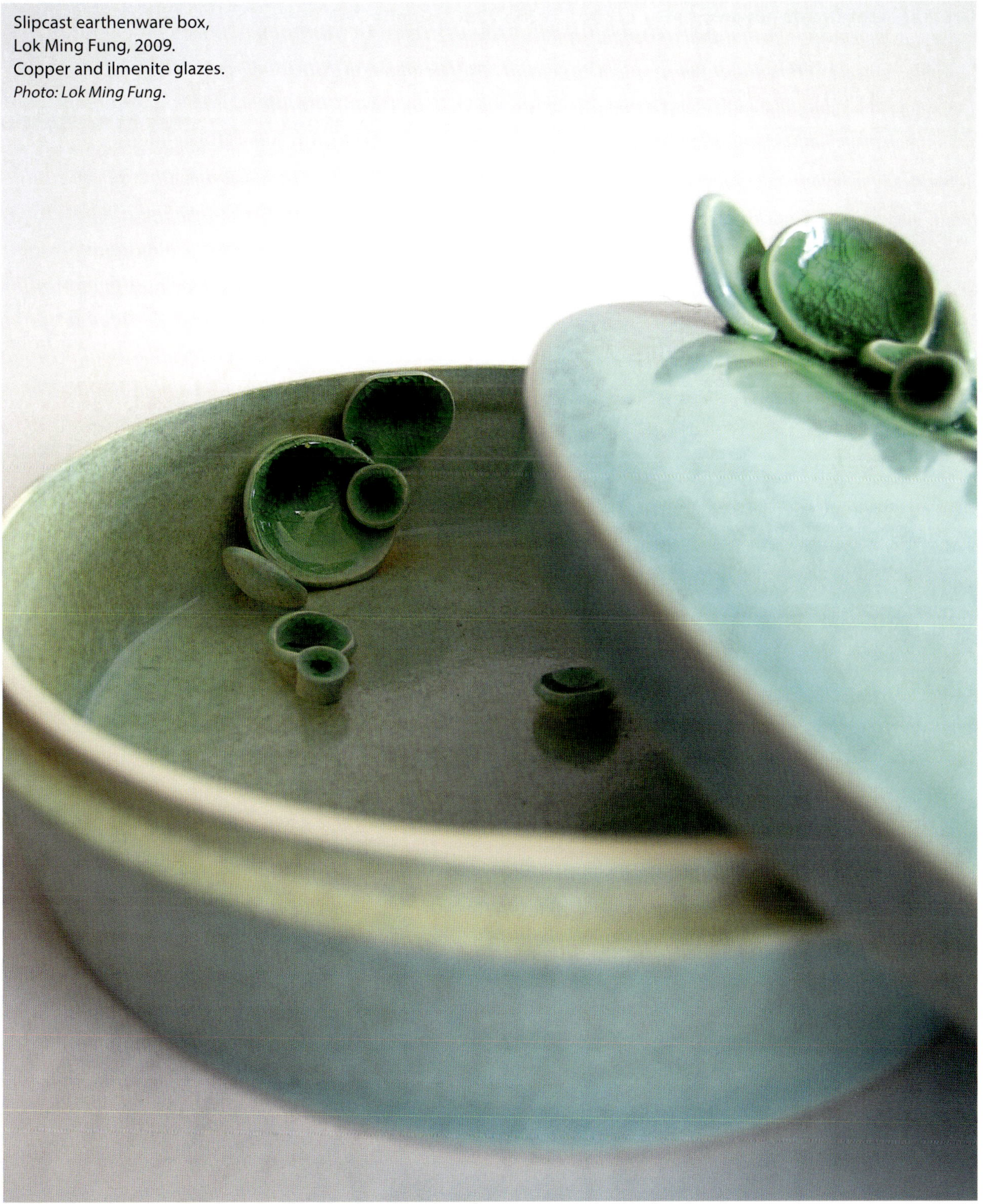

Slipcast earthenware box,
Lok Ming Fung, 2009.
Copper and ilmenite glazes.
Photo: Lok Ming Fung.

Green glazes for stoneware 1240–1280°C/2264–2336°F (cone 7–9)

Celadon runny transparent, 1260°C/2300°F (cone 8) reduced (Derek Emms)

Soda feldspar	47
Calcium borate frit	16
Whiting	14
China clay	5
Quartz	18
+	
Iron oxide	0.5

Copper green stiff transparent, 1280°C/2336°F (cone 9) reduced (Tony Hansen)

Potash feldspar	27
Whiting	21
China clay	20
Quartz	32
+	
Copper oxide	1

Chrome green runny transparent, 1260°C/2300°F (cone 8) oxidised (Stephen Murfitt)

Soda feldspar	47
Calcium borate frit	16
Whiting	14
China clay	5
Quartz	18
+	
Chromium oxide	0.2

Chrome green stiff transparent, 1280°C/2336°F (cone 9) reduced (Stephen Murfitt)

Potash feldspar	27
Whiting	21
China clay	20
Quartz	32
+	
Chromium oxide	0.2

Barium matt chartreuse, not food safe, 1240–1260°C/2264–2300°F (cone 6–8) oxidised (Emmanuel Cooper)

Potash feldspar	38
Barium carbonate	38
Lithium carbonate	3
China clay	5
Quartz	16
+	
Chromium oxide	0.2
Tin oxide	5

Magnesium matt green, 1260°C/2300°F (cone 8) oxidised (Stephen Murfitt)

Potash feldspar	34
Talc	22
Whiting	12
China clay	15
Quartz	16
+	
Copper oxide	1

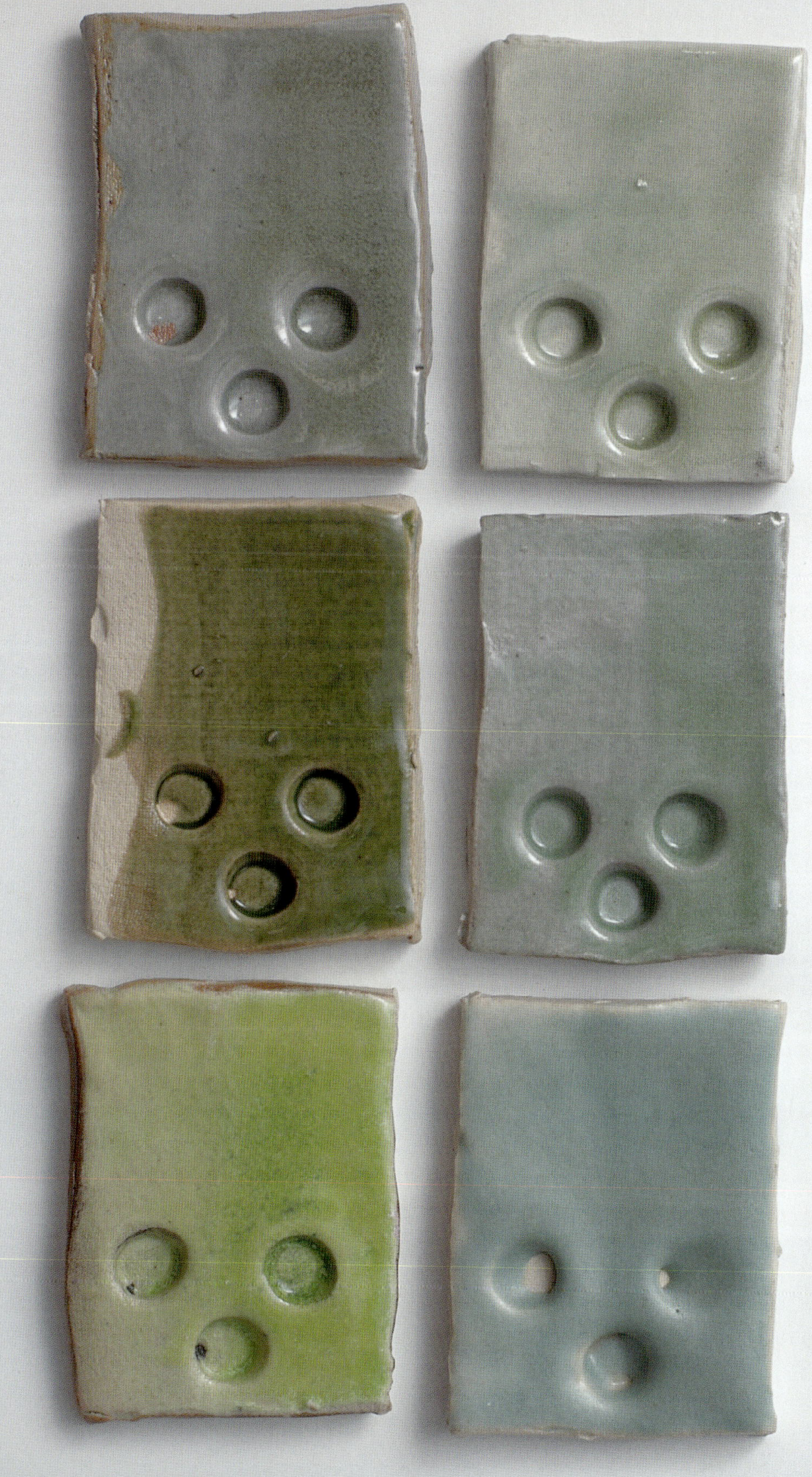

Green glazes for porcelain, 1260–1280°C/2300–2336°F cone 6–9 oxidised

Pale green runny transparent, 1260°C/2300°F (cone 8) oxidised (Stephen Murfitt)

Soda feldspar	47
Calcium borate frit	16
Whiting	14
China clay	5
Quartz	18
+	
Praseodymium oxide	6

Chrome chartreuse transparent, not food safe, 1240–1280°C/2264–2336°F (cone 6–9) oxidised (Will Levi Marshall)

Nepheline syenite	24
Barium carbonate	24
Lithium carbonate	10
Whiting	3
China clay	6
Flint	31
+	
Chromium oxide	0.3

Pale chrome green runny transparent, 1260°C/2300°F (cone 8) oxidised (Stephen Murfitt)

Soda feldspar	47
Calcium borate frit	16
Whiting	14
China clay	5
Quartz	18
+	
Chromium oxide	0.1

Nickel titanium green satin matt, 1260°C/2300°F (cone 8) oxidised (Stephen Murfitt)

Potash feldspar	33
Talc	21
Whiting	12
China clay	15
Quartz	16
Zinc oxide	3
+	
Nickel oxide	3
Titanium dioxide	5

Bright chrome green runny transparent, 1260°C/2300°F (cone 8) oxidised (Stephen Murfitt)

Soda feldspar	47
Calcium borate frit	15
Whiting	13
China clay	5
Quartz	17
+	
Chromium oxide	0.5

Dark copper green runny transparent, 1260°C/2300°F (cone 8) oxidised (Stephen Murfitt)

Soda feldspar	47
Calcium borate frit	16
Whiting	14
China clay	5
Quartz	18
+	
Copper oxide	1
Nickel oxide	0.5

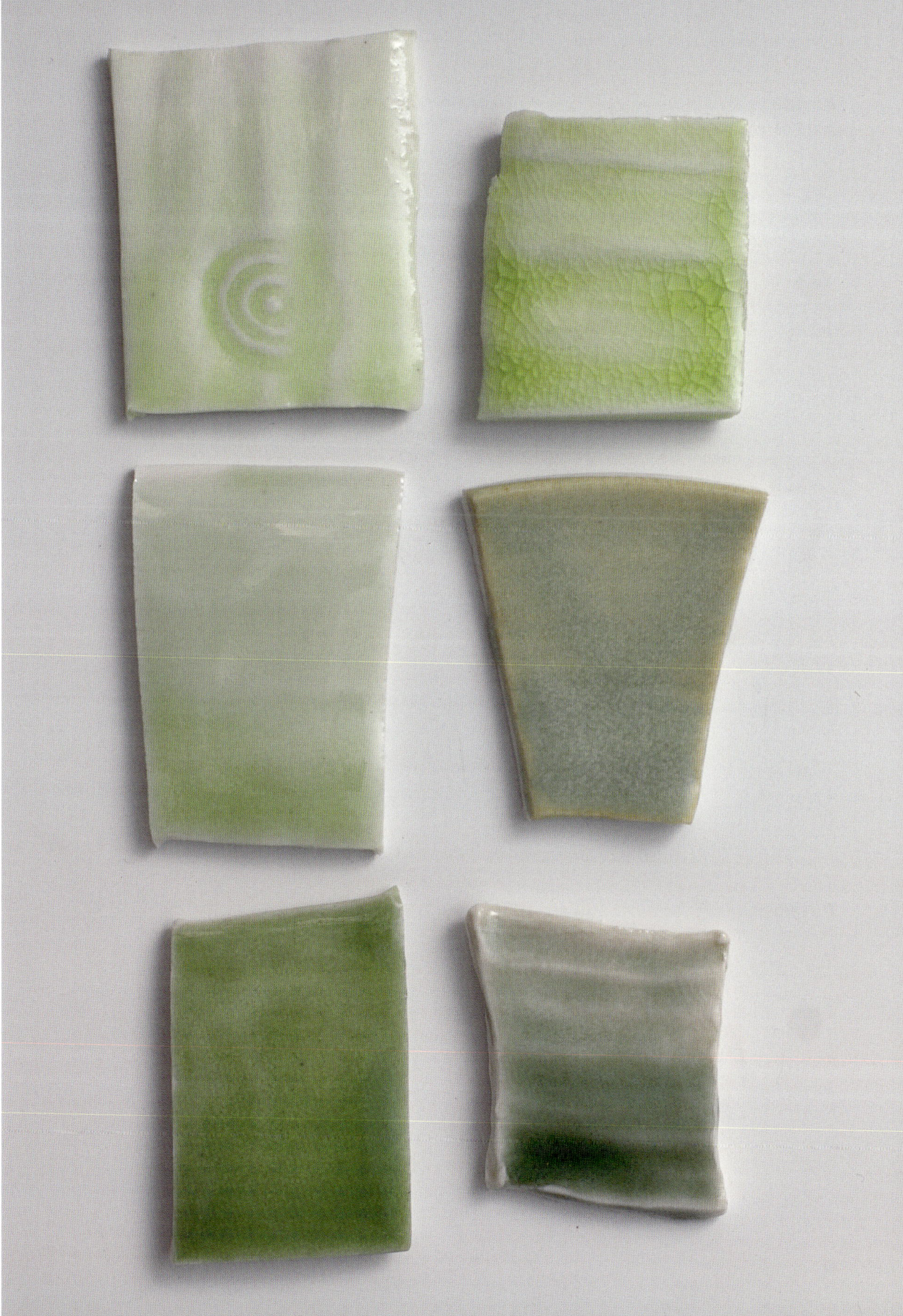

Turquoise and blue-green glazes for earthenware 1060–1100°C/1940–2012°F (cone 04–02) oxidised

Chrome green glaze, 1060°C/1940°F (cone 04) oxidised (John Solly)

Calcium borate frit	39
Soda feldspar	27
Whiting	5
China clay	6
Quartz	23
+	
Chromium oxide	0.2

Duck-egg blue glaze, 1100°C/2012°F (cone 02) oxidised

Calcium borate frit	39
Soda feldspar	27
Whiting	5
China clay	6
Quartz	23
+	
Copper oxide	1
Titanium oxide	5

Turquoise glaze, 1060°C/1940°F (cone 04) oxidised

Calcium borate frit	39
Soda feldspar	27
Whiting	5
China clay	6
Quartz	23
+	
Copper oxide	1

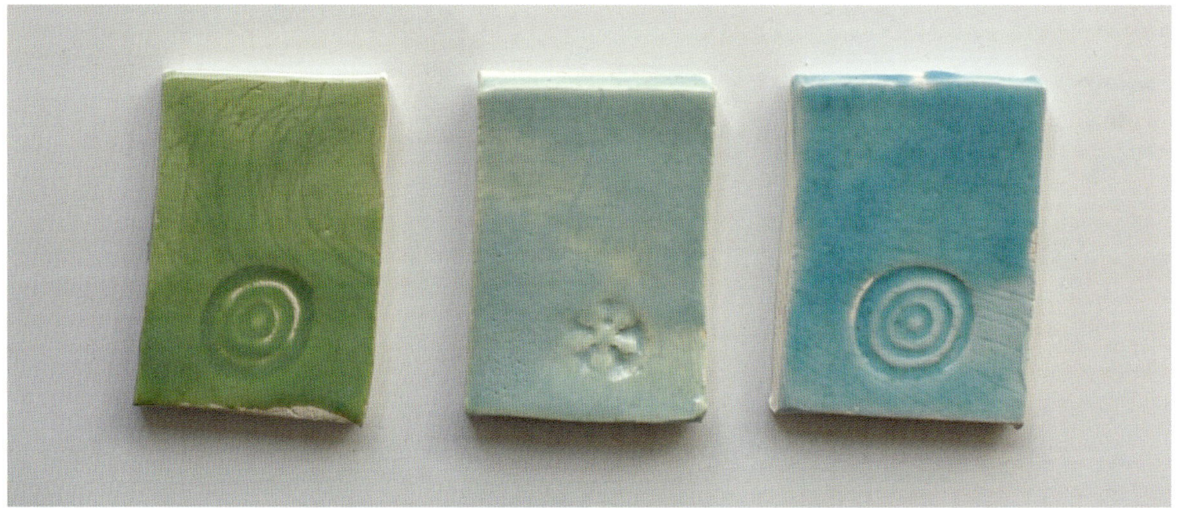

Turquoise glaze for earthenware 1060°C/1940°F (cone 04)

(Page 69, left to right: the discs show pooling)
Not food safe. To avoid crazing, use borax frit instead of high-alkaline frit.

Bright turquoise, 1060°C/1940°F (cone 04) oxidised (Lok Ming Fung)

High-alkaline frit	75
China clay	15
Flint	10
+	
Copper oxide	1.5

Dark turquoise, 1060°C/1940°F (cone 04) oxidised

High-alkaline frit	75
China clay	15
Flint	10
+	
Copper oxide	1.5
Manganese oxide	0.5

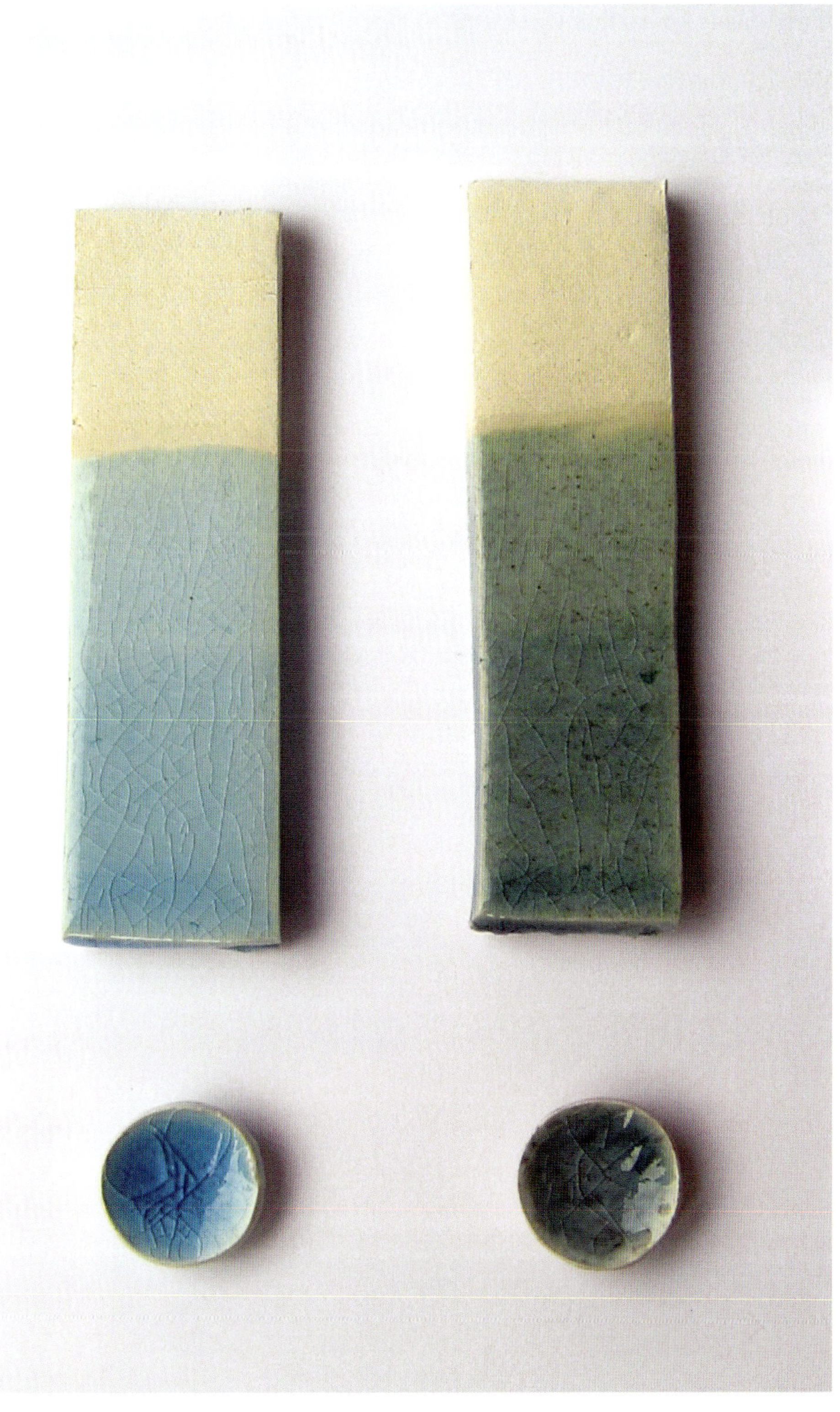

Matt glazes for earthenware 1060°C/1940°F (cone 04)

Matt duck-egg blue, 1060°C/1940°F (cone 04) oxidised (Lucy Burley)

Borax frit	45
Potash feldspar	15
Barium carbonate	10
Ball clay	15
China clay	15
+	
Copper carbonate	0.5

Matt turquoise, 1060°C/1940°F (cone 04) oxidised (Lucy Burley)

Borax frit	45
Potash feldspar	15
Barium carbonate	10
Ball clay	15
China clay	15
+	
Copper carbonate	3

Matt olive green, 1060°C/1940°F (cone 04) oxidised (Lucy Burley)

Borax frit	45
Potash feldspar	15
Barium carbonate	10
Ball clay	15
China clay	15
+	
Copper carbonate	0.75
Nickel oxide	0.75

Matt blue-green, 1060°C/1940°F (cone 04) oxidised

Borax frit	45
Potash feldspar	15
Barium carbonate	10
Ball clay	15
China clay	15
+	
Copper carbonate	2
Nickel oxide	0.4

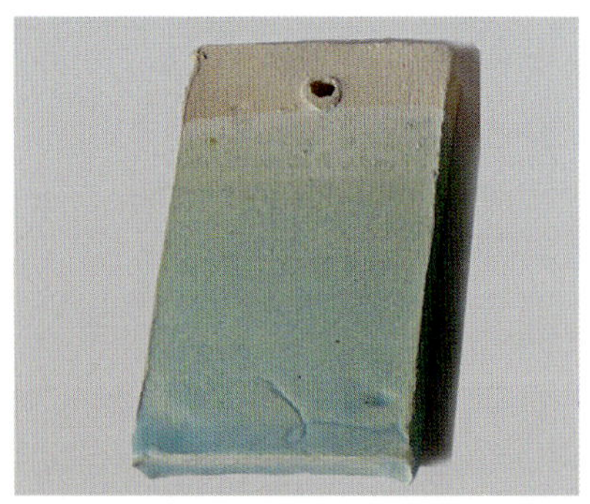

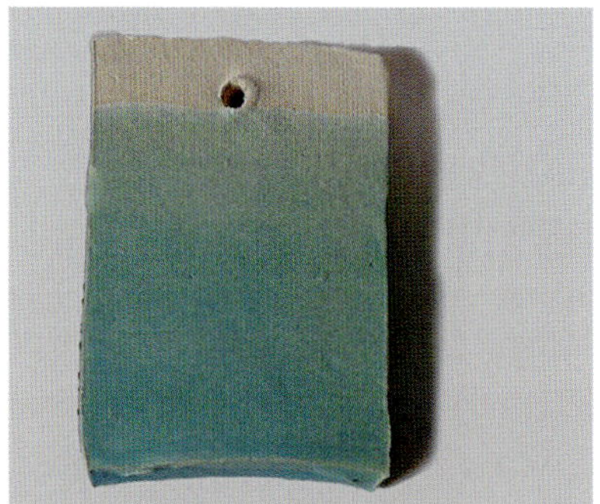

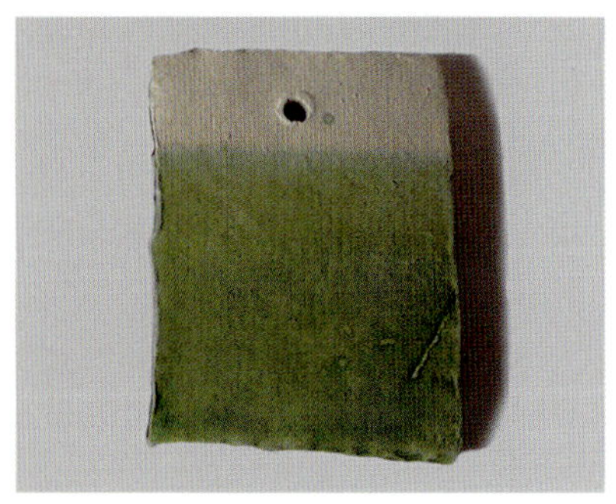

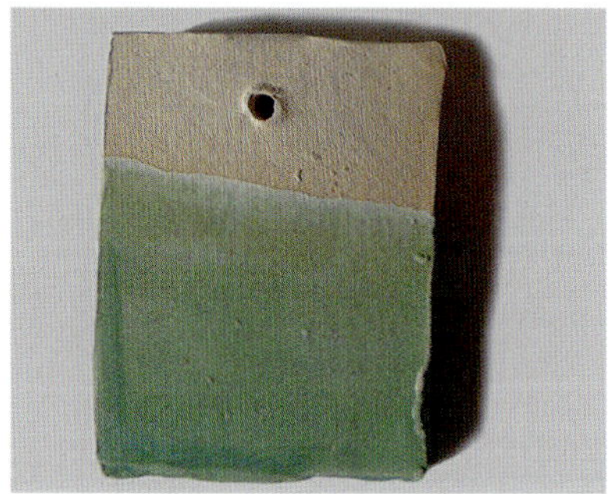

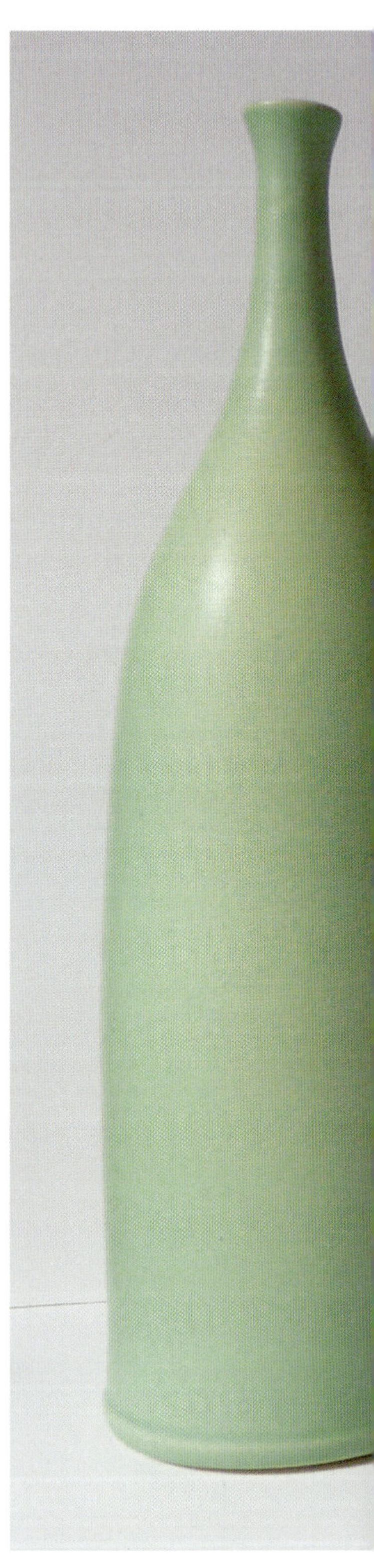

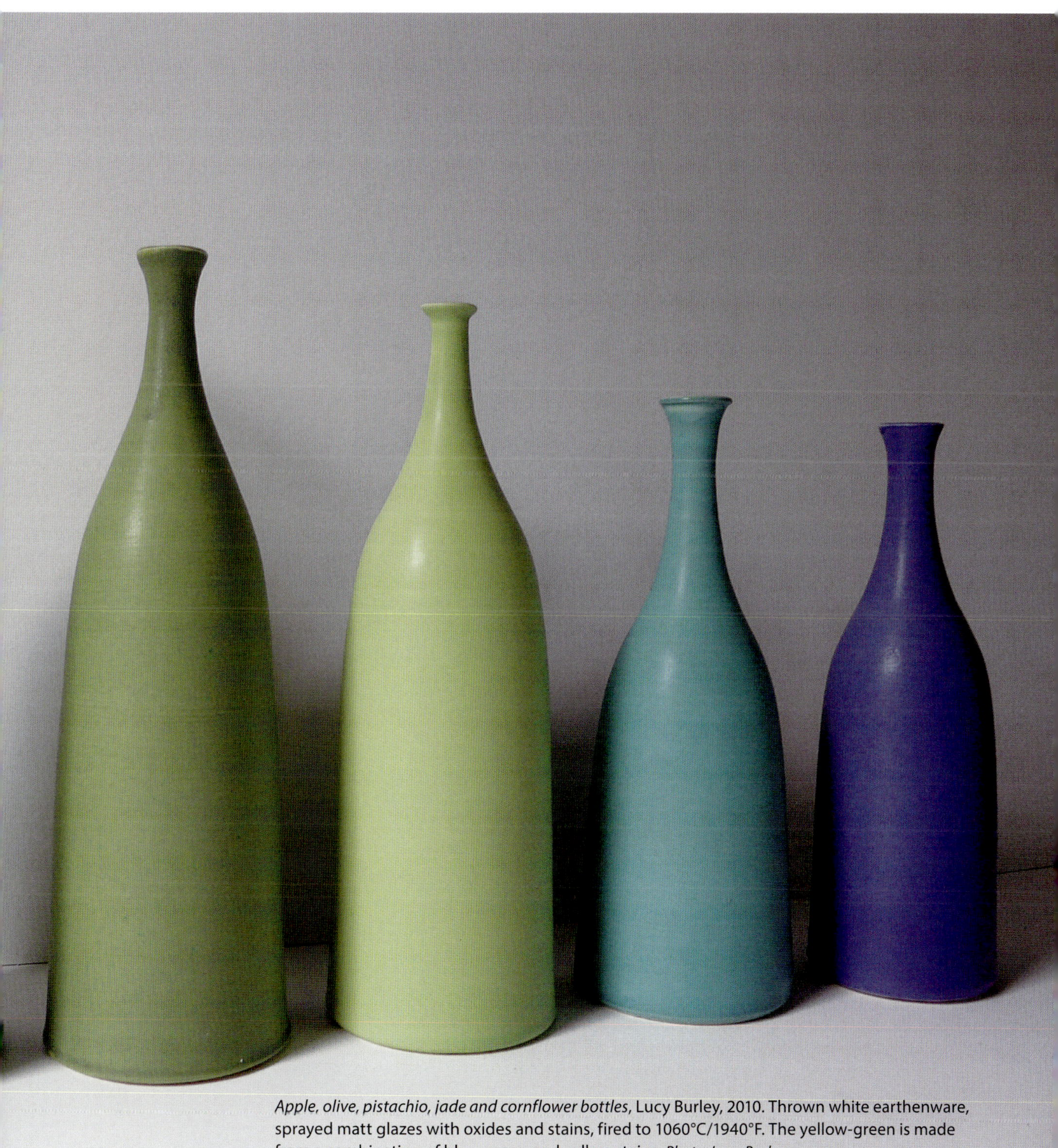

Apple, olive, pistachio, jade and cornflower bottles, Lucy Burley, 2010. Thrown white earthenware, sprayed matt glazes with oxides and stains, fired to 1060°C/1940°F. The yellow-green is made from a combination of blue, green and yellow stains. *Photo: Lucy Burley.*

Turquoise and blue-green glazes for stoneware, 1240–1280°C/2300–2336°F (cone 7–9)

Barium matt turquoise opaque, not food safe, 1240–1260°C/2264–2300°F (cone 7–9) oxidised (Emmanuel Cooper)

Potash feldspar	38
Barium carbonate	38
Lithium carbonate	3
China clay	5
Quartz	16
+	
Copper oxide	1
Tin oxide	5

Barium matt turquoise translucent, not food safe, 1240–1260°C/2264–2300°F (cone 7–8) oxidised (Emmanuel Cooper)

Potash feldspar	38
Barium carbonate	38
Lithium carbonate	3
China clay	5
Quartz	16
+	
Copper oxide	1

Magnesium matt blue-green, 1260°C/ 2300°F (cone 8) oxidised (Stephen Murfitt)

Potash feldspar	34
Talc	22
Whiting	12
China clay	15
Quartz	16
+	
Cobalt oxide	0.2
Chromium oxide	0.5

Cobalt-chrome blue-green, 1280°C/ 2336°F (cone 9) reduced (Tony Hansen)

Potash feldspar	27
Whiting	21
China clay	20
Quartz	32
+	
Cobalt oxide	0.2
Chromium oxide	0.5

Chrome green runny transparent, 1260°C/ 2300°F (cone 8) reduced (Stephen Murfitt)

Soda feldspar	47
Calcium borate frit	16
Whiting	14
China clay	5
Quartz	18
+	
Chromium oxide	0.2

Teal green runny, 1260°C/ 2300°F (cone 8) reduced

Soda feldspar	47
Calcium borate frit	16
Whiting	14
China clay	5
Quartz	18
+	
Cobalt oxide	0.2
Chromium oxide	0.5

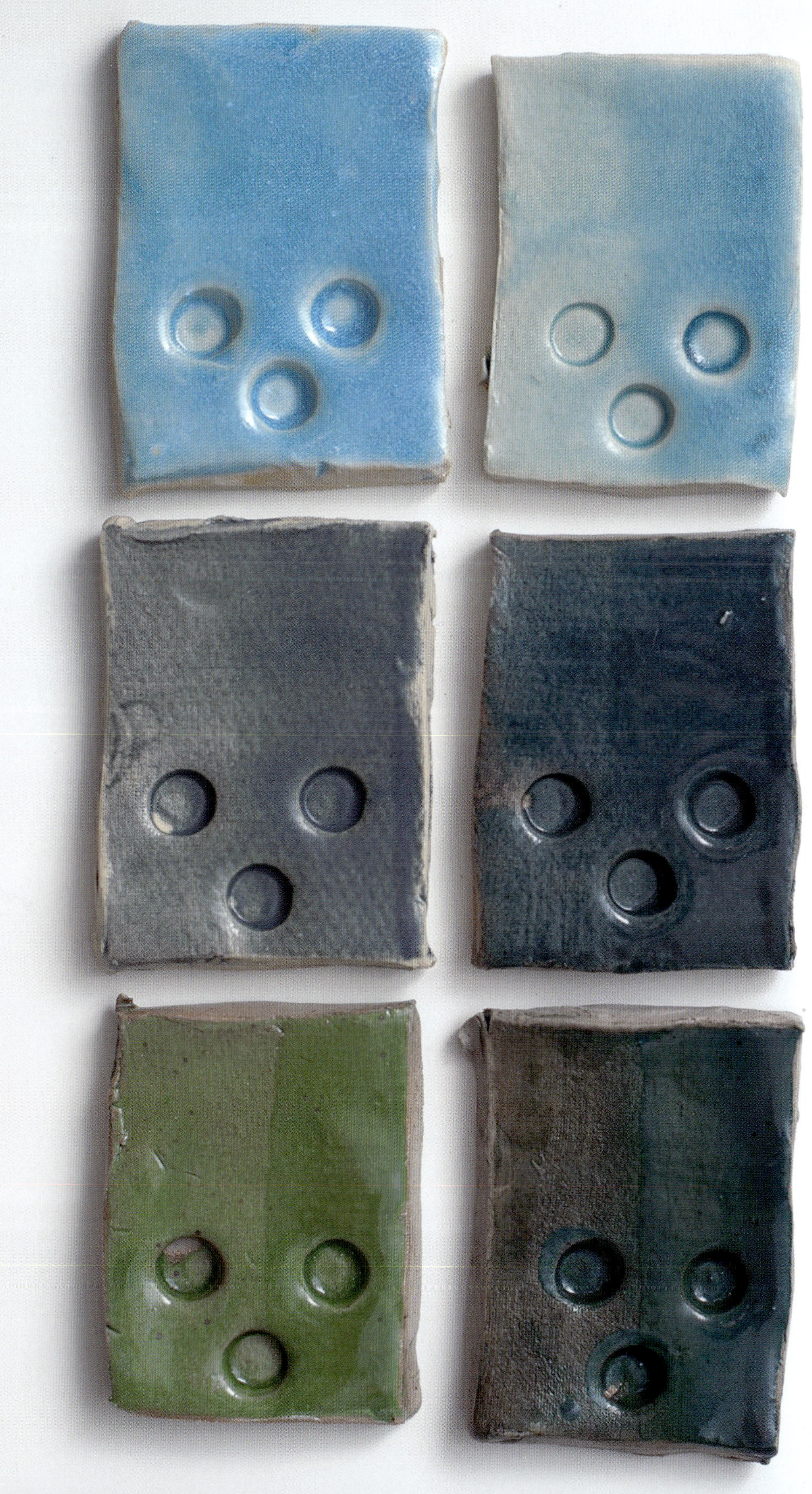

Turquoise glazes for porcelain, 1260-1280°C/2300–2336°F (cone 6–9) oxidised

Pale duck-egg blue runny (on stoneware), 1260°C/2300°F (cone 8) oxidised (Stephen Murfitt)

Soda feldspar	47
Calcium borate frit	16
Whiting	14
China clay	5
Quartz	18
+	
Copper oxide	0.1
Tin oxide	5

Turquoise opaque runny, 1260°C/2300°F (cone 8) oxidised

Soda feldspar	47
Calcium borate frit	16
Whiting	14
China clay	5
Quartz	18
+	
Copper oxide	1
Tin oxide	5

Turquoise transparent runny, 1260°C/2300°F (cone 8) oxidised

Soda feldspar	47
Calcium borate frit	16
Whiting	14
China clay	5
Quartz	18
+	
Copper oxide	1

Sea-green crystalline matt, 1240–1260°C/2264–2300°F (cone 6–8) oxidised (Michael Bailey)

Soda feldspar	42
Dolomite	22
Whiting	3
Zinc oxide	5
China clay	4
Bentonite	2
Quartz	22
+	
Copper oxide	1

Barium turquoise satin matt, not food-safe, 1260°C/2300°F (cone 8) oxidised (Emmanuel Cooper)

Nepheline syenite	56
Barium carbonate	26
Lithium carbonate	2
China clay	6
Quartz	8
Calcium borate frit	2
+	
Copper oxide	2

Sea-green transparent runny, 1260°C/2300°F (cone 8) oxidised

Soda feldspar	47
Calcium borate frit	16
Whiting	14
China clay	5
Quartz	18
+	
Copper oxide	2

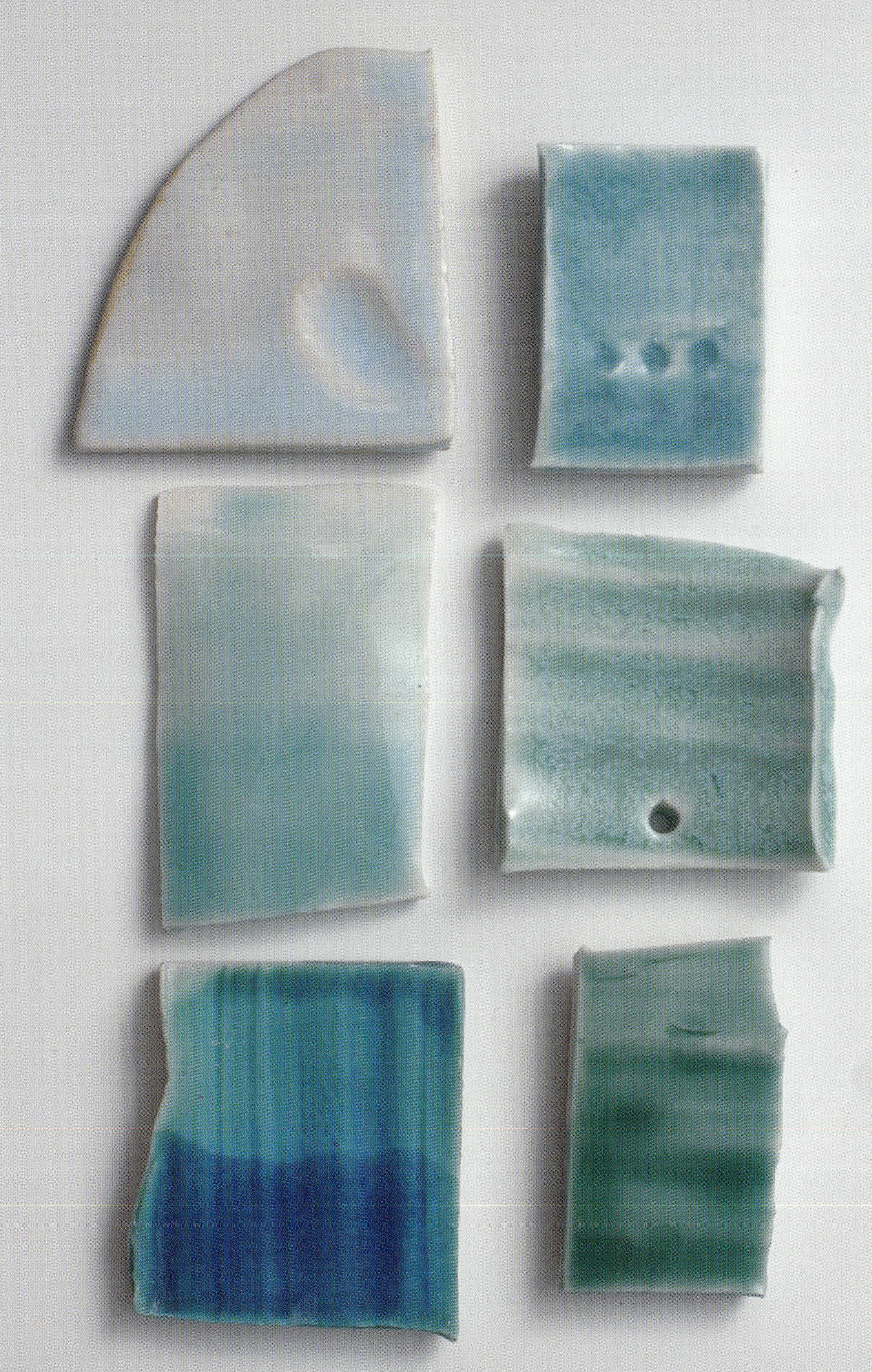

Purple glazes

Purple can be made by adding a small amount of cobalt to a chrome-pink tin glaze, or by adding manganese and cobalt to an alkaline glaze (containing sodium, barium or strontium). Cobalt turns lavender-blue in magnesium glazes (containing talc or dolomite), and an intense purple-blue can be obtained in high-cobalt barium matt glazes. Purple can also be obtained from copper oxide in barium matt earthenware glazes (see frontispiece). Manganese dioxide will produce plum purples, particularly with cobalt in high-alkaline, low-alumina glazes. Neodymium oxide produces a pale violet in alkaline glazes, particularly those containing barium or lithium, which increase the solubility of the neodymium. Nickel gives dark aubergine purple in barium glazes. If cobalt or rutile is added to a copper-red glaze, purple can be obtained in reduction.

Recipe for mulberry underglaze (19th century) (from *Pottery Gazette*, London, 1880s, Smith, Greenwood & Co)

Manganese dioxide	4.5 lbs
Tin oxide	2 lbs
Flint	1 lb
Cornish stone	1 lb
Cobalt oxide	1.5 lbs

Calcine in biscuit oven[3] (1120°C/2048°F, cone 02). The same colour can be obtained if manganese and cobalt are added to a suitable base glaze.

[3] In industry, the biscuit firing is to a higher temperature than the glaze or glost firing.

Porcelain bowl, Richard Baxter, 2010. Sprayed cobalt slip, barium matt glaze, fired in oxidation to 1220°C (2228°F). *Photo: Richard Baxter.*

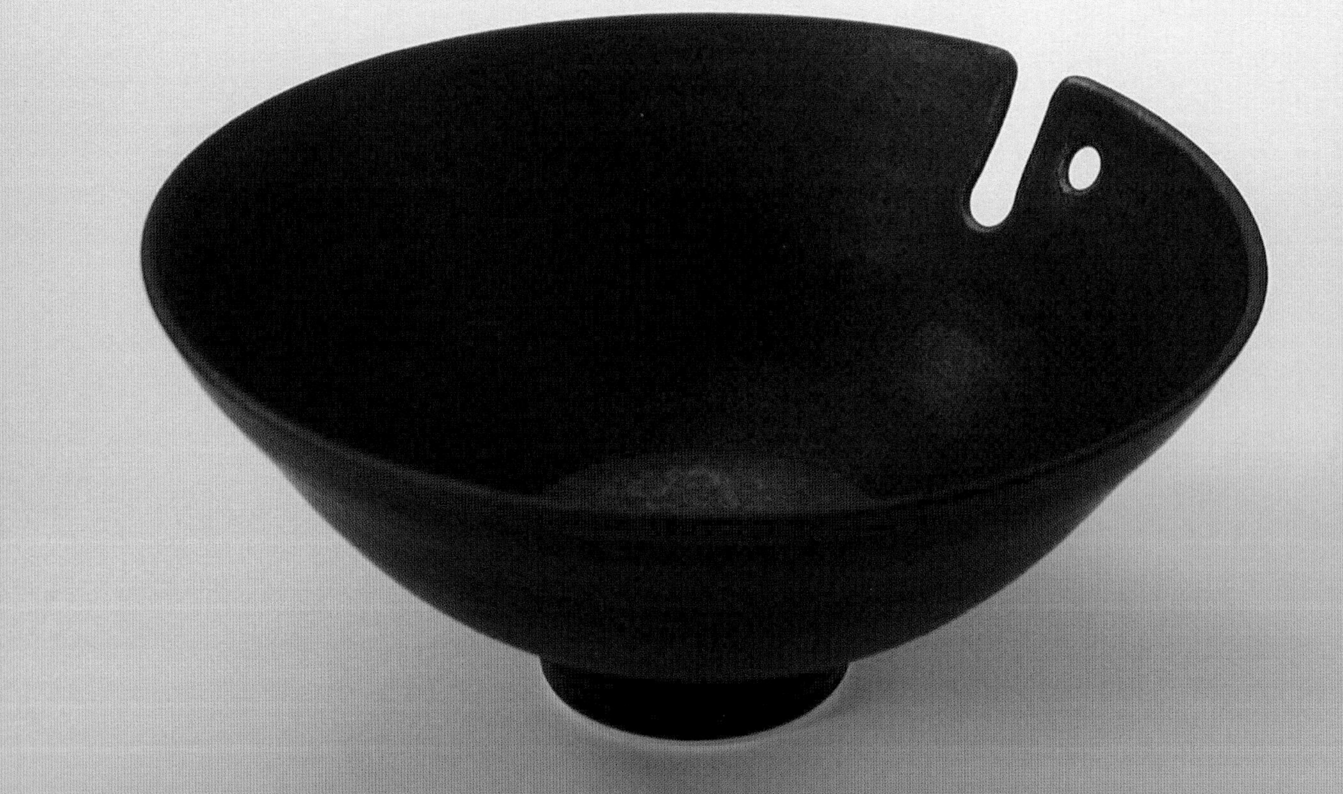

Purple glazes for earthenware 1000–1100°C/1832–2012°F (cone 04) oxidised

Red-purple glaze, 1060°C/1940°F (cone 04) oxidised (John Solly)

Calcium borate frit	39
Soda feldspar	27
Whiting	5
China clay	6
Quartz	23
+	
Red stain (CdSe)	5
Cobalt carbonate	0.3

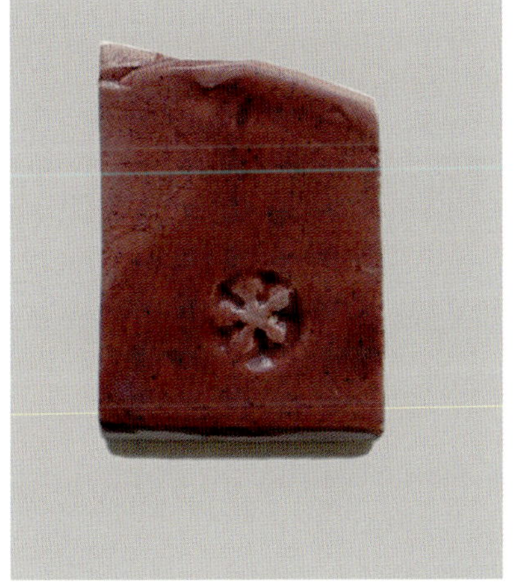

Purple glaze, 1060°C/1940°F (cone 04) oxidised

Calcium borate frit	39
Soda feldspar	27
Whiting	5
China clay	6
Quartz	23
+	
Red stain (CdSe)	5
Cobalt carbonate	0.5

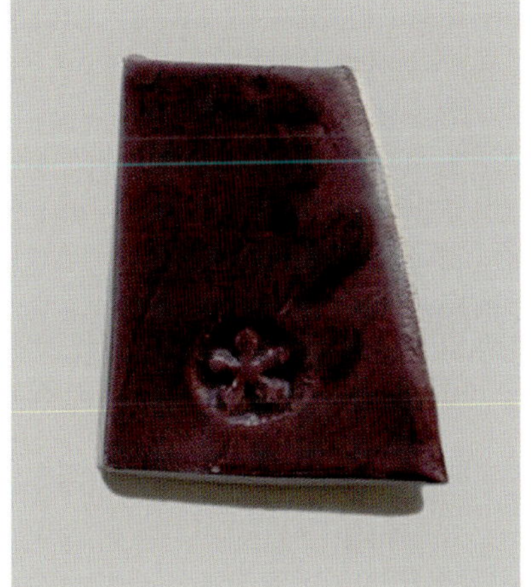

Dark purple glaze, 1060°C/1940°F (cone 04) oxidised

Calcium borate frit	39
Soda feldspar	27
Whiting	5
China clay	6
Quartz	23
+	
Manganese dioxide	0.5
Cobalt oxide	0.1

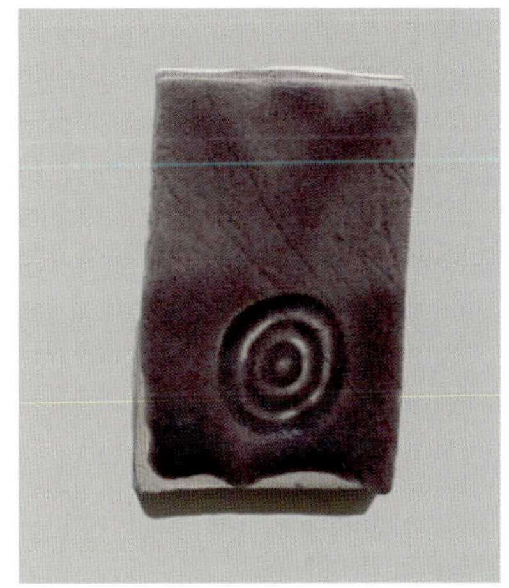

Matt plum purple, 1060°C/1940°F (cone 04) oxidised (Lucy Burley)

Borax frit	45
Potash feldspar	15
Barium carbonate	10
Ball clay	15
China clay	15
+	
Blue stain (CoZnSi)	1
Lilac stain (CrSn)	2
Crimson stain (CrSn)	3

(Potterycrafts Lilac P4182 and Crimson P4131)

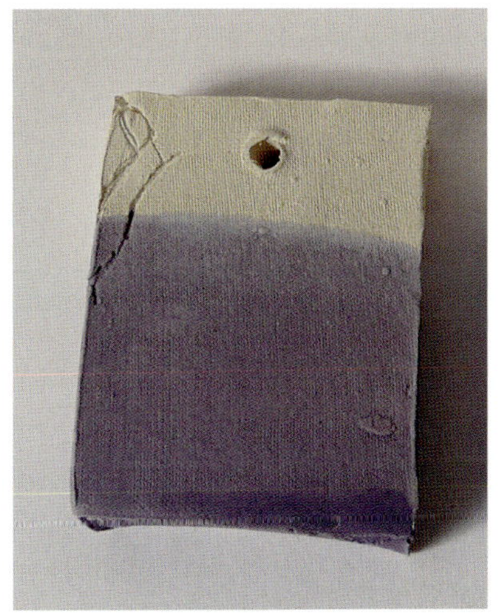

Purple and grey glazes for stoneware 1260–1280°C/2300–2336°F (cone 8–9)

Pale violet blue transparent 1280°C/2336°F (cone 9) oxidised

Potash feldspar	27
Whiting	21
China clay	20
Quartz	32
+	
Neodymium oxide	5

Pale lavender blue transparent, 1280°C/2336°F (cone 9) reduced

Potash feldspar	27
Whiting	21
China clay	20
Quartz	32
+	
Neodymium oxide	5

Violet blue magnesium matt, 1260°C/2300°F (cone 8) oxidised

Potash feldspar	34
Talc	22
Whiting	12
China clay	15
Quartz	16
+	
Cobalt oxide	0.1
Manganese dioxide	0.5

Lavender blue magnesium matt, 1260°C/2300°F (cone 8) reduced (Stephen Murfitt)

Potash feldspar	34
Talc	22
Whiting	12
China clay	15
Quartz	16
+	
Cobalt oxide	0.1

Grey magnesium matt, 1260°C/2300°F (cone 8) oxidised

Potash feldspar	34
Talc	22
Whiting	12
China clay	15
Quartz	16
+	
Cobalt oxide	0.1
Copper oxide	0.5

Purple grey matt, 1260°C/2300°F (cone 8) reduced

Potash feldspar	34
Talc	22
Whiting	12
China clay	15
Quartz	16
+	
Cobalt oxide	0.1
Copper oxide	0.5

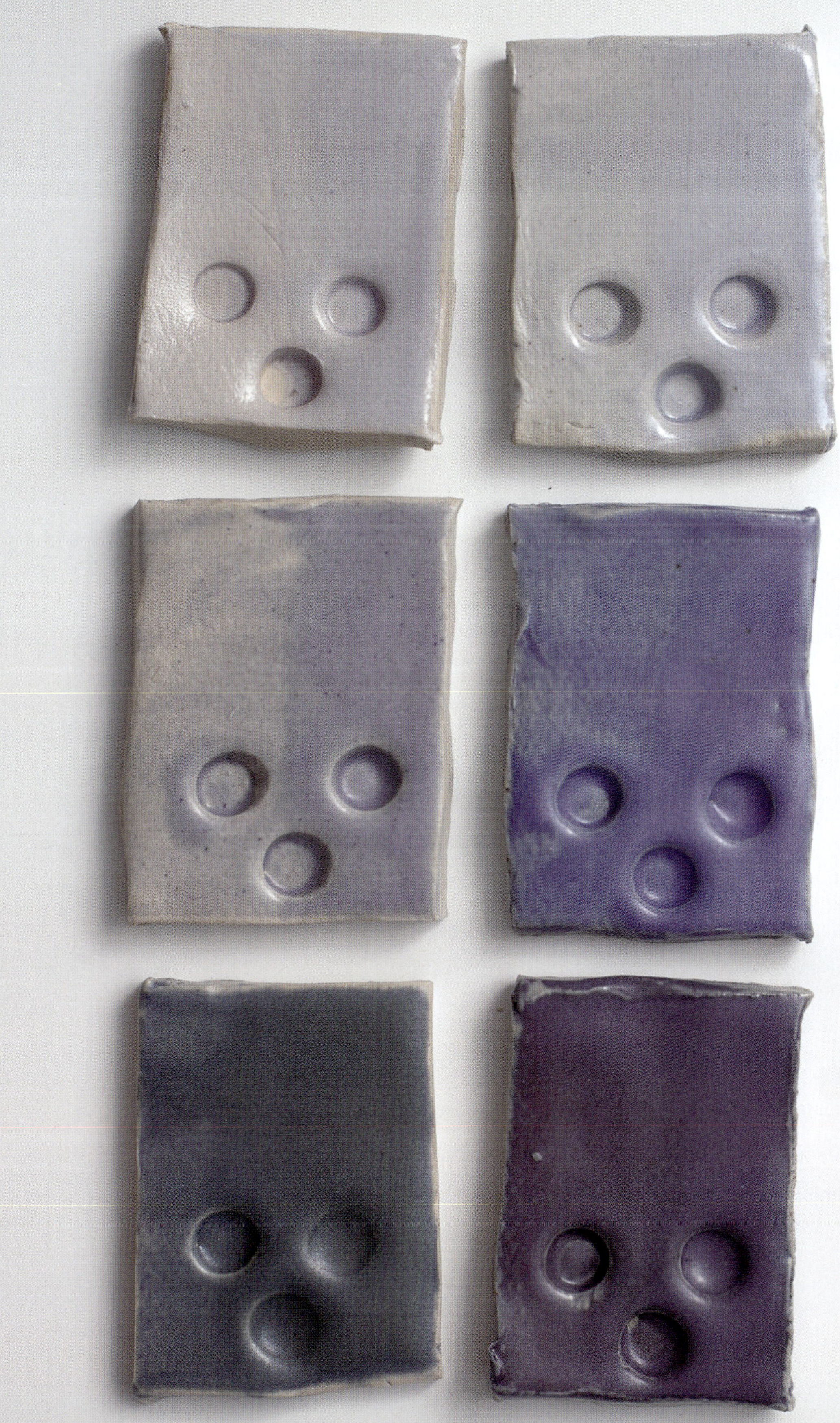

Purple glazes for porcelain 1240–1280°C/2246–2336°F (cone 6–8) oxidised

Pale purple-blue runny, 1240–1260°C/2264–2300°F (cone 6–8) oxidised

Soda feldspar	47
Calcium borate frit	16
Whiting	14
China clay	5
Quartz	18
+	
Cobalt oxide	0.1
Manganese dioxide	0.5
Tin oxide	5

Pale violet runny, 1240–1260°C/2264–2300°F (cone 6–8) oxidised

Soda feldspar	47
Calcium borate frit	16
Whiting	14
China clay	5
Quartz	18
+	
Neodymium oxide	6

Lavender blue magnesium matt, 1260°C/2300°F (cone 8) oxidised (Stephen Murfitt)

Potash feldspar	33
Talc	21
Whiting	12
China clay	15
Quartz	16
Zinc oxide	3
+	
Cobalt oxide	0.5

Rutile-tin-cobalt purple runny, 1240–1260°C/2264–2300°F (cone 6–8) oxidised

Soda feldspar	47
Calcium borate frit	16
Whiting	14
China clay	5
Quartz	18
+	
Rutile	2
Tin oxide	4
Cobalt oxide	0.05

Cobalt-manganese purple matt, 1260°C/2300°F (cone 8) oxidised (David Leach)

Potash feldspar	43
Talc	13
Calcium borate frit	12
Dolomite	7
China clay	5
Bentonite	2
Quartz	18
+	
Cobalt oxide	1
Manganese dioxide	3

Nickel purple matt, not food safe, 1240–1260°C/2264–2300°F (cone 6–8) oxidised (Emmanuel Cooper)

FFF feldspar	36
Barium carbonate	36
Lithium carbonate	3
China clay	5
Quartz	16
Zinc oxide	3
+	
Nickel oxide	1.5

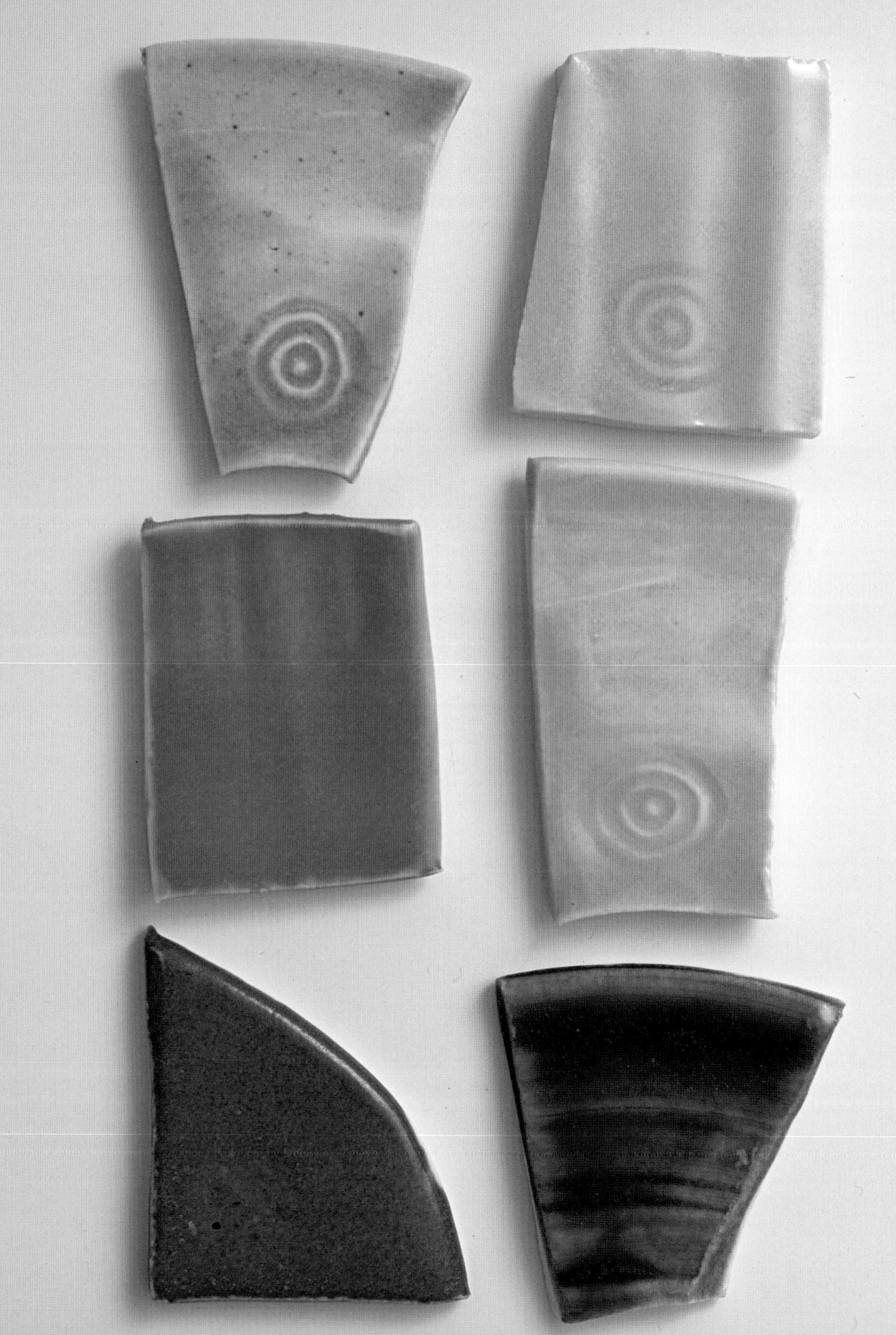

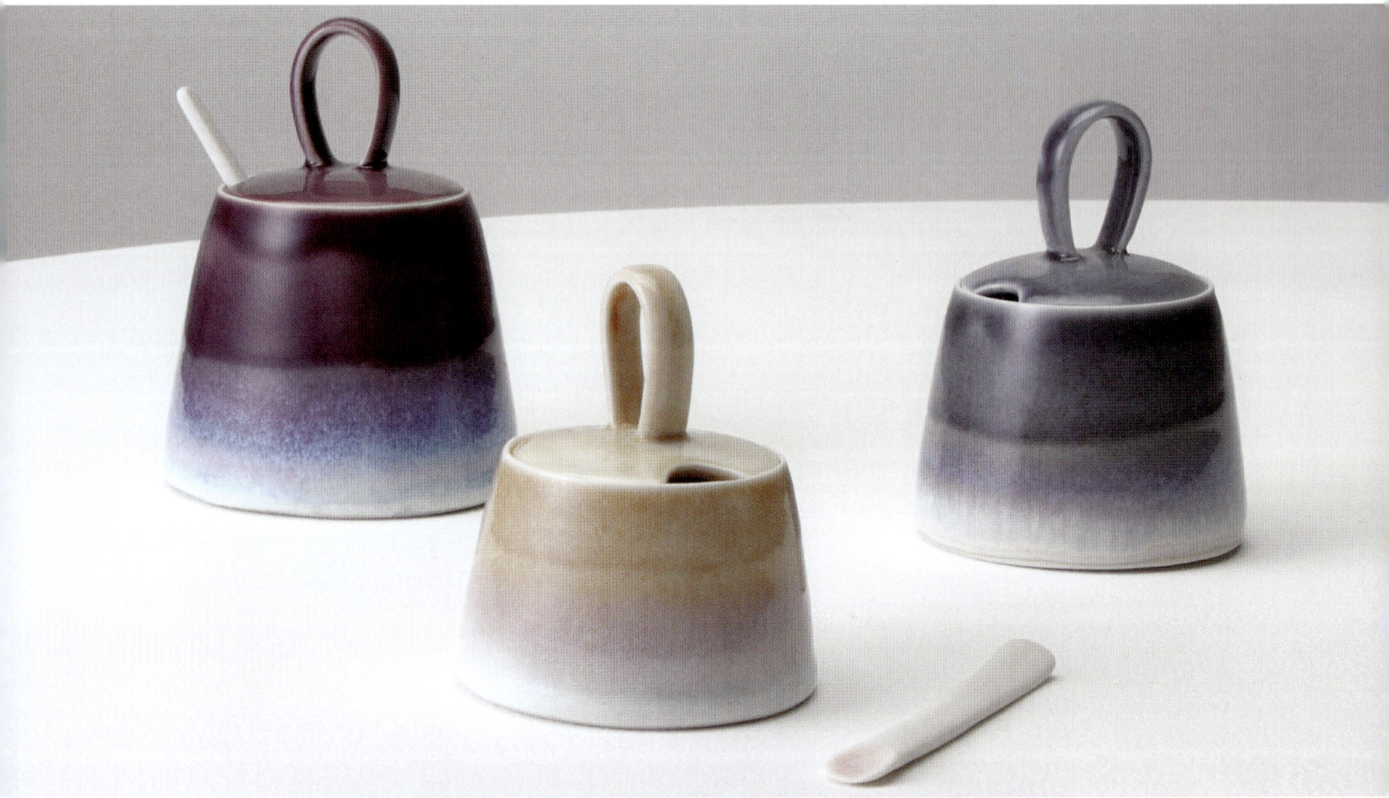

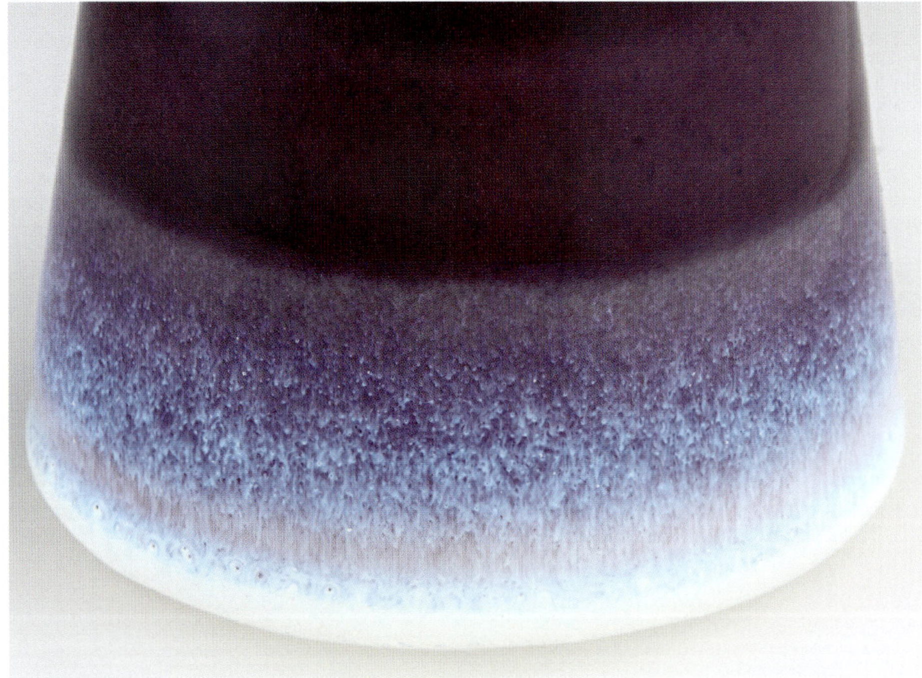

Tutone lidded pots, Lou Taylor, 2010. Thrown porcelain, glazes with blended stains and ox *Photo: Matthew Booth.*

LEFT: Detail of *Tutone* gl Louisa Taylor, 2010. Re stain and cobalt, dipp in rutile-based Chun-t glaze, 1260°C (2300°F) oxidised. *Photo: Matthe Booth.*

(Similar to glaze show p.57 top right)

Pink glazes

The usual way to produce pink in glazes is to use chromium and tin, or a pink stain which is likely to contain the same materials, together with calcium and silica. Around 0.1% chromium and 5% tin oxide will produce pink in glazes that are high in calcium (more than 15% whiting or 0.7 calcium in the unity molecular formula) and that contain no zinc oxide or magnesia. The boron content should not be too high – no more than a third of the calcium content. The colour depends on the ratio of chrome to tin: 1:25 gives pink, 1:20 gives maroon and 1:5 gives green. Chromium is volatile at high temperatures and will cause pink flashing on tin-opacified pots nearby in the kiln. To avoid this, white glazes can be opacified with zirconium silicate and should also contain no zinc, which turns brown in the presence of chromium. However, in high zinc, high-alumina glazes (0.4-0.7 ZnO and 0.4 Al_2O_3 in UMF) a pink colour will form with 1% chromium oxide. Chrome-tin pinks should be fired to temperatures below 1260°C (2300°F/cone 8); otherwise, the colour evaporates. To avoid this, the kiln can be fired slowly to around 1240°C (2822°F) and held for 15 to 30 minutes to soak. Chrome-tin pinks are only possible in oxidation, but copper oxide can produce a pink colour in reducing conditions.

Recipe for chrome-tin pink underglaze (19th century) (from *Pottery Gazette*, London, 1880s, Smith, Greenwood & Co)

Tin oxide	40 lbs
Whiting	20 lbs
Chrome oxide	1.5 lbs

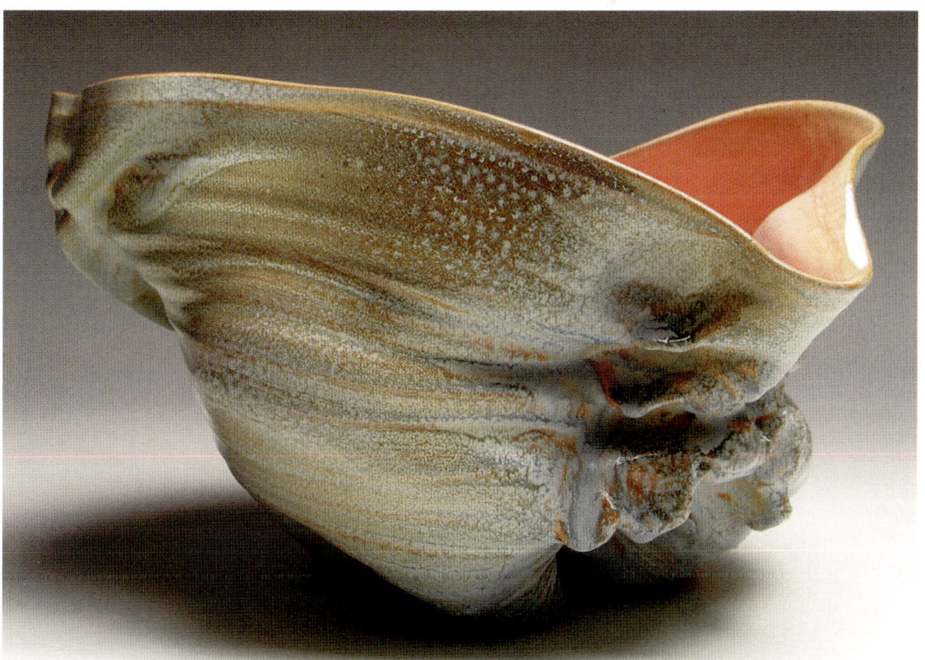

Clay-e-motion vessel, Anne Marie Laureys, 2004. Layered glazes, stains and oxides, fired to 1140–1180°C (2034–2156°F), ht: 33cm (13in). *Photo: courtesy of Peter Claeys, Belgium.*

Calcine in biscuit oven (1120°C/2048°F, cone 02), giving plenty of air. The same colour can be obtained if tin and chrome are added to a suitable base glaze containing calcium.

Rutile will also produce pink with tin oxide (about 2% rutile to 5% tin) in oxidation. Rutile often contains impurities, including chromium, which explains the pink colour obtained with tin oxide. The glaze should be high in calcium and silica and low in alumina. The pink colour is paler and less grainy than that obtained using pure chromium oxide, owing to the more finely dispersed particles of chromium in the rutile. Samples of rutile obtained from different sources will contain different amounts of iron and chromium.

Erbium oxide can be used to make a pale transparent pink. Glazes high in alkaline fluxes such as barium, sodium and lithium help to dissolve the rare-earth oxides. Above 8%, these oxides remain suspended in the glaze, and the colour stays the same but becomes more opaque. An opaque coral pink can be obtained using a red stain together with zirconium silicate.

In barium zinc glazes containing nickel, a bright crystalline pink is possible. This glaze is steel blue where applied thinly, and pink where thick (see p.89). Adjusting the ratio of barium to zinc, or adding cobalt, will create purple. Barium matt glazes are not usually food safe, and should not be used on functional pottery.

Bowl, Kerry Hastings, 2010. Coiled, grogged stoneware coloured with chromium oxide, tin glaze, fired to 1140°C (2084°F). *Photo: Sussie Ahlburg.*

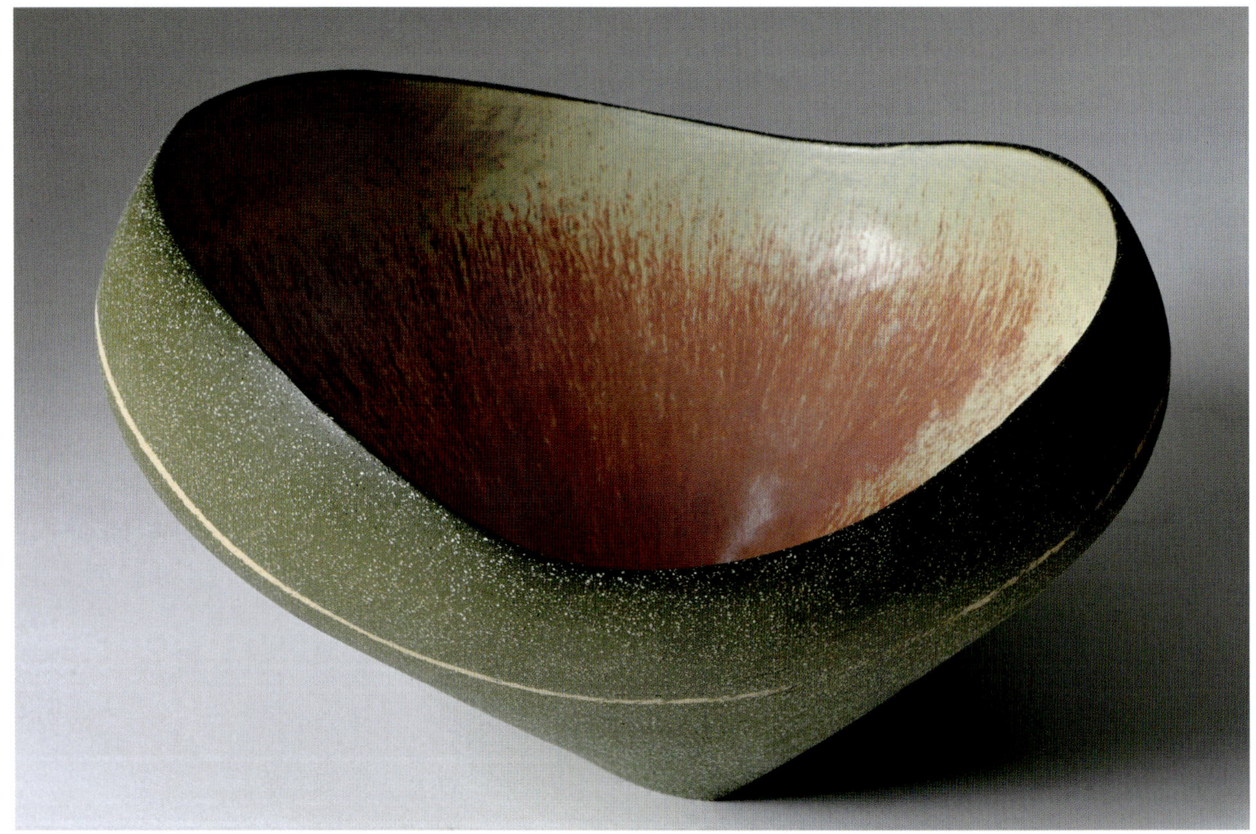

Pink glazes for earthenware 1000–1100°C/1832–2012°F (cone 06–02) oxidised

Pink opaque, 1060°C/1940°F (cone 04) oxidised

Calcium borate frit	39
Soda feldspar	27
Whiting	5
China clay	6
Quartz	23
+	
Red stain (CdSeZrSi)	0.5
Zirconium silicate	5

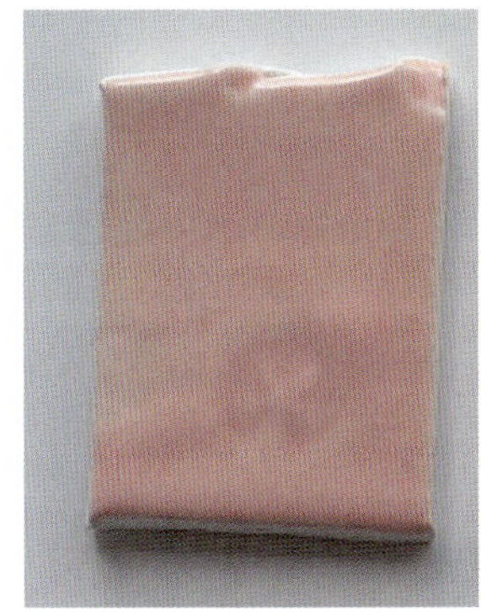

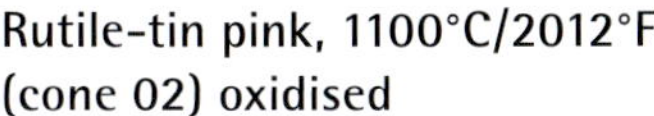

Rutile-tin pink, 1100°C/2012°F (cone 02) oxidised

Calcium borate frit	24
Soda feldspar	27
Whiting	20
China clay	6
Quartz	23
+	
Rutile	2
Tin oxide	5

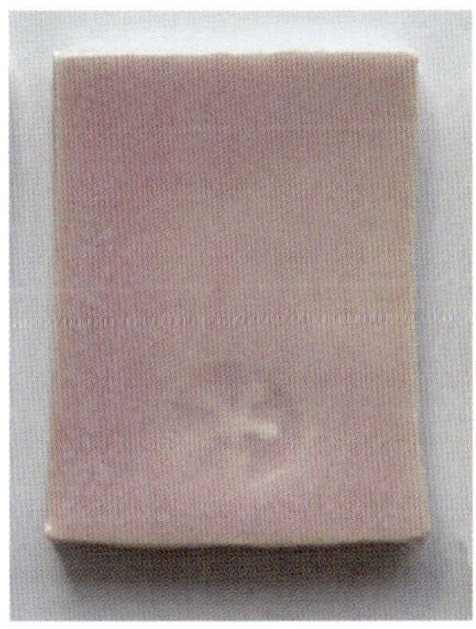

Chrome-tin pink, 1100°C/2012°F (cone 02) oxidised

Calcium borate frit	34
Soda feldspar	24
Whiting	17
China clay	5
Quartz	20
+	
Chromium	0.1
Tin oxide	4

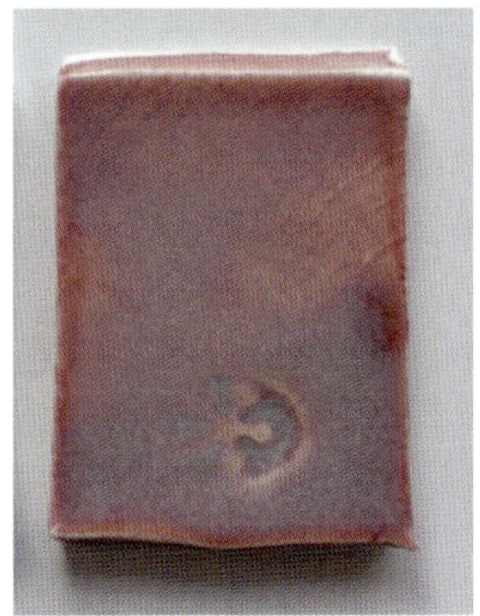

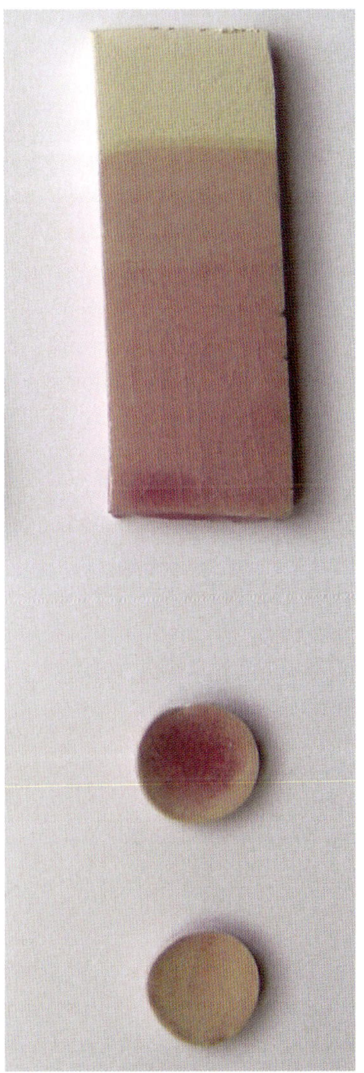

Chrome-tin stain pink, not food safe. To avoid crazing, use borax frit instead of high-alkaline frit.

(The disc shows pooling of thickly applied glaze.)

High-alkaline frit	75
China clay	15
Flint	10
+	
Chrome-tin pink stain (Potterycrafts Lilac stain P4182)	5

Pink and cream glazes for stoneware 1240–1280°C/2264–2336°F (cone 6–9)

Rutile-tin pink runny opaque, 1240–1260°C/2264–2300°F (cone 6–8) oxidised

Soda feldspar	47
Calcium borate frit	16
Whiting	14
China clay	5
Quartz	18
+	
Rutile	2
Tin oxide	5

Chrome-tin pink, 1260°C/2300°F (cone 8) oxidised

Potash feldspar	27
Whiting	21
China clay	20
Quartz	32
+	
Chromium oxide	0.2
Tin oxide	5

Copper red, 1280°C/2336°F (cone 9) reduced

Potash feldspar	27
Whiting	21
China clay	20
Quartz	32
+	
Copper oxide	1
Tin oxide	5

Cream magnesium matt, 1260°C/2300°F (cone 8) oxidised (Stephen Murfitt)

Potash feldspar	34
Talc	22
Whiting	12
China clay	15
Quartz	16
+	
Rutile	2
Tin oxide	5

Speckled cream magnesium matt, 1260°C/2300°F (cone 8) oxidised

Potash feldspar	34
Talc	22
Whiting	12
China clay	15
Quartz	16
+	
Red iron oxide	0.5

Pale orange barium matt, not food safe, 1240–1260°C/2264–2300°F (cone 6–8) oxidised

Potash feldspar	38
Barium carbonate	38
Lithium carbonate	3
China clay	5
Quartz	16
+	
Cerium oxide	5

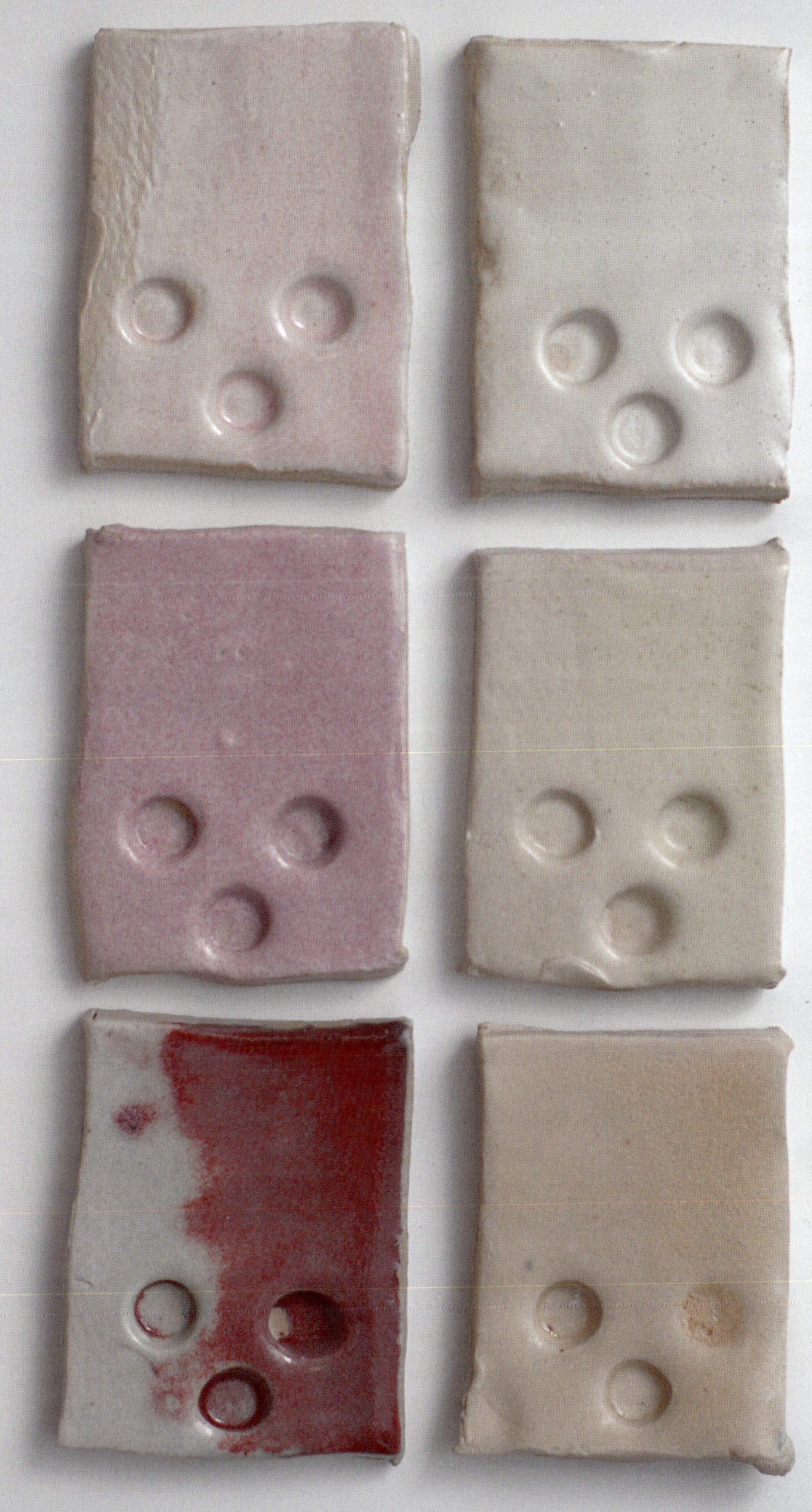

Pink glazes for porcelain 1240–1260°C/2264–2300°F (cone 6–8) oxidised

Erbium pink runny transparent, 1240–1260°C/2264–2300°F (cone 6–8) oxidised

Soda feldspar	47
Calcium borate frit	16
Whiting	14
China clay	5
Quartz	18
+	
Erbium oxide	6

Chrome-tin red-pink, 1280°C/2336°F (cone 9) oxidised (Emmanuel Cooper)

Cornish stone	50
Whiting	29
China clay	15
Quartz	5
+	
Chromium oxide	0.1
Tin oxide	2

Rutile-tin pink, 1260°C/2300°F (cone 8) oxidised

Nepheline syenite	26
Whiting	12
Lithium carbonate	10
Barium carbonate	3
Calcium borate frit	5
Quartz	44
+	
Rutile	1.5
Tin oxide	4

Manganese brown-pink, not food safe, 1240–1260°C/2264–2300°F (cone 6–8) oxidised (Emmanuel Cooper)

Potash feldspar	38
Barium carbonate	38
Lithium carbonate	3
China clay	5
Quartz	16
+	
Manganese dioxide	2

Chrome-tin pink runny, 1240–1260°C/2246–2300°F (cone 6–8) oxidised

Soda feldspar	47
Calcium borate frit	16
Whiting	14
China clay	5
Quartz	18
+	
Chromium oxide	0.1
Tin oxide	8

Nickel pink matt, not food safe, 1260°C/2300°F (cone 8) oxidised (Emmanuel Cooper)

Potash feldspar	33
Barium carbonate	40
Zinc oxide	16
China clay	5
Quartz	6
+	
Nickel oxide	1.5

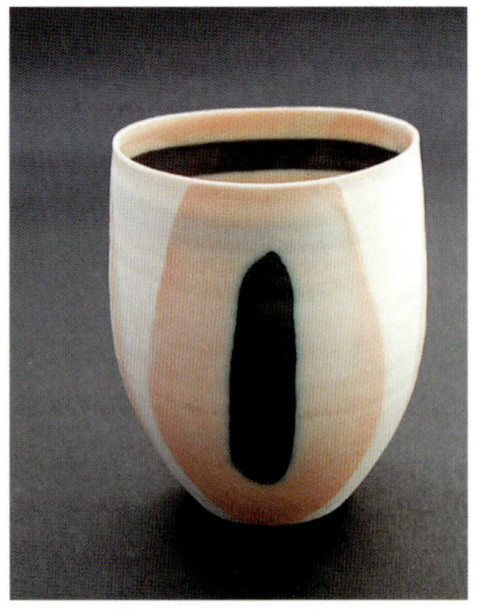

Pink vessel, Richard Baxter, 2010. Thrown porcelain vessel, barium matt glaze with 8% red stain, applied manganese and copper oxide, fired to 1220°C (2228°F), ht: 11cm (4¼in). *Photo: Richard Baxter.*

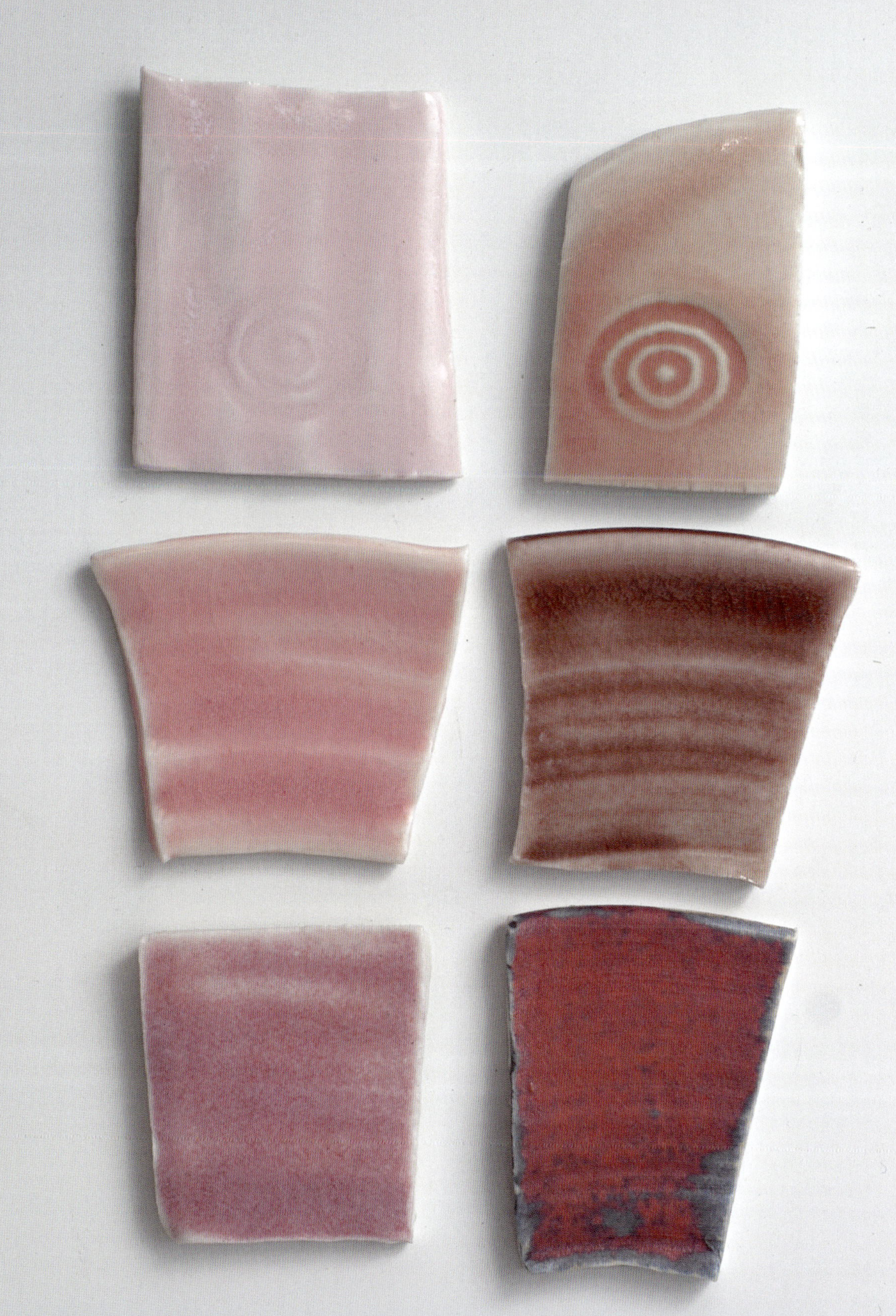

Red and orange glazes

Copper red can only be obtained in reduction, and the colour depends on glaze thickness, kiln atmosphere and position in the kiln. The best reds occur in runny, alkaline glazes containing less than 1% copper carbonate and 5% tin oxide. The oxblood red colour is often streaked and mottled, and is caused by colloidal particles of copper metal suspended in the glaze. Local reduction of the glaze is possible in an electric kiln if very finely ground silicon carbide is added to the glaze. The silicon carbide reduces the glaze but not the clay body.

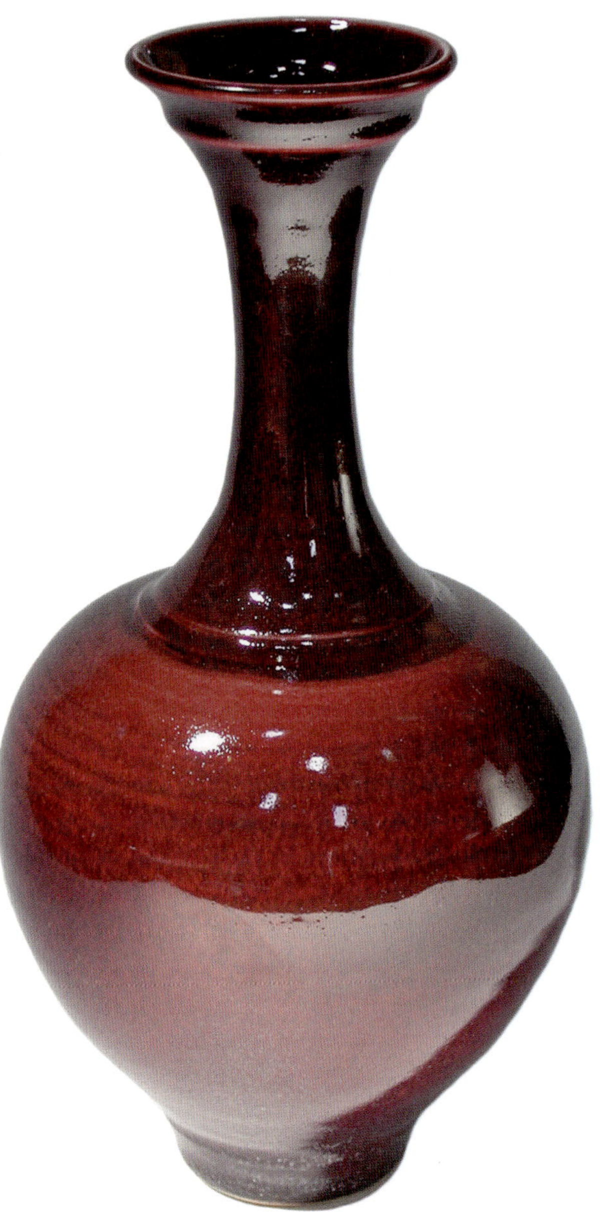

Bridget Drakeford, 2009.
Thrown porcelain bottle,
copper-red glaze.
Photo: Irene Sanderson.

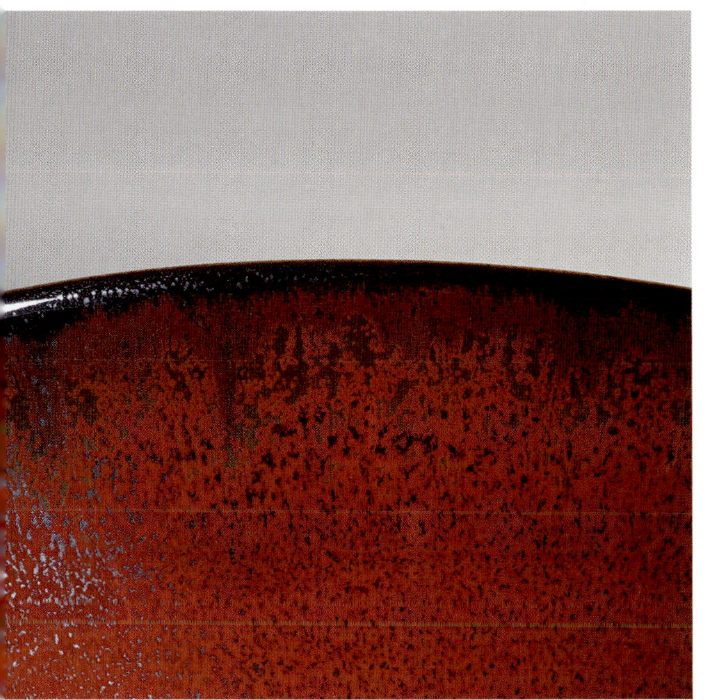

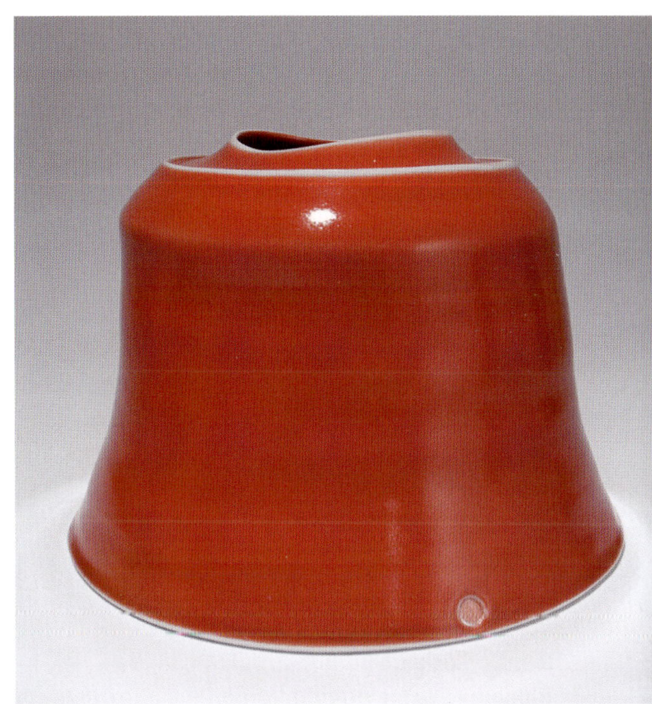

ABOVE LEFT: *Two Tone Bowl* rim, Suleyman Saba, 2009. Iron red glaze detail. Magnesium glaze with 8% iron oxide, fired in oxidation to 1280°C (2336°F). *Photo: courtesy of Stephen Brayne.*

ABOVE RIGHT: *Medium Red*, Tanya Gomez, 2010. Thrown porcelain, red stain. *Photo: Dominic Tschudin.*

Copper-red glaze, 1260°C/2300°F (cone 8) reduced (Bridget Drakeford)

Nepheline syenite	36
Whiting	9
Barium carbonate	9
High-alkaline frit	9
Talc	4
China clay	5
Silica	28
+	
Copper carbonate	0.5
Tin oxide	4

Saturated iron orange-red is obtained in oxidation in magnesia glazes containing 15% bone ash and 8–12% red iron oxide. Small amounts of iron and titanium (or rutile) give a pale yellow-orange in oxidation, particularly with tin in high calcia and alumina glazes. Cerium oxide can produce orange-yellows in combination with titanium or rutile. Bright orange can be made in high-zinc glazes (with more than 10% zinc oxide) using small amounts of iron and chromium oxides.

In lead glazes with low alumina, chromium oxide can be used to make red and orange at temperatures around 900–950°C/1652–1742°F, although these glazes are very runny and are not food safe. Cadmium sulphide and cadmium selenide are used to make red and orange stains. Cadmium sulphide gives a bright yellow, and the addition of increasing amounts of cadmium selenide gives oranges and reds. These can be used at high temperatures if they are encapsulated in a zirconium silicate crystal matrix, although deep red is only possible at earthenware temperatures. (See pp. 95 and 132.)

Orange is often obtained in wood, salt and soda firings by using a flashing slip containing clay and nepheline syenite. Thinly applied Shino glazes (thick white glazes made from feldspar and clay) are often orange-red when wood-fired. The iron in the clay reacts with the sodium in the glaze or kiln atmosphere, and turns orange-red if it is reduced and then re-oxidised on cooling.

Tangerine glaze, 1260°C/2300°F (cone 6-8) oxidised (Jeannine Vrins)

Nepheline syenite 40
Wollastonite 22
Zinc oxide 10
Kaolin 5
Silica 23
+
Red iron oxide 1.8
Chromium oxide 0.3

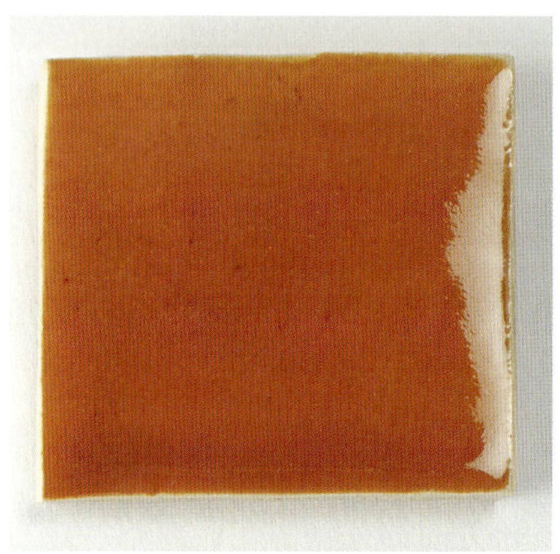

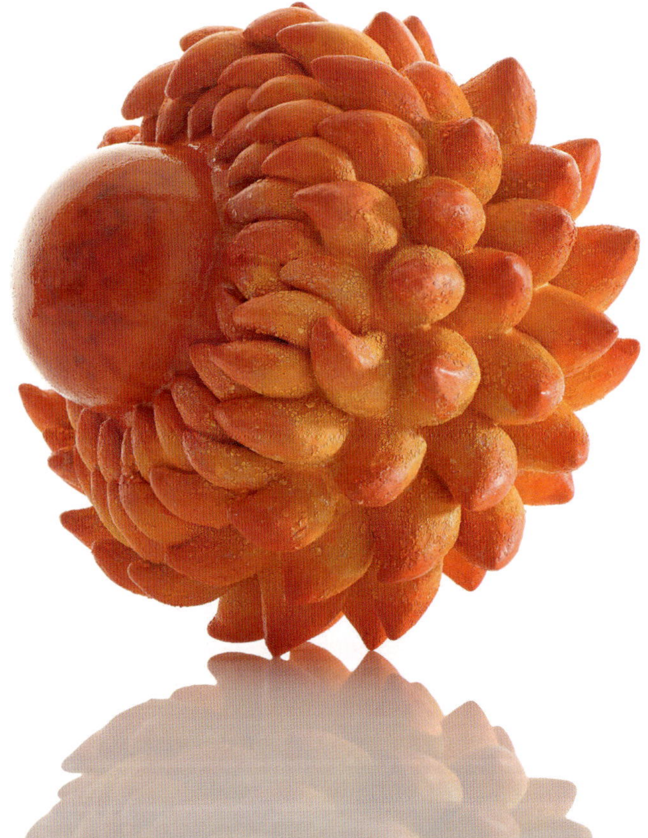

LEFT: *Red Hot Creature,* Tessa Eastman, 2017. L360xW360xH330mm. *Private Collection. Sylvain Deleu Photography.*

RIGHT: *Flower Lamp,* Jeannine Vrins, 2019. *Photo courtesy of the artist.*

Flower lamp, Jeannine Vrins, 2019, Belgium, stoneware with tangerine glaze, nepheline syenite 40, silica 23, wollastonite 22, zinc oxide 10, kaolin 5, red iron oxide 1.8, chromium oxide 0.3 fired to cone 8.

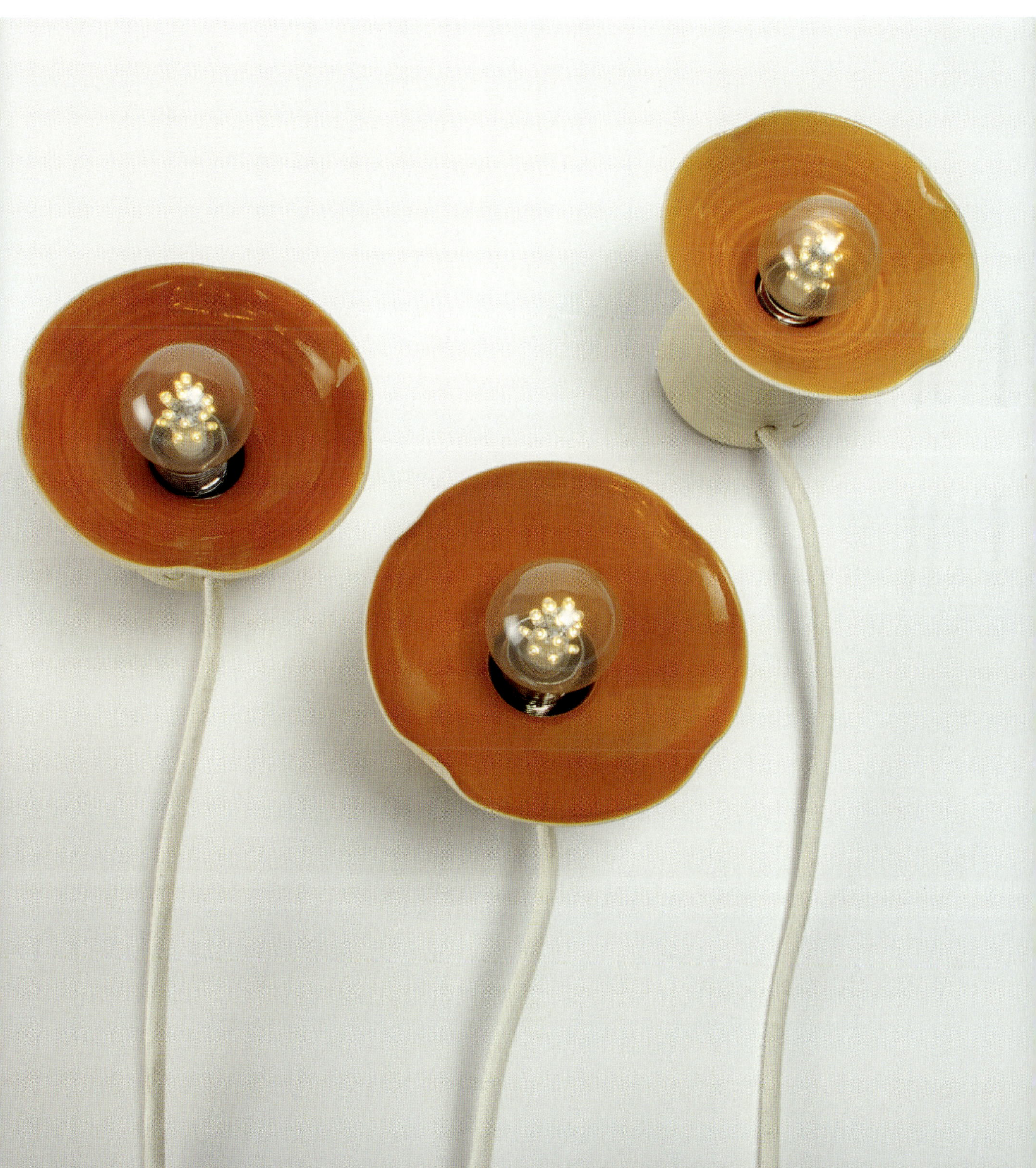

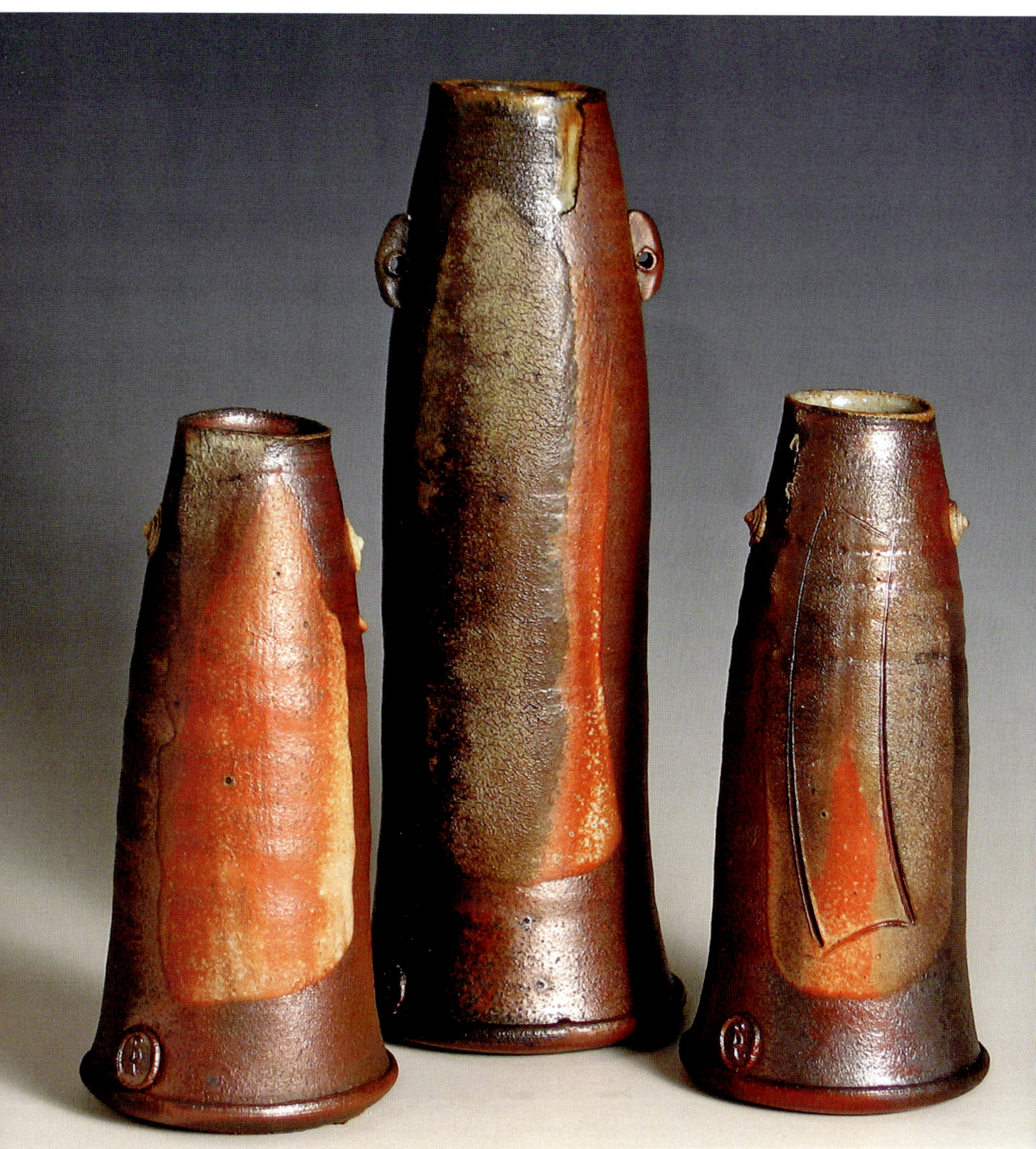

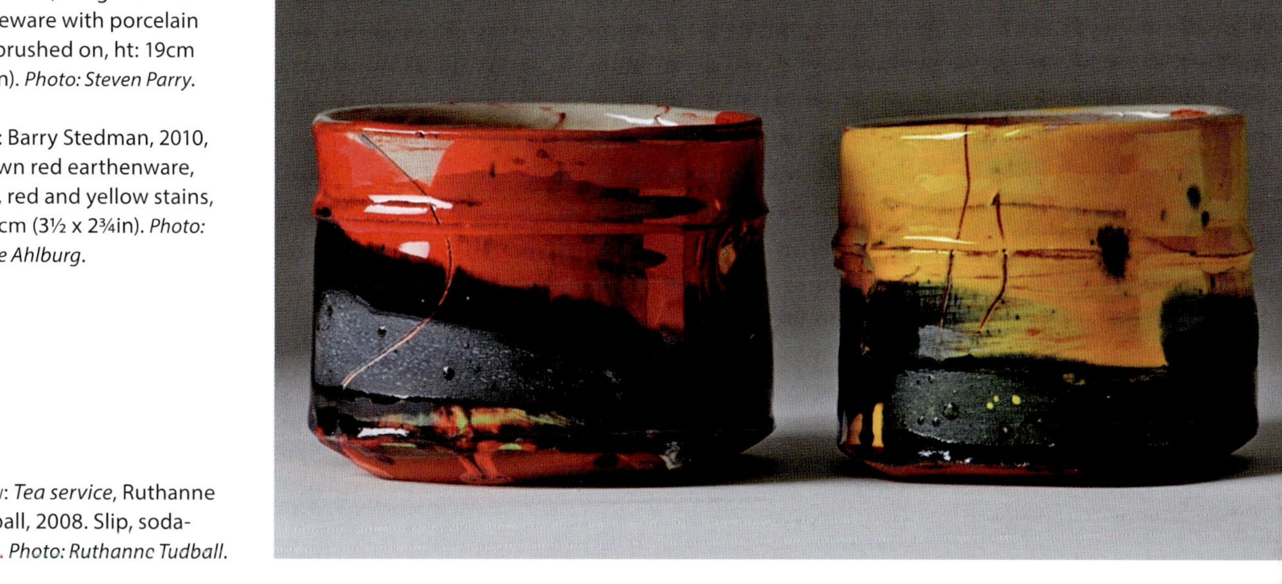

LEFT: Stephen Parry, three thin vases, anagama-fired stoneware with porcelain slip brushed on, ht: 19cm (7½in). *Photo: Steven Parry.*

RIGHT: Barry Stedman, 2010, thrown red earthenware, slips, red and yellow stains, 9 x 7cm (3½ x 2¾in). *Photo: Sussie Ahlburg.*

BELOW: *Tea service*, Ruthanne Tudball, 2008. Slip, soda-fired. *Photo: Ruthanne Tudball.*

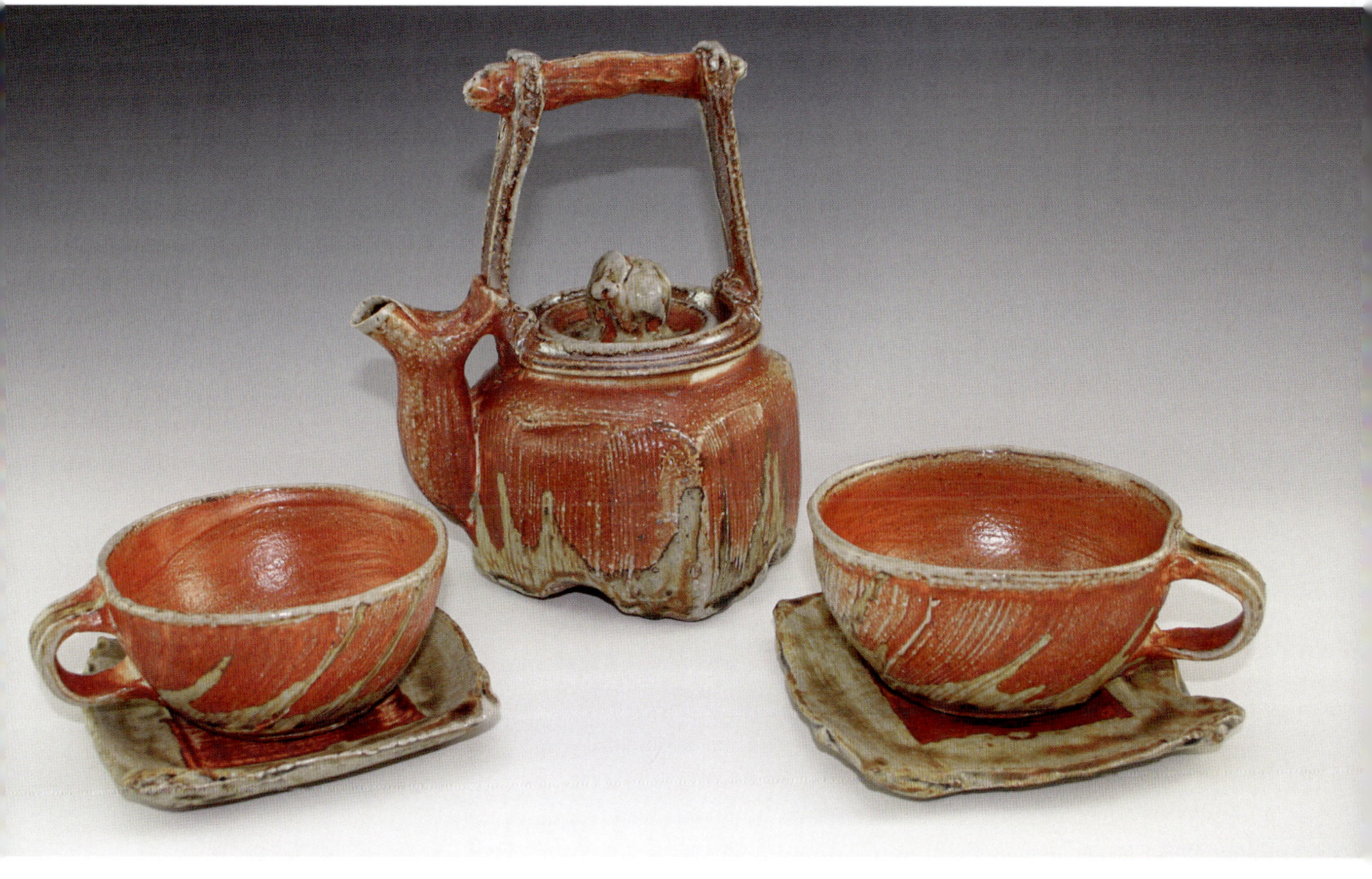

Red and orange glazes for earthenware 1000–1100°C/1832–2012°F (cone 06–02)

Orange glaze, 1060°C/1940°F (cone 04) oxidised

Calcium borate frit	39
Soda feldspar	27
Whiting	5
China clay	6
Quartz	23
+	
Red stain	1.25
Yellow stain	3.75

Cadmium selenium zirconium silicate stains ($CdSeZrSiO_4$)

Red glaze, 1060°C/1940°F (cone 04) oxidised

Calcium borate frit	39
Soda feldspar	27
Whiting	5
China clay	6
Quartz	23
+	
Red stain	5

Cadmium selenium zirconium silicate stain ($CdSeZrSiO_4$)

Red and orange glazes for stoneware and porcelain, 1240–1280°C/2264–2336°F (cone 6–10) oxidised

Coral red, 1280°C/2336°F (cone 9) oxidised

Potash feldspar	27
Whiting	21
China clay	20
Quartz	32
+	
Red stain (CdSeZrSi)	4

Iron red (on stoneware), 1240–1260°C/2264–2300°F (cone 6–8) oxidised (Michael Bailey)

Potash feldspar	47
Bone ash	15
Lithium carbonate	4
Talc	17
China clay	4
Bentonite	2
Quartz	11
+	
Red iron oxide	11.5

Chrome-tin maroon, 1280°C/2336°F (cone 9) oxidised

Cornish stone	29
Dolomite	18
Whiting	16
China clay	12
Quartz	20
Bone ash	4
+	
Chromium oxide	0.5
Tin oxide	7

Chrome-tin red, 1260°C/2300°F (cone 8) oxidised (Jonathan Keep)

FFF feldspar	47
Whiting	24
China clay	6
Quartz	12
Calcium borate frit	6
Lithium carbonate	6
+	
Chromium oxide	0.1
Tin oxide	6

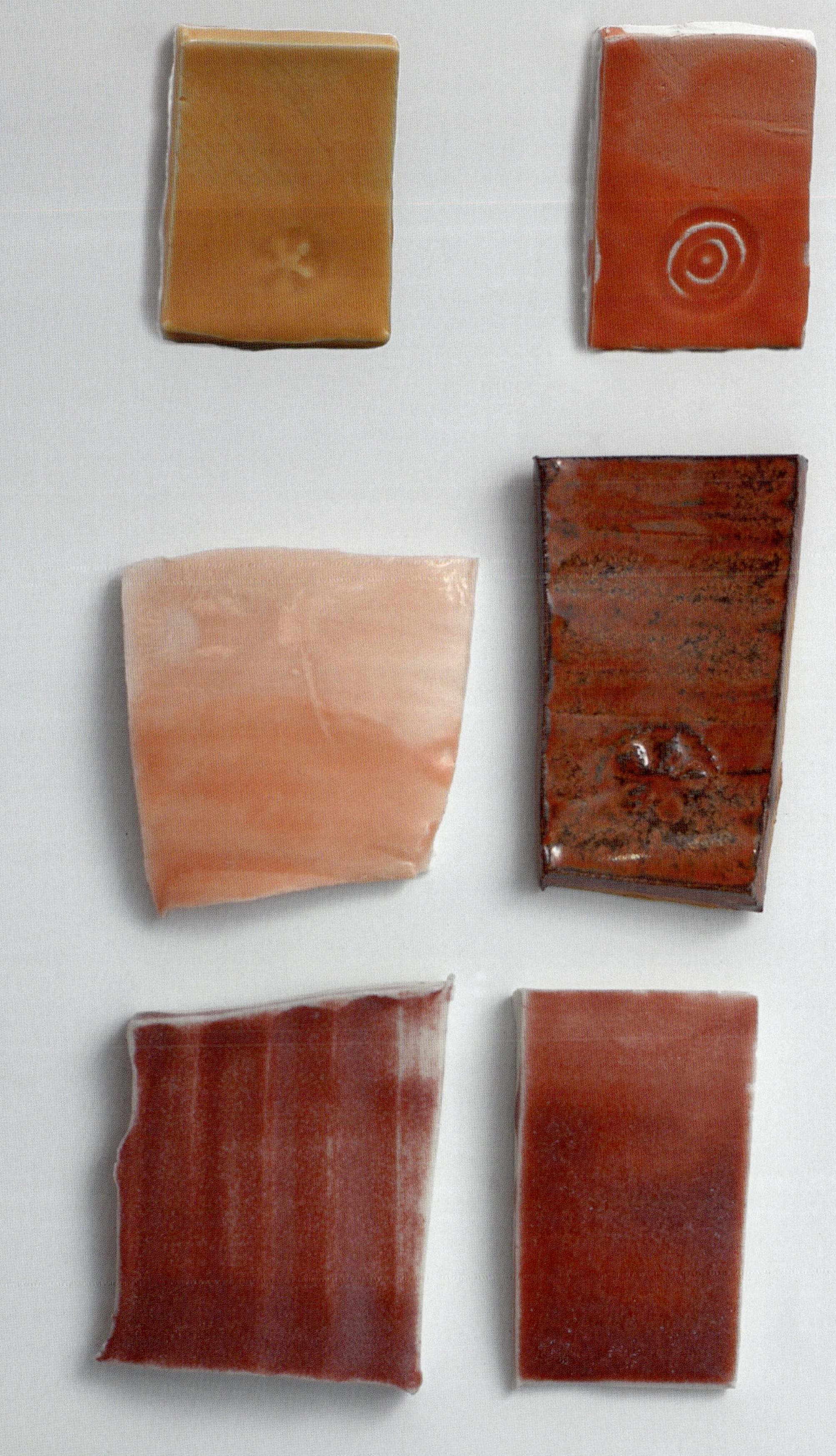

Yellow glazes

Slip Trailed Baluster Jugs, Hannah McAndrew, 2010. Earthenware covered with white slip and lead glaze. The decoration is trailed with a black slip containing iron and manganese. *Photo: courtesy of Shannon Tofts.*

When fired in oxidation, a small amount (1–5%) of iron oxide gives a honey- or amber-yellow colour. Iron oxide in a barium glaze high in zirconium will also give a yellow colour in reduction. Iron oxide was used in low-fired yellow porcelain glazes in Imperial China, and also in lead slipware glazes in 17th-century England and France. Lead antimonate was used to give a bright yellow on low-temperature Maiolica ware made in Renaissance Italy. Vanadium and tin oxide are also used to make a yellow stain that can be used at higher temperatures than antimony, but which does not give such a bright yellow. Chromium oxide gives yellow in low-temperature lead glazes fired to around 1050°C (1922°F). Uranium oxide was used as a high-temperature yellow colourant in the early 20th century, but it is now unavailable owing to its radioactivity. Cerium and titanium give a creamy yellow, as does rutile. A small amount (1–3%) of nickel and 10% titanium can produce a mustard yellow.

To obtain bright yellows, it is necessary to use a commercial stain. Praseodymium oxide and zirconium silicate are often used to make yellow stains, although they are not as strong as cadmium-sulphide yellows, which are bright orange-yellow. Zinc sulphide is added to cadmium sulphide to make light primrose-yellow stains.

BELOW: *Yellow parade with grey bowl*, Gwyn Hanssen Pigott, 2008. Reduction-fired porcelain. *Photo: courtesy of Brian Hand.*

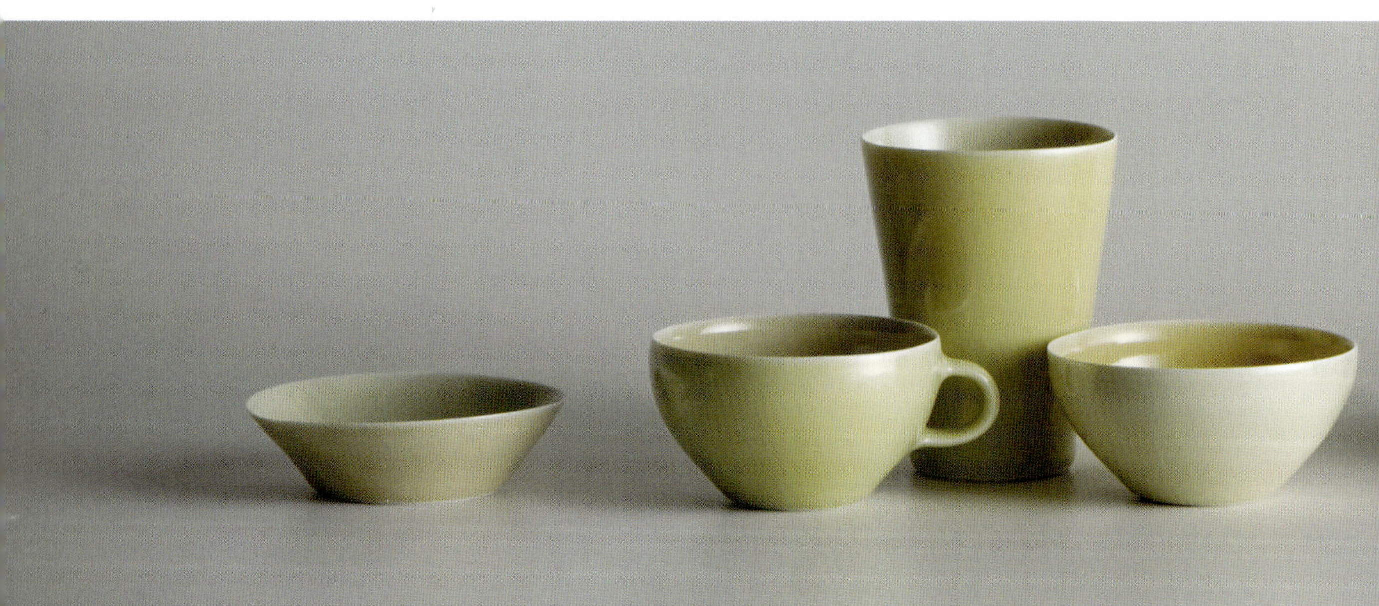

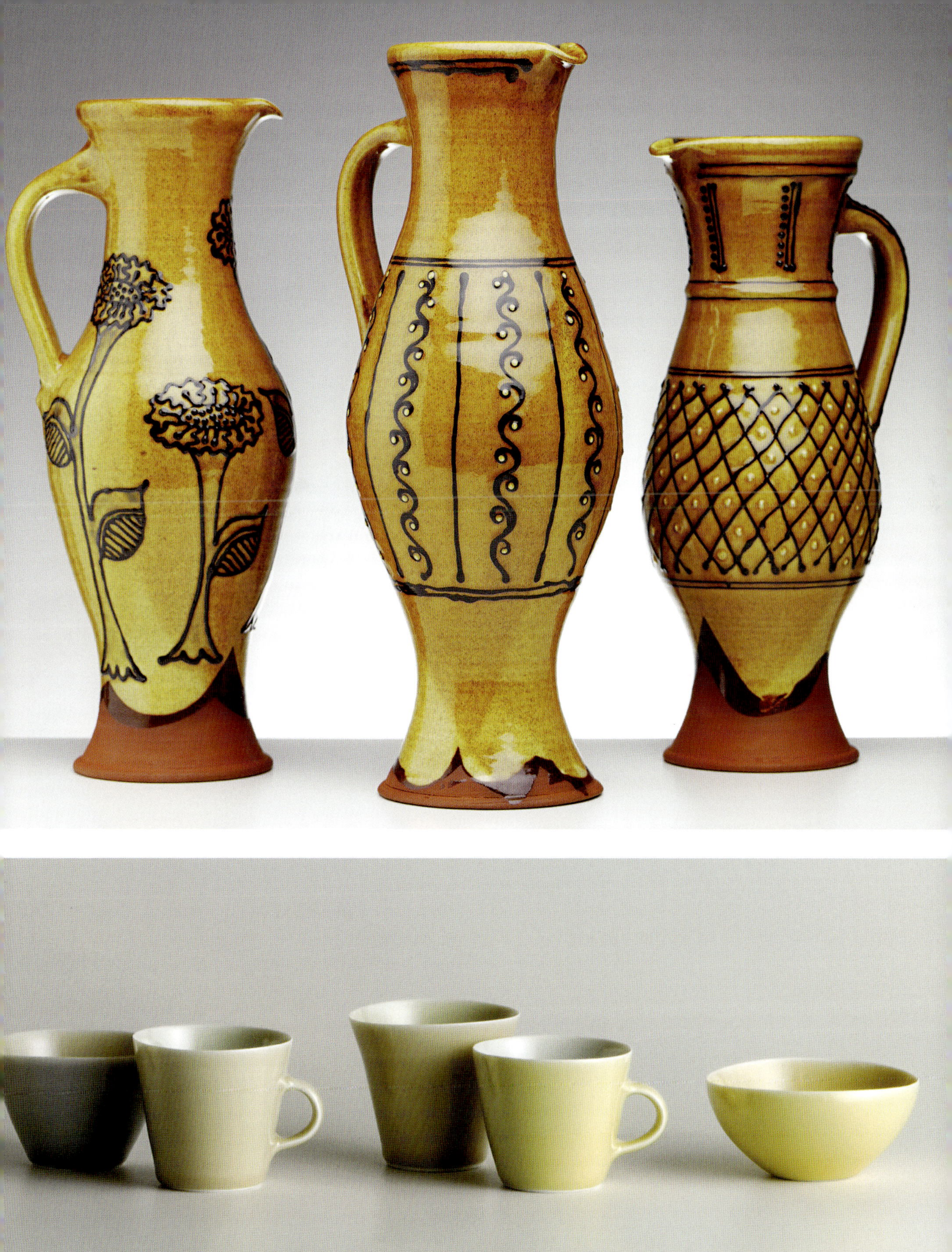

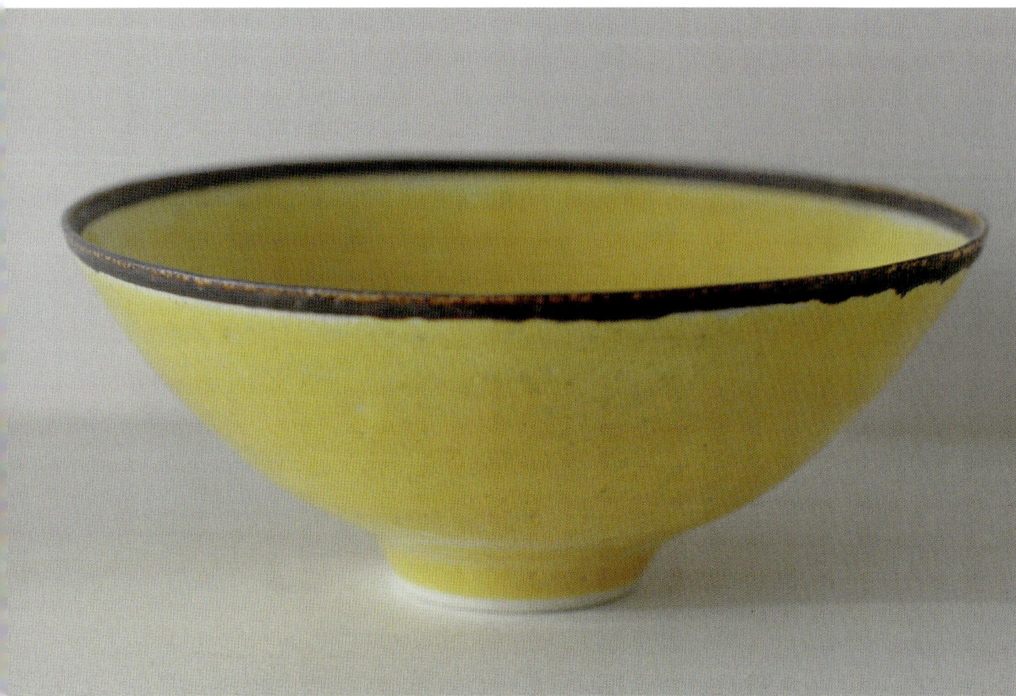

Bowl, Lucie Rie, 1970s. Uranium-yellow porcelain bowl with manganese on rim. Private collection. *Photo: Henry Bloomfield*.

BELOW: *Porcelain bowl*, Avril Farley, 2005. Zinc-silicate crystalline glaze, cerium oxide and rutile glaze. *Photo: Martin Avery*.

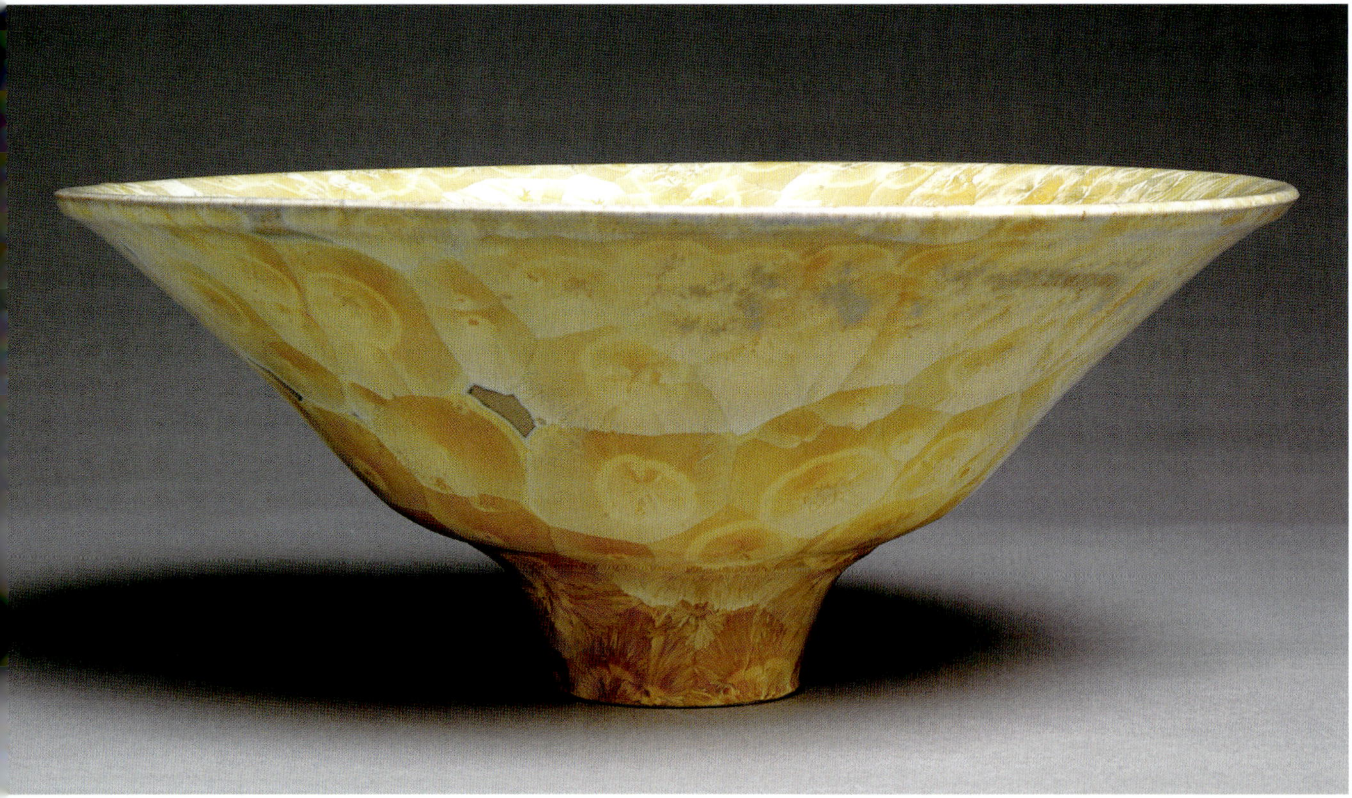

Yellow glazes for earthenware 1000–1100°C/1832–2012°F (cone 06–02)

Cadmium yellow glaze, 1060°C/1940°F (cone 04) oxidised (John Solly)

Calcium borate frit	39
Soda feldspar	27
Whiting	5
China clay	6
Quartz	23
+	
Yellow stain	5

Cadmium sulphide zirconium silicate stain ($CdSZrSiO_4$)

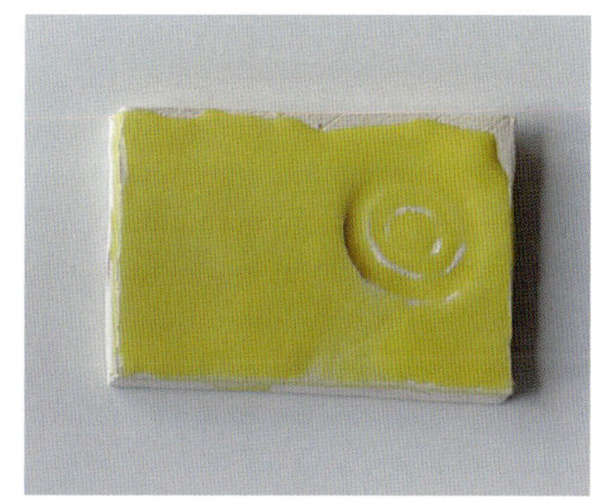

Praseodymium-zirconium yellow, not food safe. To avoid crazing, use borax frit instead of high alkaline frit. (Lok Ming Fung)

High-alkaline frit	75
China clay	15
Flint	10
+	
Yellow stain	5

Zirconium praseodymium silicate stain ($ZrPrSiO_4$)
(Potterycrafts Canary yellow P4140)

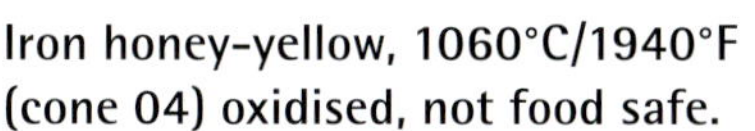

Iron honey-yellow, 1060°C/1940°F (cone 04) oxidised, not food safe.

High-alkaline frit	75
China clay	15
Flint	10
+	
Red iron oxide	10

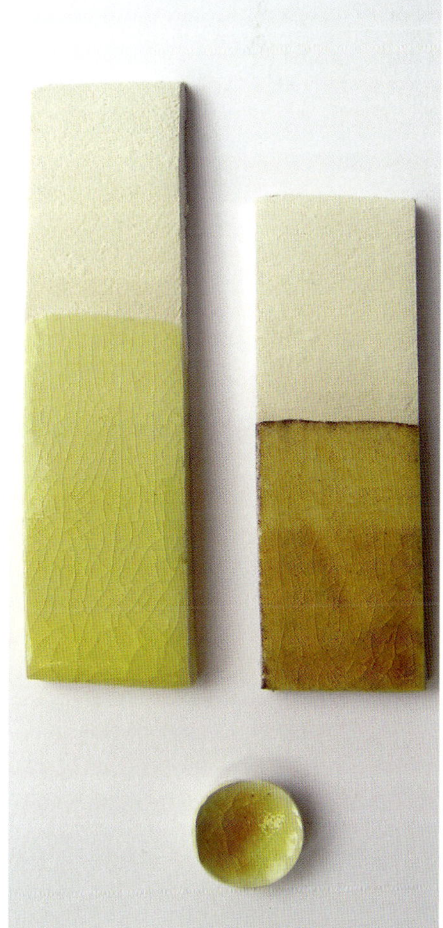

Praseodymium-zirconium yellow, from Lok Ming Fung. Left to right: stain yellow, iron yellow. Disc: iron yellow over stain yellow, showing glazes overlapping.

Yellow glazes for stoneware and porcelain, 1240–1280°C/2264–2336°F (cone 6–10) oxidised

Yellow-cream transparent, 1280°C/2336°F (cone 9) oxidised

Potash feldspar	26
Whiting	20
China clay	19
Quartz	30
Calcium borate frit	5
+	
Rutile	2.5

Bright yellow, 1280°C/2336°F (cone 9) oxidised

Potash feldspar	27
Whiting	21
China clay	20
Quartz	32
+	
Yellow stain	4

(Cadmium sulphide zirconium silicate stain ($CdSZrSiO_4$))

Orange-yellow opaque, 1260°C/2300°F (cone 8) oxidised

Potash feldspar	34
Talc	22
Whiting	12
China clay	15
Quartz	16
+	
Rutile	7
Tin oxide	5

Barium yellow matt, 1240–1260°C/2264–2300°F (cone 6–8) oxidised (John Britt)

Nepheline syenite	42.5
Dolomite	15.5
Barium carbonate	24
China clay	9
Quartz	9
+	
Zirconium silicate	19
Red iron oxide	3.5

Tan-yellow transparent, 1280°C/2336°F (cone 9) oxidised

Potash feldspar	27
Whiting	21
China clay	20
Quartz	32
+	
Rutile	5

Nickel-titanium yellow matt, 1260°C/2300°F (cone 8) oxidised

Potash feldspar	33
Talc	21
Whiting	12
China clay	15
Quartz	16
Zinc oxide	3
+	
Nickel oxide	3
Titanium dioxide	10

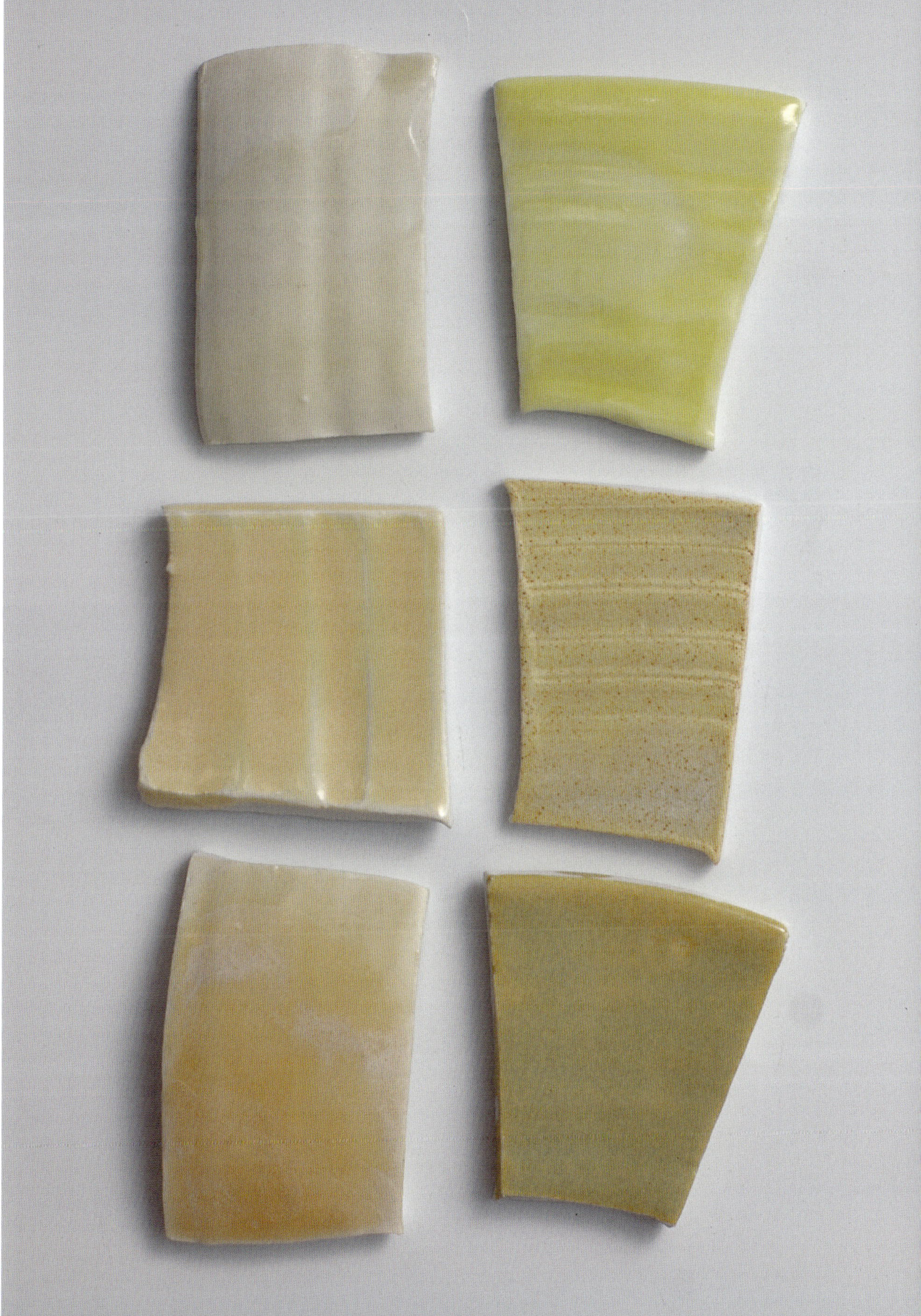

Brown and grey glazes

RIGHT: *Large tenmoku bowls*, Sue Paraskeva, 2010. Feldspar glaze containing 13% red iron oxide, fired in reduction to 1260°C (2300°F). *Photo: Sue Paraskeva.*

The most popular brown glazes used in studio pottery are the Oriental tenmoku and kaki, both derived from large amounts (8–12%) of iron oxide. Tenmoku is a dark brown-black glaze which breaks to rust on rims, best fired in reduction. Kaki is a rust-red saturated iron glaze containing bone ash, which gives the brightest red-browns in oxidation (see p.91). Commercial brown stains, made from iron-zinc chromite, are usually less interesting than the variegated browns obtained from iron oxide. Red earthenware contains iron oxide and is red-brown when covered with a clear glaze. Rich dark browns can be obtained from iron and manganese. Manganese dioxide can be used on its own as a brown-black pigment. Small amounts of iron and titanium (or rutile) give a yellow-brown colour, while manganese yields a pink-brown colour in glazes. Pale browns can be achieved with small amounts of nickel. Darker shades may be obtained by adding cobalt.

Recipe for brown underglaze (19th century) (from *Pottery Gazette*, London, 1880s, Smith, Greenwood & Co)

Zinc oxide	1 lb
Iron chromate	3 lbs

Calcine in glost oven (1050°C/1922°F, cone 04). The same colour can be obtained if iron, chrome and zinc are added to a suitable base glaze (see p.106, bottom right).

BELOW: *Inge tray, jug and plate*, Lars P. Soendergaard Gregersen, 2003. Thrown porcelain, matt glazes, fired in oxidation in a gas kiln. *Photo courtesy of the artist.*

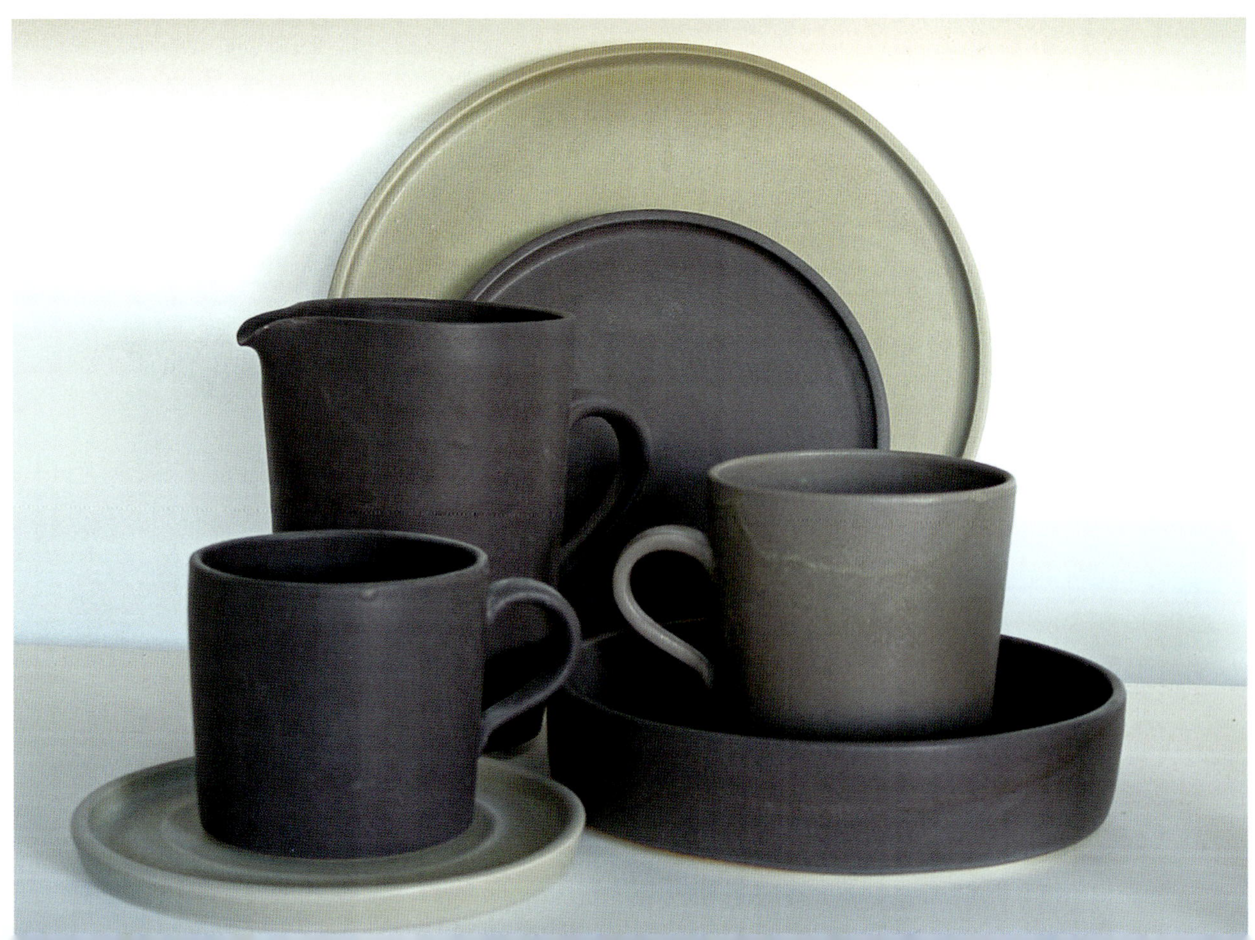

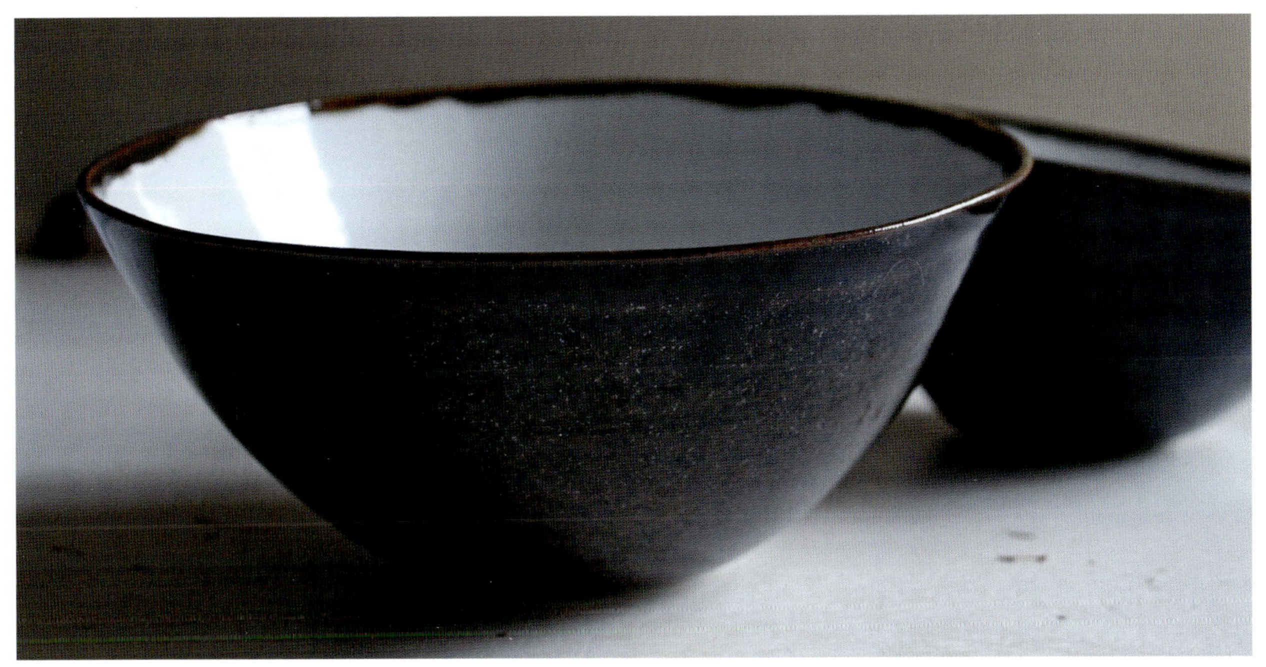

Brown glazes for earthenware, 1000–1100°C/1832–2012°F (cone 06–02)

Yellow-brown glaze, 1060°C/1940°F (cone 04) oxidised (John Solly)

Calcium borate frit	39
Soda feldspar	27
Whiting	5
China clay	6
Quartz	23
+	
Rutile	2

Grey-brown glaze, 1060°C/1940°F (cone 04) oxidised

Calcium borate frit	39
Soda feldspar	27
Whiting	5
China clay	6
Quartz	23
+	
Ilmenite	5

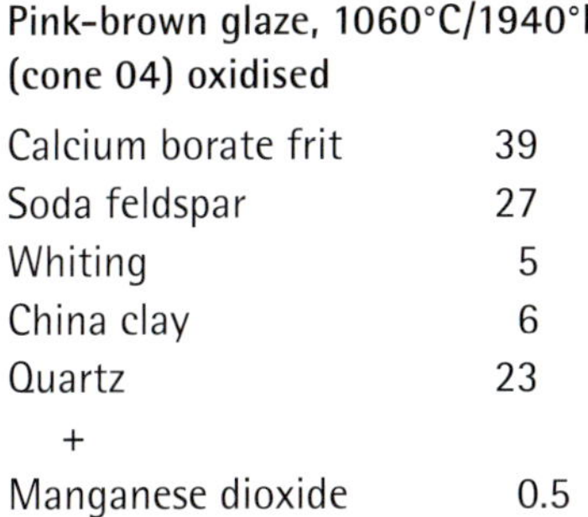

Pink-brown glaze, 1060°C/1940°F (cone 04) oxidised

Calcium borate frit	39
Soda feldspar	27
Whiting	5
China clay	6
Quartz	23
+	
Manganese dioxide	0.5

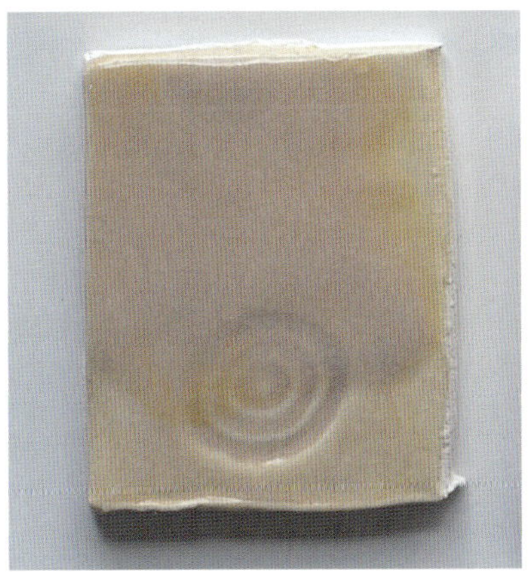

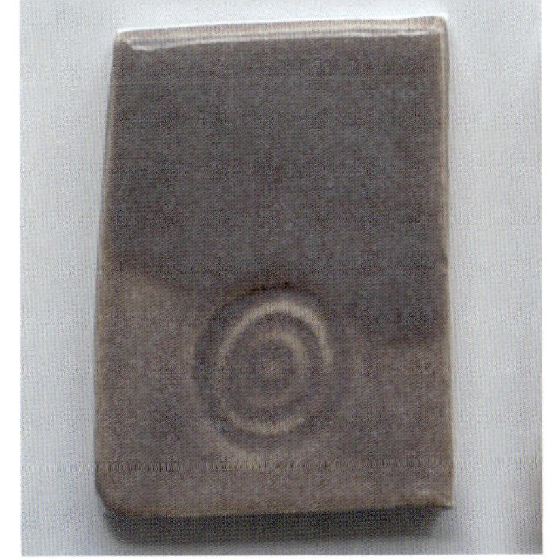

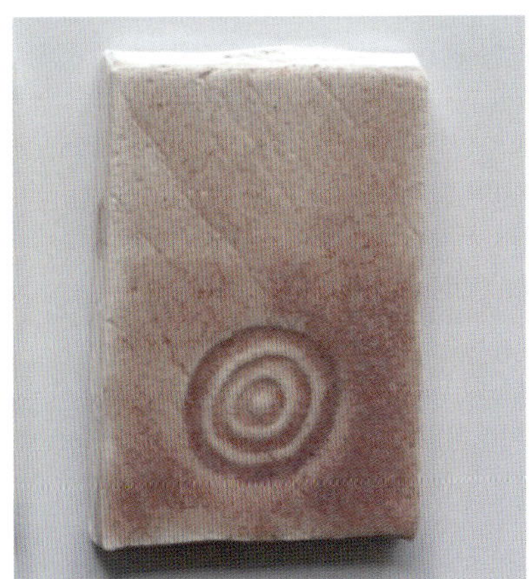

Cream and brown glazes for stoneware and porcelain, 1240–1280°C/ 2264–2336°F (cone 6–9) oxidised

Yellow-brown transparent, 1280°C/2336°F (cone 9) oxidised

Potash feldspar	27
Whiting	21
China clay	20
Quartz	32
+	
Ilmenite	5

Speckled cream matt, 1240–1260°C/ 2264–2300°F (cone 6–8) oxidised

Soda feldspar	44
Dolomite	23
Whiting	3
China clay	4
Bentonite	2
Quartz	23
+	
Tin oxide	1
Rutile	5

Pale brown transparent, 1280°C/2336°F (cone 9) oxidised

Potash feldspar	27
Whiting	21
China clay	20
Quartz	32
+	
Nickel oxide	0.3

Dark brown transparent, 1280°C/2336°F (cone 9) oxidised

Potash feldspar	27
Whiting	21
China clay	20
Quartz	32
+	
Nickel oxide	0.3
Cobalt oxide	0.1
Ilmenite	5

Brown matt, 1260°C/2300°F (cone 8) oxidised

FFF feldspar	32
Talc	20
Whiting	12
Zinc oxide	3
China clay	16
Quartz	17
+	
Red iron oxide	8

Red-brown matt, 1260°C/2300°F (cone 8) oxidised

FFF feldspar	32
Talc	20
Whiting	12
Zinc oxide	3
China clay	16
Quartz	17
+	
Red iron oxide	8
Chromium oxide	0.5

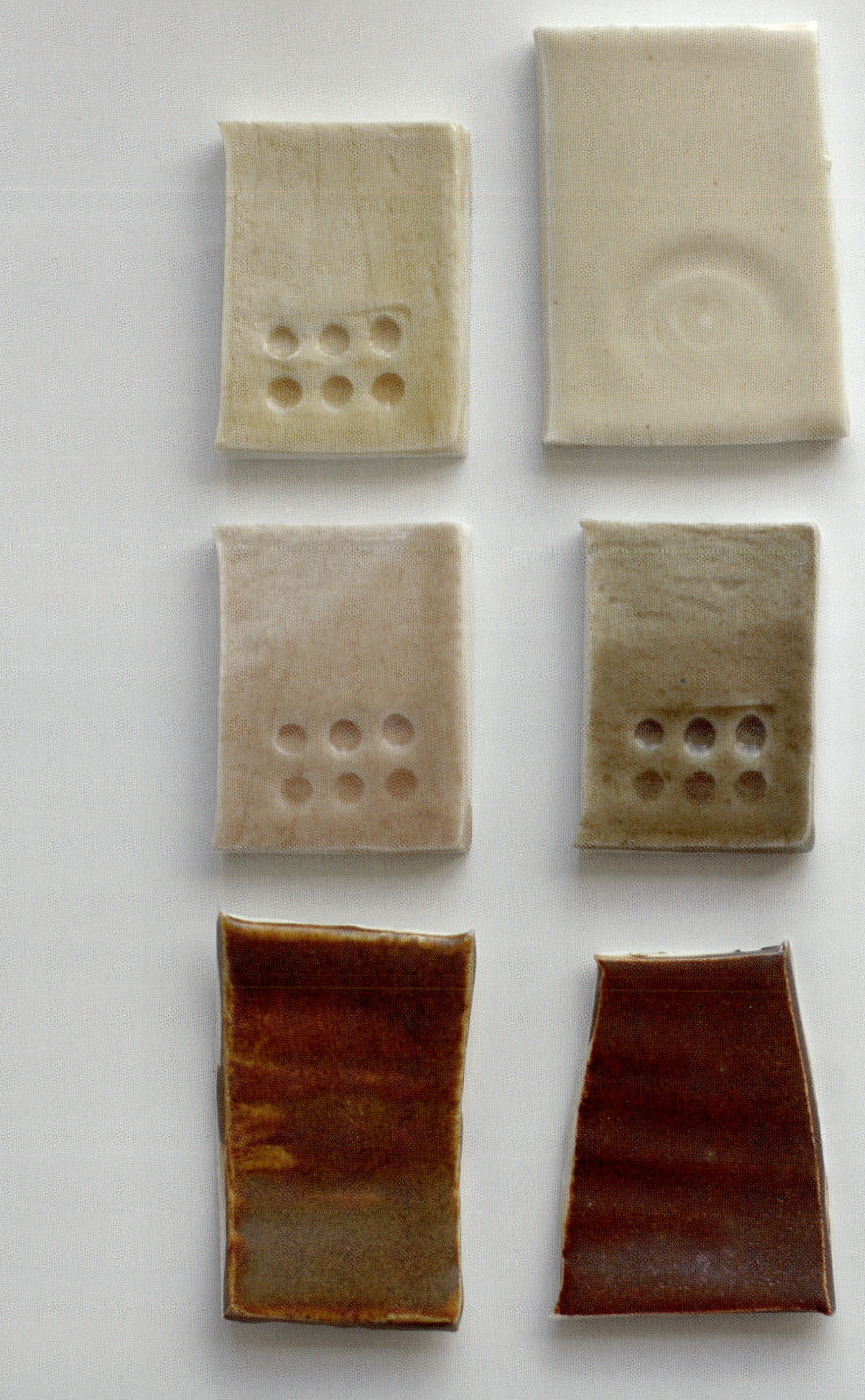

White, black and grey glazes

RIGHT: *Cow parsley jugs*, Ken Eardley, 2004. Earthenware, paper resist, underglaze colours. *Photo: Sussie Ahlburg.*

Potters make white glazes by adding an opacifier such as tin oxide, titanium oxide or zirconium silicate to a transparent glaze. Most matt glazes are semi-opaque, but they can be made whiter by adding an opacifier. On porcelain, there is no need to make the glaze opaque, as the clay body is already white.

Potters can make black by adding iron, cobalt, manganese and chromium oxides in the ratio 2:2:2:1 to a glossy or matt glaze. Without chromium (which is refractory and does not completely dissolve in the glaze), a very dark midnight blue is obtained. Cobalt sometimes causes problems, bleeding colour into adjacent areas of transparent glaze. Cobalt-free black stains (containing iron and chromium) can be used to avoid this. Nickel is sometimes added to black stains, particularly for glazes containing zinc, which turns chromium brown. Grey glazes can be made using small amounts of nickel and cobalt.

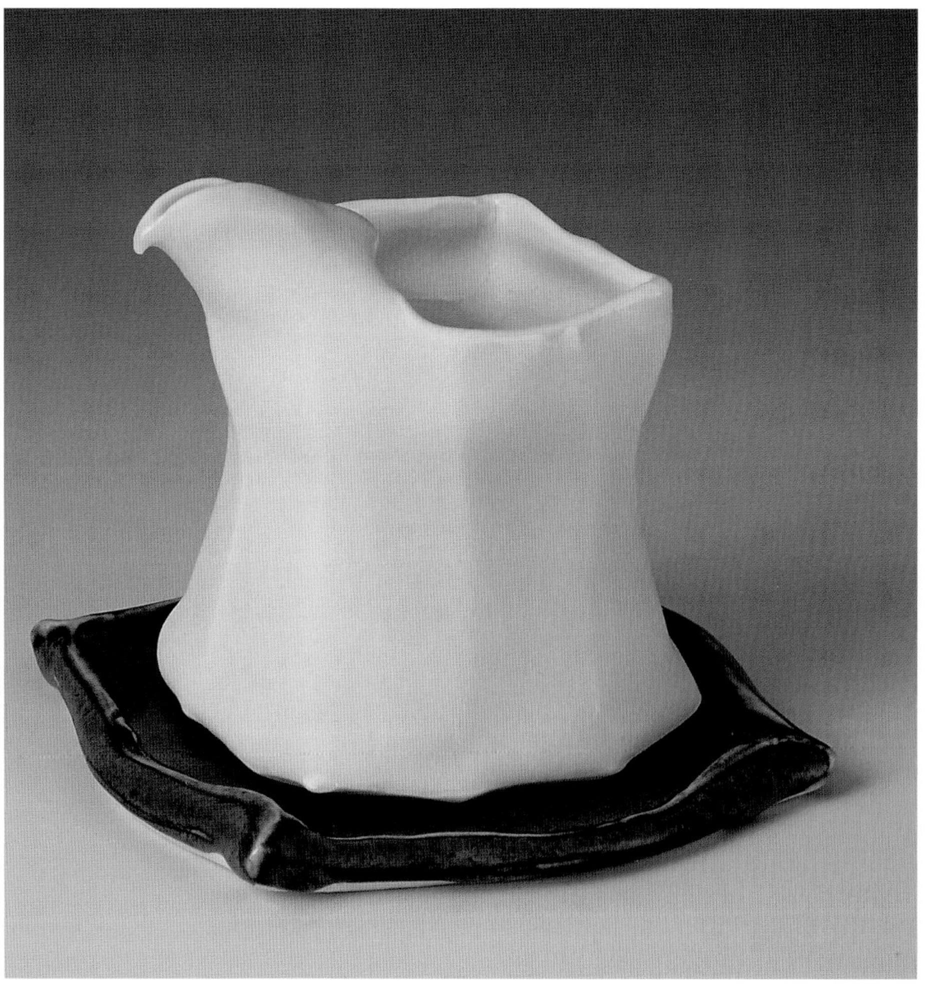

LEFT: *Soy Joy*, Joanna Howells, 2008. Thrown porcelain, satin matt white and iron black glazes, reduction-fired. *Photo: Joanna Howells.*

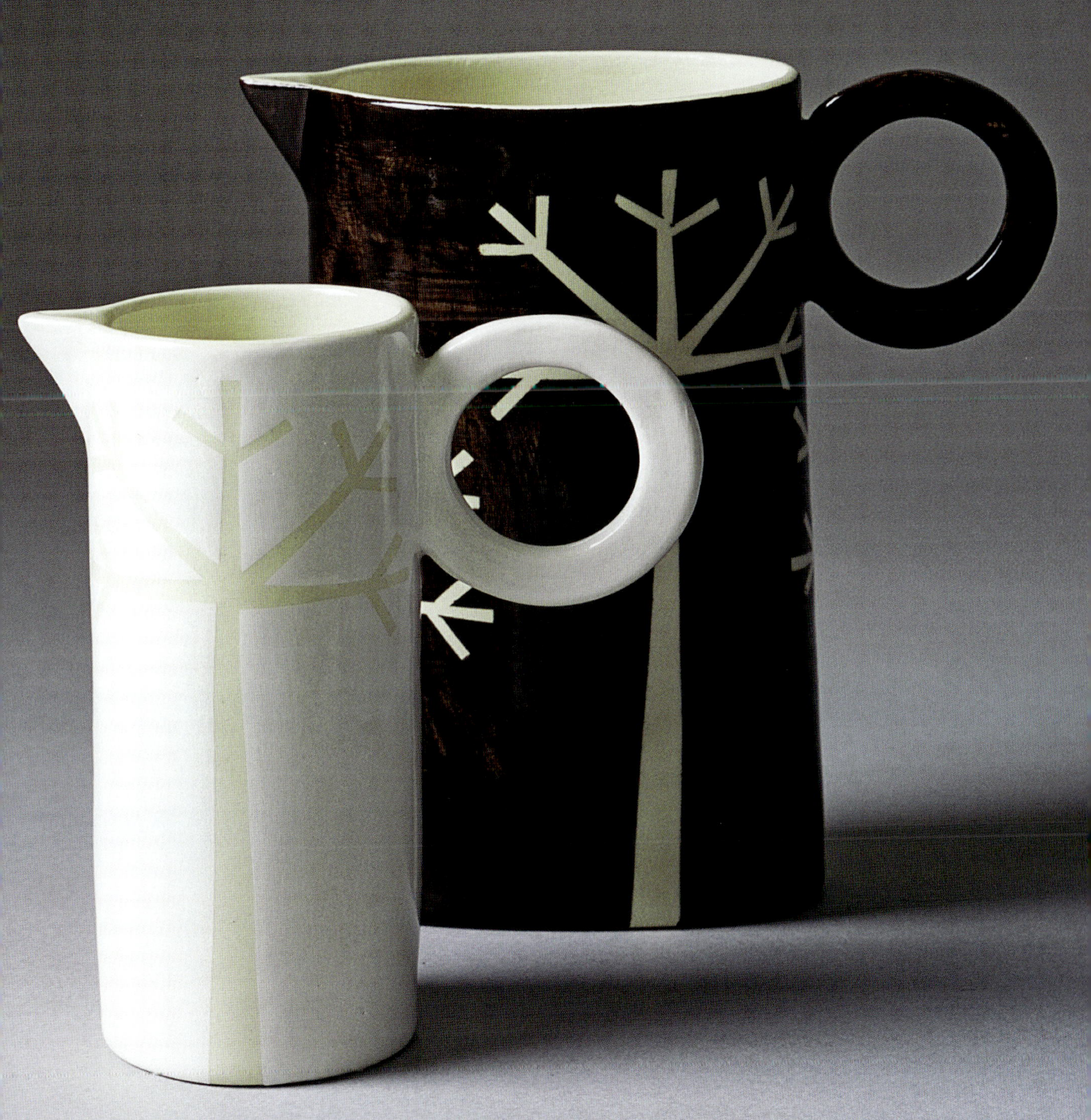

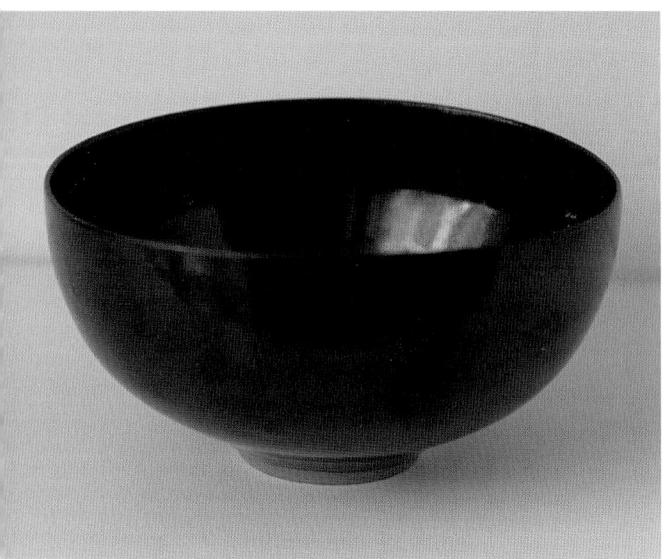

Small Bowl, Lucie Rie, 1970s. Thrown stoneware bowl, glossy black glaze. Private collection. *Photo: Henry Bloomfield.*

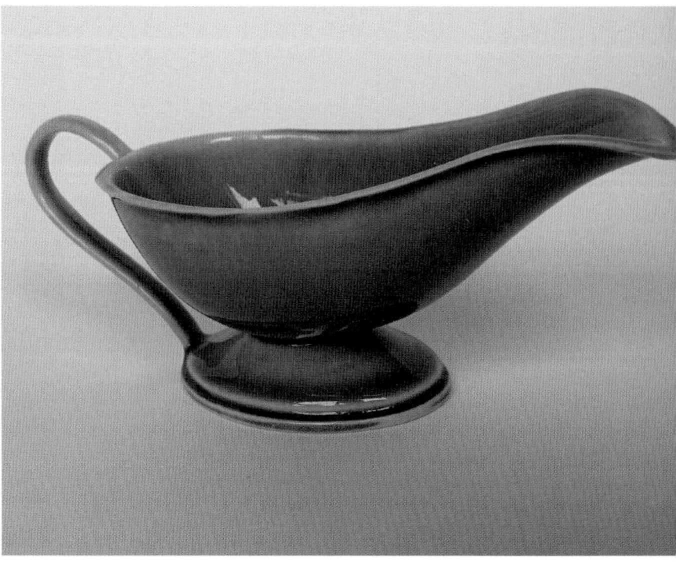

Gravy jug, Adam Harvey, 2010. Slip cast Parian semi-porcelain, manganese and cobalt alkaline glaze containing lithium, fired to 1170°C (2138°F) with a 40-minute soak. *Photo: Adam Harvey.*

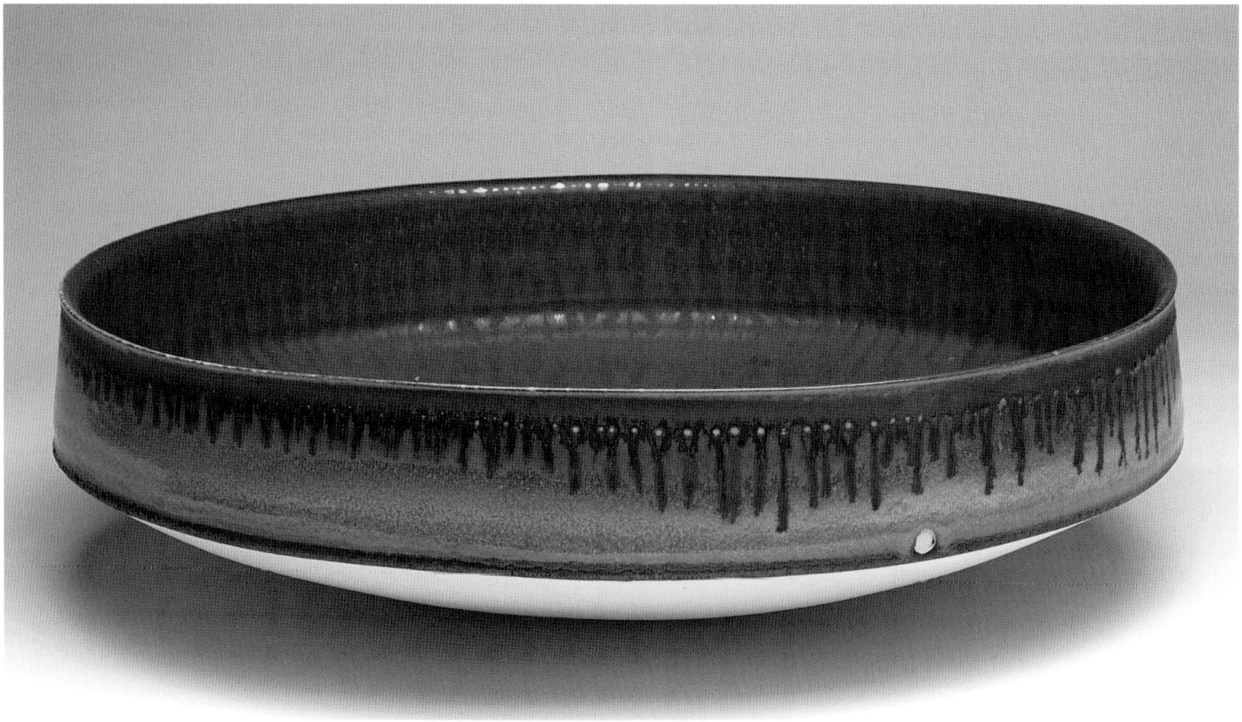

Nocturnal, Tanya Gomez, 2008. Thrown porcelain paper clay, black metallic glaze, w: 60cm (23½in). *Photo: Ray Fowler.*

White glazes for earthenware 1060–1100°C/1940–2012°F (cone 04–02)

Transparent glaze, 1060°C/1940°F (cone 04) oxidised (John Solly)

Calcium borate frit	39
Soda feldspar	27
Whiting	5
China clay	6
Quartz	23

Opaque white glaze, 1060°C/1940°F (cone 04) oxidised

Calcium borate frit	39
Soda feldspar	27
Whiting	5
China clay	6
Quartz	23
+	
Zirconium silicate	5

Matt white glaze, 1100°C/2012°F (cone 02) oxidised

Calcium borate frit	24
Soda feldspar	27
Whiting	20
China clay	6
Quartz	23

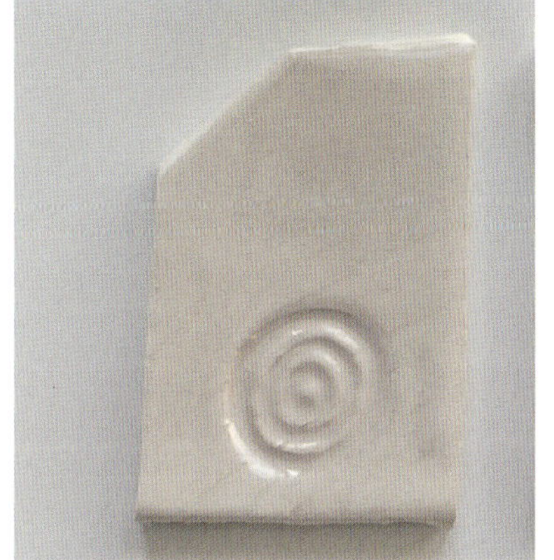

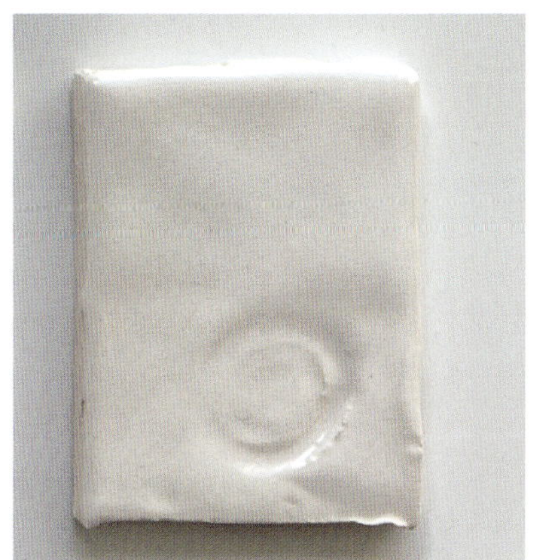

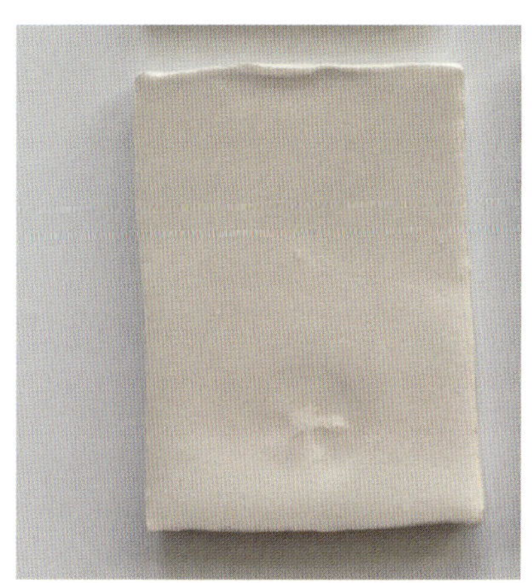

Black glaze for earthenware, 1060–1100°C/1940–2012°F (cone 04–02)

Glossy black glaze, 1100°C/2012°F (cone 02) oxidised

Calcium borate frit	44
Talc	8
Whiting	8
China clay	12
Quartz	28
+	
Red iron oxide	2
Manganese dioxide	2
Cobalt oxide	2
Chromium oxide	1

Grey glazes for earthenware 1060°C/1940°F (cone 04)

Matt pale grey, 1060°C/1940°F (cone 04) oxidised (Lucy Burley)

Borax frit	45
Potash feldspar	15
Barium carbonate	10
Ball clay	15
China clay	15
+	
Blue stain (CoZnSi)	0.5
Nickel oxide	0.12

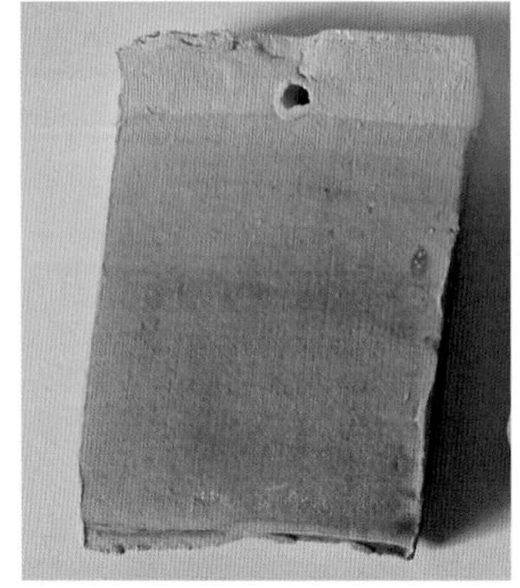

Matt grey, 1060°C/1940°F (cone 04) oxidised

Borax frit	45
Potash feldspar	15
Barium carbonate	10
Ball clay	15
China clay	15
+	
Blue stain (CoZnSi)	1
Nickel oxide	0.25

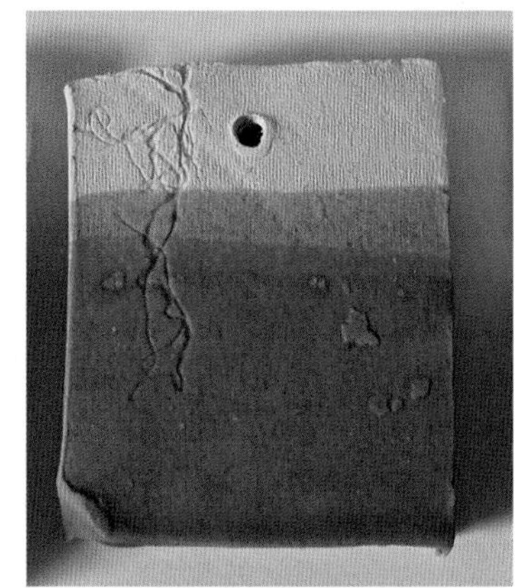

Matt purple grey, 1060°C/1940°F (cone 04) oxidised

Borax frit	45
Potash feldspar	15
Barium carbonate	10
Ball clay	15
China clay	15
+	
Blue stain (CoZnSi)	1
Lilac stain (CrSn)	5
Nickel oxide	0.25

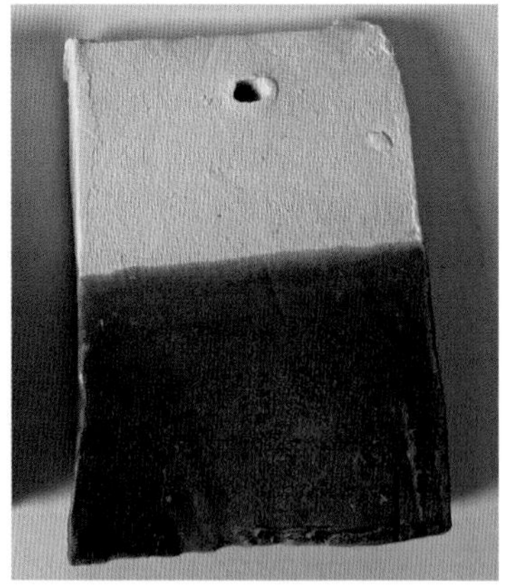

Shades of grey bottles, Lucy Burley, 2009. Thrown white earthenware, sprayed matt glazes with stains and oxides, fired to 1060°C (1940°F). *Photo: Lucy Burley.*

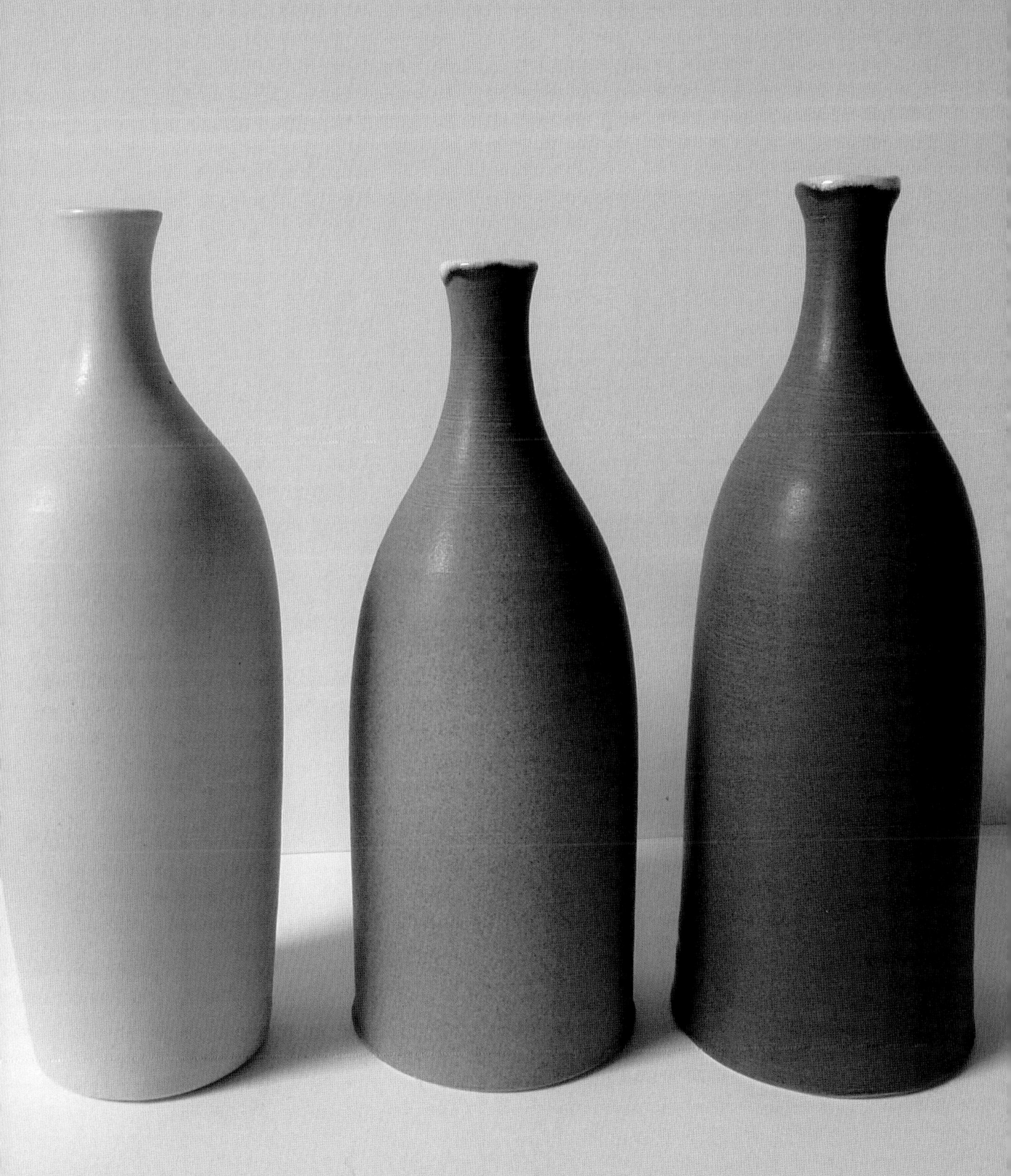

White, grey and black glazes for stoneware and porcelain, 1240–1280°C/2264–2336°F (cone 6–10) oxidised

Crystalline matt white, 1240–1260°C /2264–2300°F (cone 6–8) oxidised (Michael Bailey)

Soda feldspar	43
Whiting	23
Zinc oxide	6
China clay	7
Quartz	22
+	
Titanium oxide	5

Satin matt translucent, 1260°C/2300°F (cone 8) oxidised (Stephen Murfitt)

FFF feldspar	32
Talc	20
Whiting	12
Zinc oxide	3
China clay	16
Quartz	17

Glossy transparent, 1240–1260°C /2264–2300°F (cone 6–8) oxidised (Stephen Murfitt)

Potash feldspar	34
Calcium borate frit	14
Whiting	11
China clay	13
Quartz	23
Dolomite	5

Alkaline transparent, 1260°C/2300°F (cone 8) oxidised (Emmanuel Cooper)

Nepheline syenite	26
Whiting	12
Lithium carbonate	10
Barium carbonate	3
Calcium borate frit	5
Flint	44

Pale grey satin matt translucent, 1260°C/2300°F (cone 8) oxidised

Potash feldspar	33
Talc	21
Whiting	12
China clay	15
Quartz	16
Zinc oxide	3
+	
Cobalt oxide	0.1
Nickel oxide	0.2

Grey transparent, 1280°C/2336°F (cone 9) oxidised

Potash feldspar	27
Whiting	21
China clay	20
Quartz	32
+	
Cobalt oxide	0.1
Nickel oxide	0.3

Blue-grey magnesium matt, 1280°C/ 2336°F (cone 9) oxidised

Potash feldspar	40
Dolomite	16
Bone ash	8
China clay	24
Flint	8
Calcium borate frit	5
+	
Cobalt oxide	0.3
Nickel oxide	0.5

Glossy black, 1280°C/2336°F (cone 9) oxidised

Potash feldspar	27
Whiting	21
China clay	20
Quartz	32
+	
Manganese dioxide	2
Red iron oxide	2
Cobalt oxide	2
Chromium oxide	1

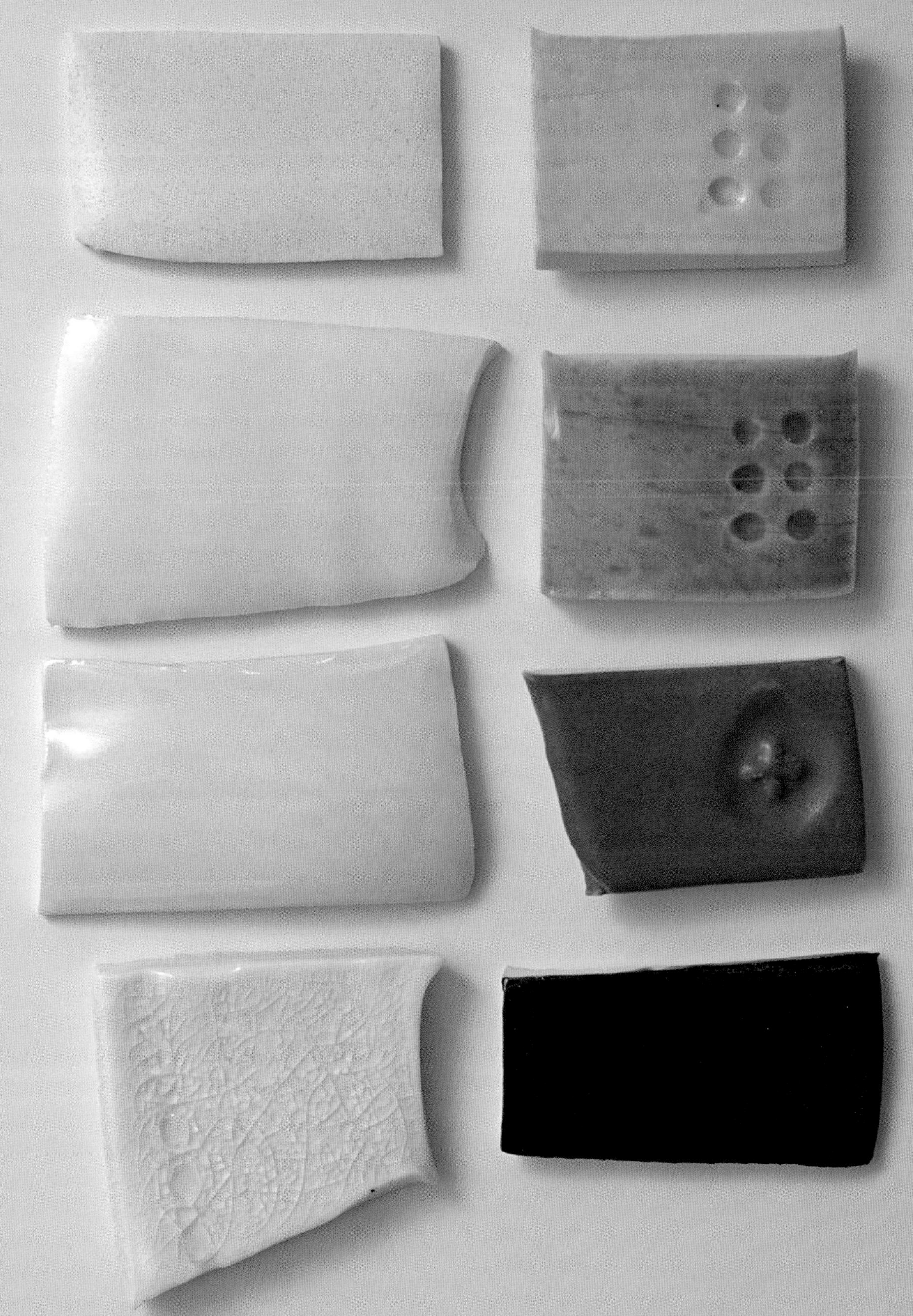

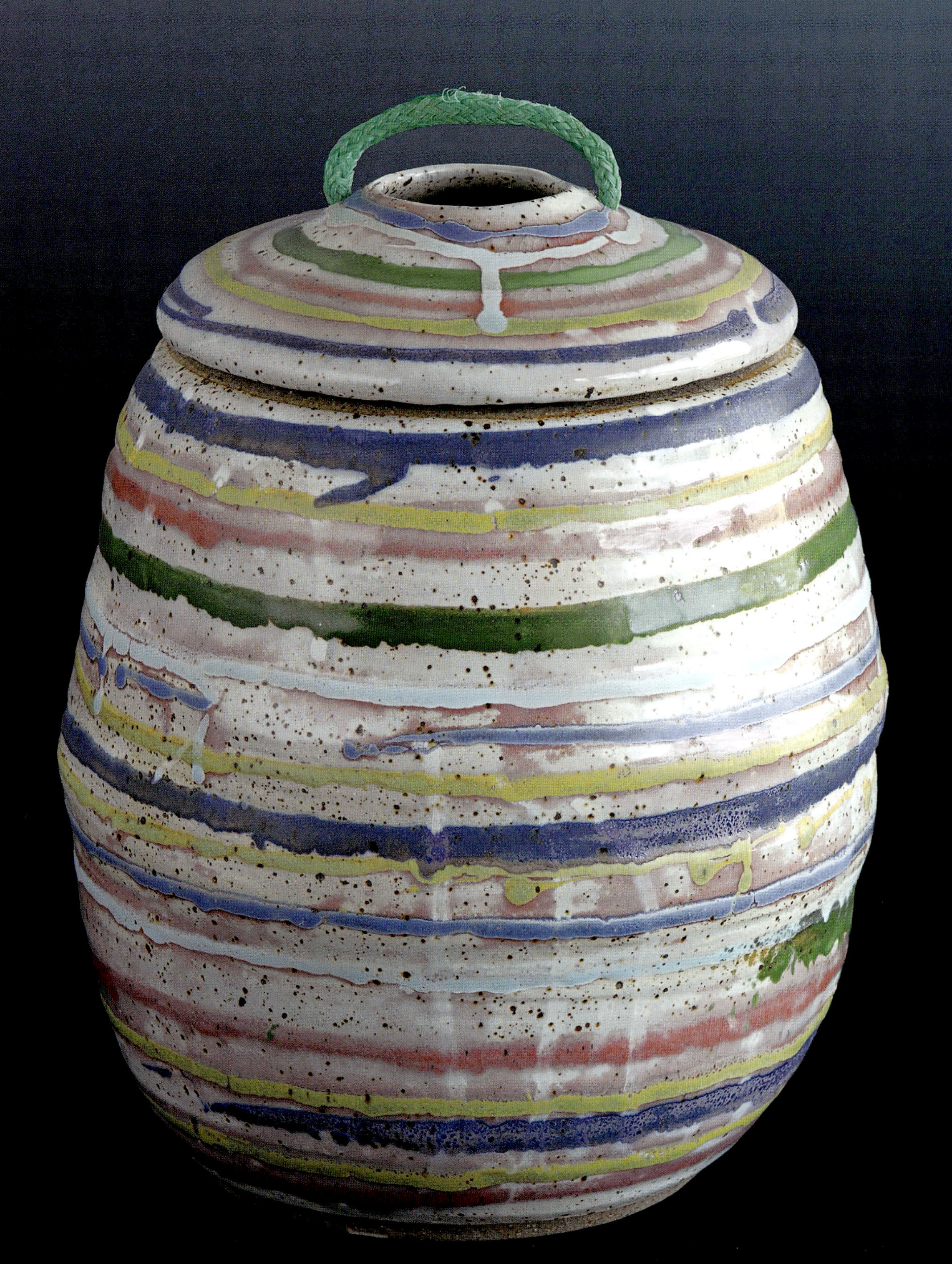

6

Mixing glazes

LEFT: *Lidded Jar*, Chris Barnes, 2009. Stoneware with white slip, white base glaze, transparent reactive glaze, and bands of coloured glazes. Blue is cobalt in dolomite glaze. Yellow is iron in barium-zirconium glaze. Red is copper in borax glaze. Green is chromium in potassium glaze. Pale duck-egg blue is copper in barium-zirconium glaze. Mid-blue is cobalt and copper in barium-zirconium glaze, fired in reduction to cone 9. The copper in the barium-zirconium glaze has diffused into the transparent glaze beneath to form a soft red fringe. *Photo: courtesy of Val Corbett.*

Weighing

The weighing of glaze ingredients, particularly colouring oxides, requires the ability to measure small amounts, down to 0.1g. A triple beam balance scale is the most accurate, but digital scales can also be used. Smaller amounts can be measured by dividing 0.1g into portions with a straight edge. The powdered glaze ingredients are weighed and added carefully to a bucket that is half-full of water. If the least dense ingredients, such as China clay, talc and whiting, are added before the denser materials, such as feldspar, nepheline syenite, quartz and frit, there is less chance they will settle in a hard layer at the bottom.

Sieving

The glaze must be left for a few hours to slake the dry materials, and then it can be sieved several times through an 80s-mesh sieve using a brush or rubber spatula. Glazes containing small amounts of cobalt or iron oxide may require sieving again through a 120s-mesh or 200s-mesh sieve to avoid specks of colour, or grinding in a ball mill or mortar and pestle.

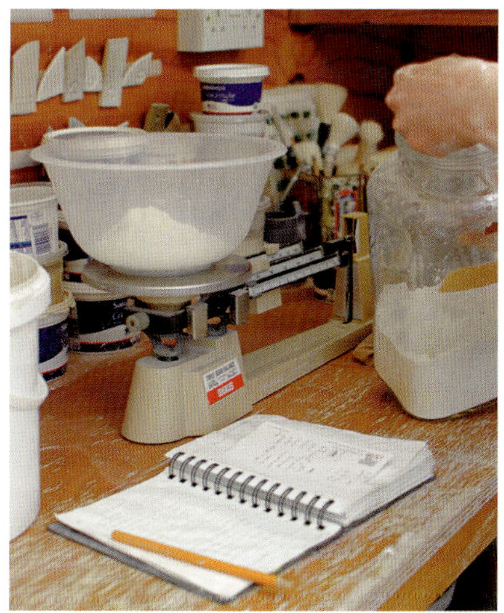

Weighing the glaze ingredients on a triple-beam balance.

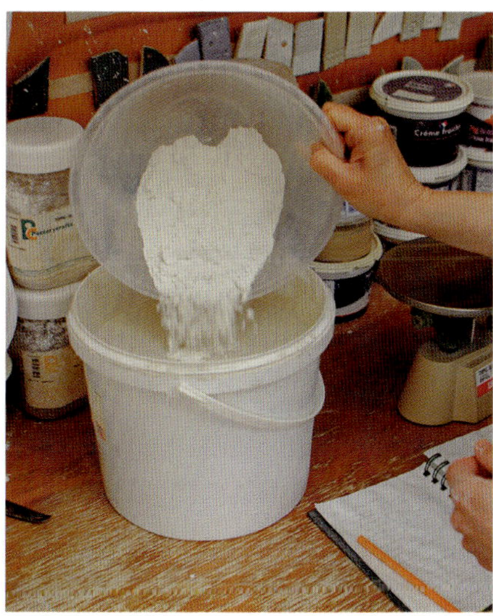

Adding ingredients to water.

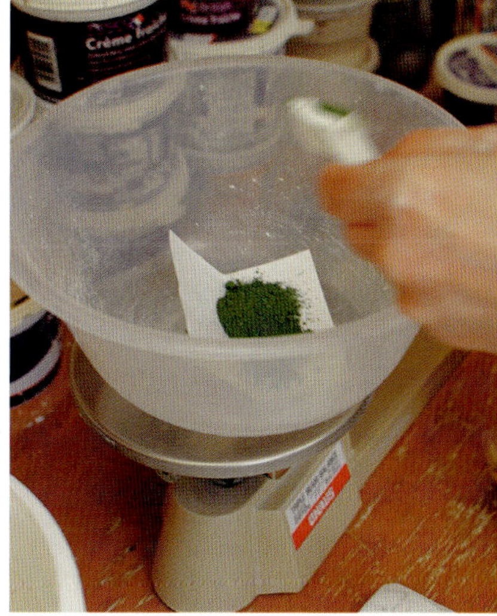

Weighing out colouring oxide.

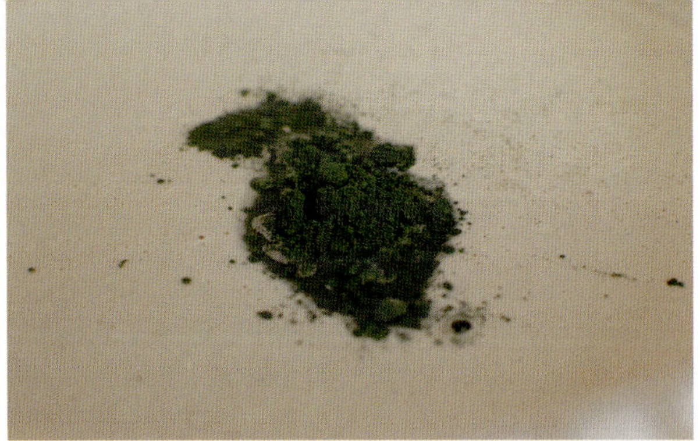

1 Colouring oxide added to glaze and left to slake for several hours.

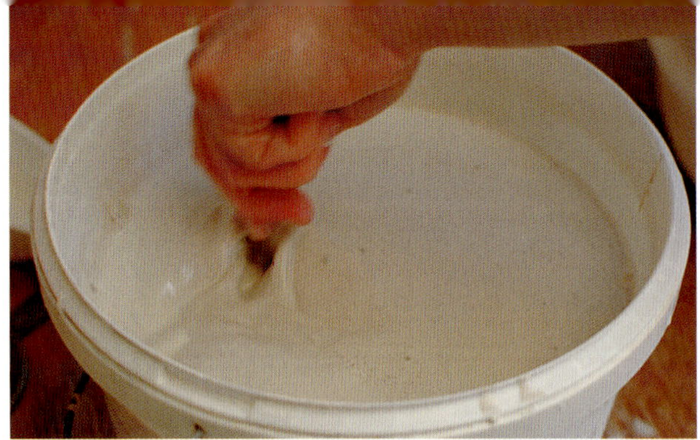

2 Stirring the glaze.

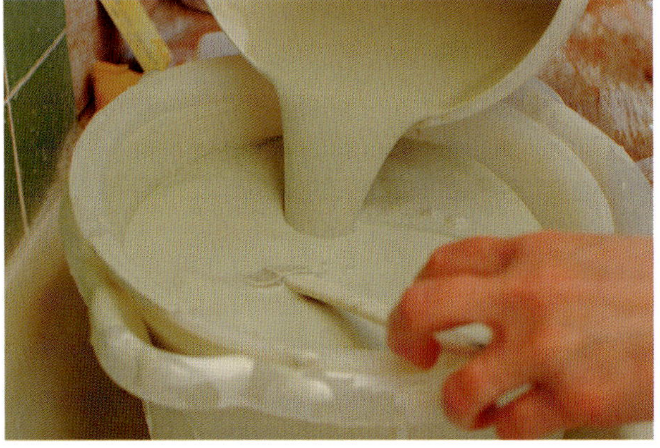

3 Sieving the glaze through an 80s-mesh sieve to disperse colouring oxide.

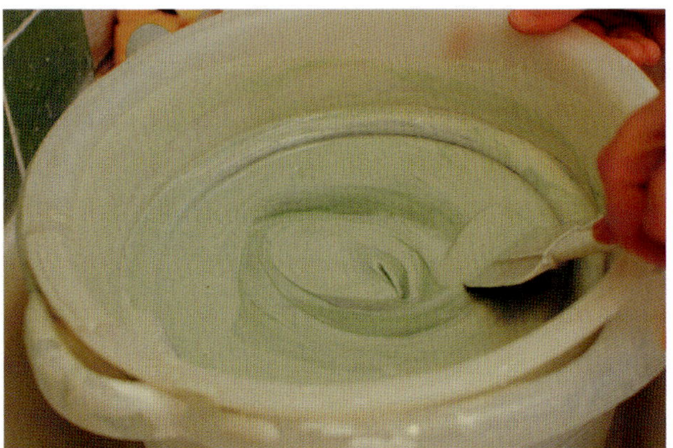

4 Pushing the glaze through a sieve with a spatula. This is repeated several times until the colour is evenly dispersed.

After sieving the glaze, the thickness should be assessed. Most glazes should be between the thickness of milk and the thickness of single cream. For consistency, a hydrometer can be used to measure the specific gravity, or the water level can be marked on the bucket to use each time a new batch of a particular glaze is made. To measure the specific gravity without using a hydrometer, just weigh 100ml glaze and divide the weight by 100, for example, if 100ml glaze weighs 140g, the specific gravity is 1.4. If the glaze is too thin, it should be left overnight to settle, then the water should be removed from the top. To test the glaze, a tile can be dipped and the glaze thickness measured with a pin. Most glazes should be applied about a millimetre (1/32in) thick. Some glazes, such as ash glazes and Chun blues, require a thicker application of several millimetres.

Glaze additives

Most glazes contain some clay, which helps to suspend the glaze in water, but glazes containing less than 5% clay may require the addition of bentonite, a plastic clay which aids suspension. Only a small amount is required (around 2% bentonite), which can be substituted for the same amount of China clay in the recipe. If the glaze settles out in a hard layer, remove the water, dig out the glaze, mix the water back in and add a small amount (a teaspoon) of magnesium sulphate (Epsom salts) dissolved in warm water. This will flocculate the glaze and make the particles clump together. However, if the glaze becomes too thick and cracks when it dries on the pot, even when water is added (as can happen in bone ash glazes), you can deflocculate it by adding a few drops of sodium silicate or Dispex. To help the glaze adhere to the pot, particularly when brushing on glazes, gum arabic or CMC (carboxy methyl cellulose) can be added.

Health and safety

Many glaze colourants are toxic and should be handled with care. Toxic substances should be disposed of safely, in landfill, and not down the drain. Gloves should be worn when mixing glazes, particularly those containing strong alkalis such as wood ash or lithium carbonate. Some glaze materials, such as Cornish stone (containing fluorspar, which decomposes to fluorine) and manganese dioxide, give off toxic fumes in the kiln, so kiln rooms should be well-ventilated. Welder's glass should be used when peering through spy holes. A fire extinguisher should be kept near the kiln.

Highly toxic glaze materials	*Toxic glaze materials*
Lead	Cobalt
Barium	Copper
Cadmium-selenium	Lithium
(red, orange and yellow stains)	Boron
Antimony	Zinc
Vanadium	
Uranium	
Nickel	
Chromium	
Manganese	

Silica dust is a health hazard, and a respirator mask should be used when handling dry powdered quartz, flint, clay, feldspar, talc, wollastonite and frits. Glaze materials should be kept in lidded containers. Surfaces and floors should be sponged or mopped. Towels, aprons and overalls should be washed regularly. Food or drink should not be consumed in the workshop.

Some glazes may not be food safe, particularly those containing lead or barium. Acid foods can dissolve the glaze, leaching out heavy metals. If the glaze contains a high-enough proportion of silica and alumina and is fired to maturity, the glaze should be resistant to acid attack and leaching. (Limits for stable glazes are given in Appendix 3, p.148.) A properly formulated glass is actually a good way to encapsulate toxic materials; nuclear waste is fired in a black borosilicate glass before being encased in stainless steel and concrete. By law, domestic earthenware sold in the UK and the USA must not leach lead or cadmium (found in red, orange and yellow stains), but it would be preferable

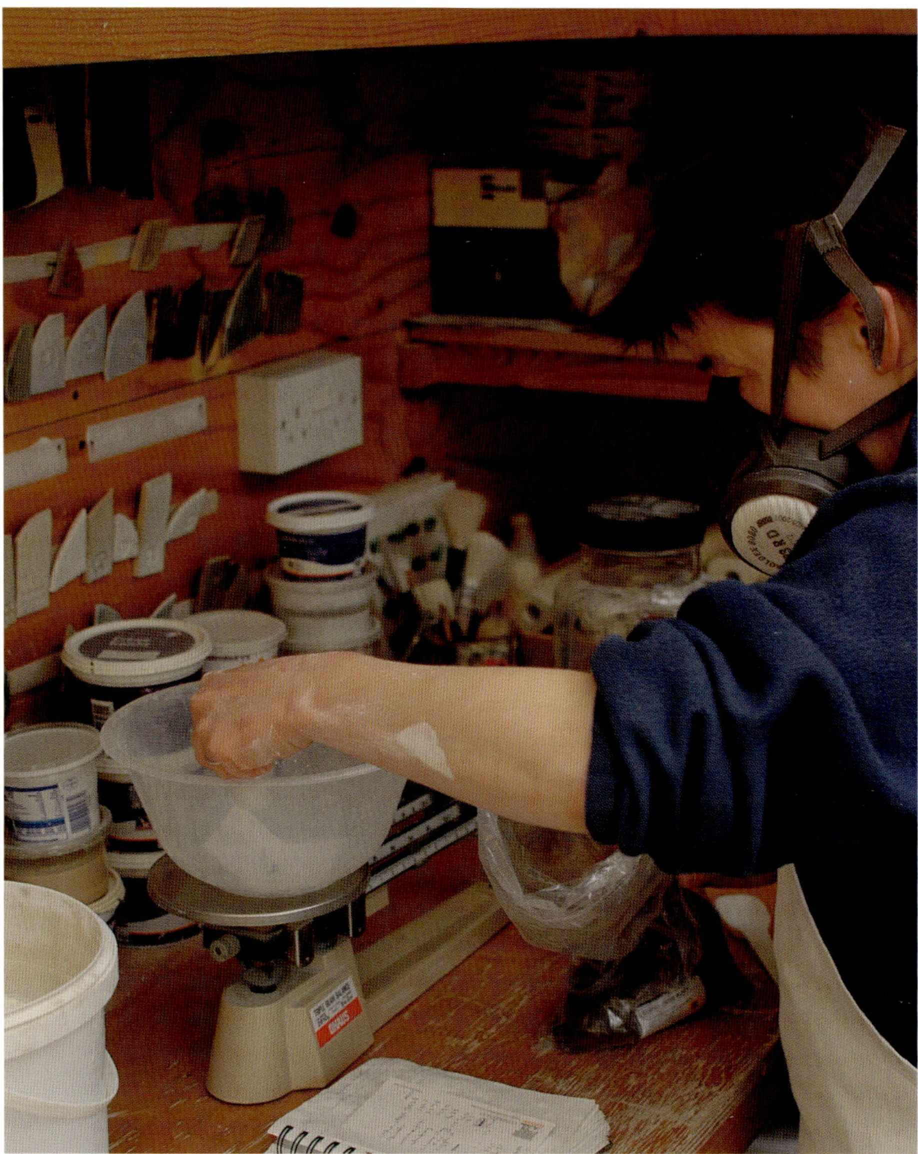

to avoid leaching of any metal oxide, including barium, copper or manganese. Matt and crazed glazes have the greatest surface area for acid attack. They can be tested by soaking in vinegar (5% acetic acid) overnight and checking for any changes. Alkali attack can be tested by leaving a sample in the dishwasher for several weeks, or boiling in a solution of 5% sodium carbonate for a few hours. Many potters no longer use lead glazes, but instead use glazes made from frits containing alkalis and boron.

Tests given here to check for leaching may not be conclusive and to be totally sure, potters making functional ware should send samples to be tested by a qualified laboratory (some can be found on p.156).

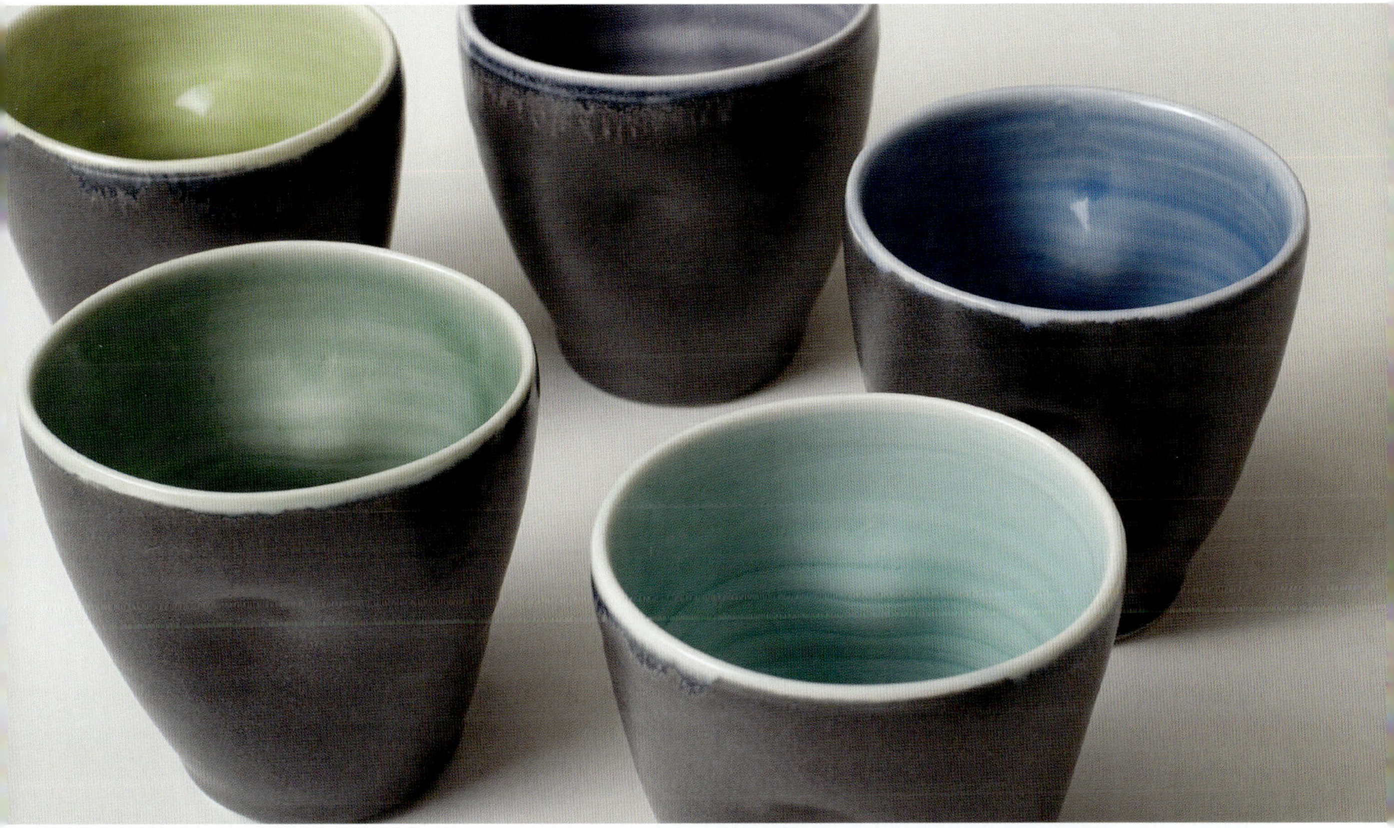

ABOVE: *Dimpled Cups*, Linda Bloomfield, porcelain with satin matt glaze on the outside and coloured glazes on the inside. *Photo Henry Bloomfield.*

RIGHT: *Nesting Bowls*, Linda Bloomfield, satin matt on the outside, coloured glazes on the inside. *Photo Henry Bloomfield.*

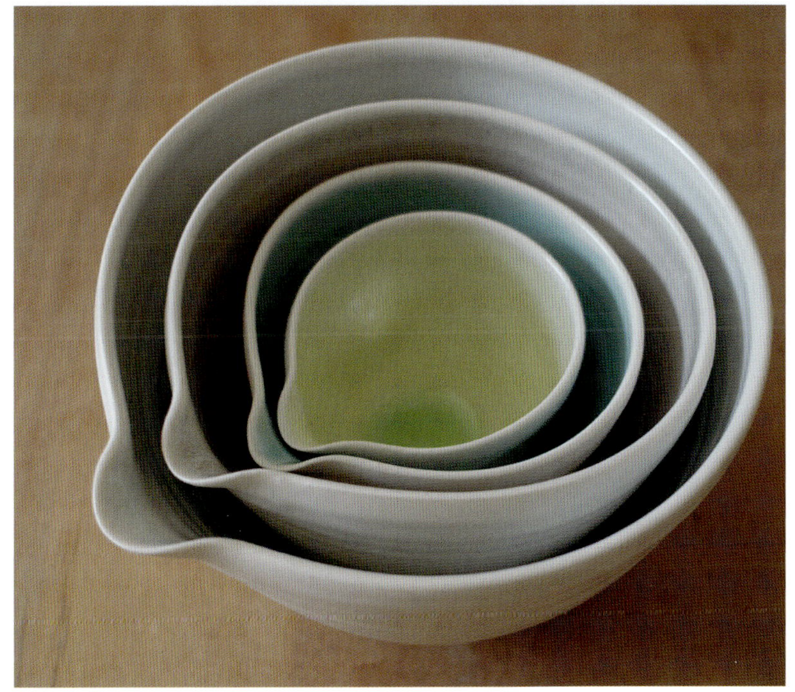

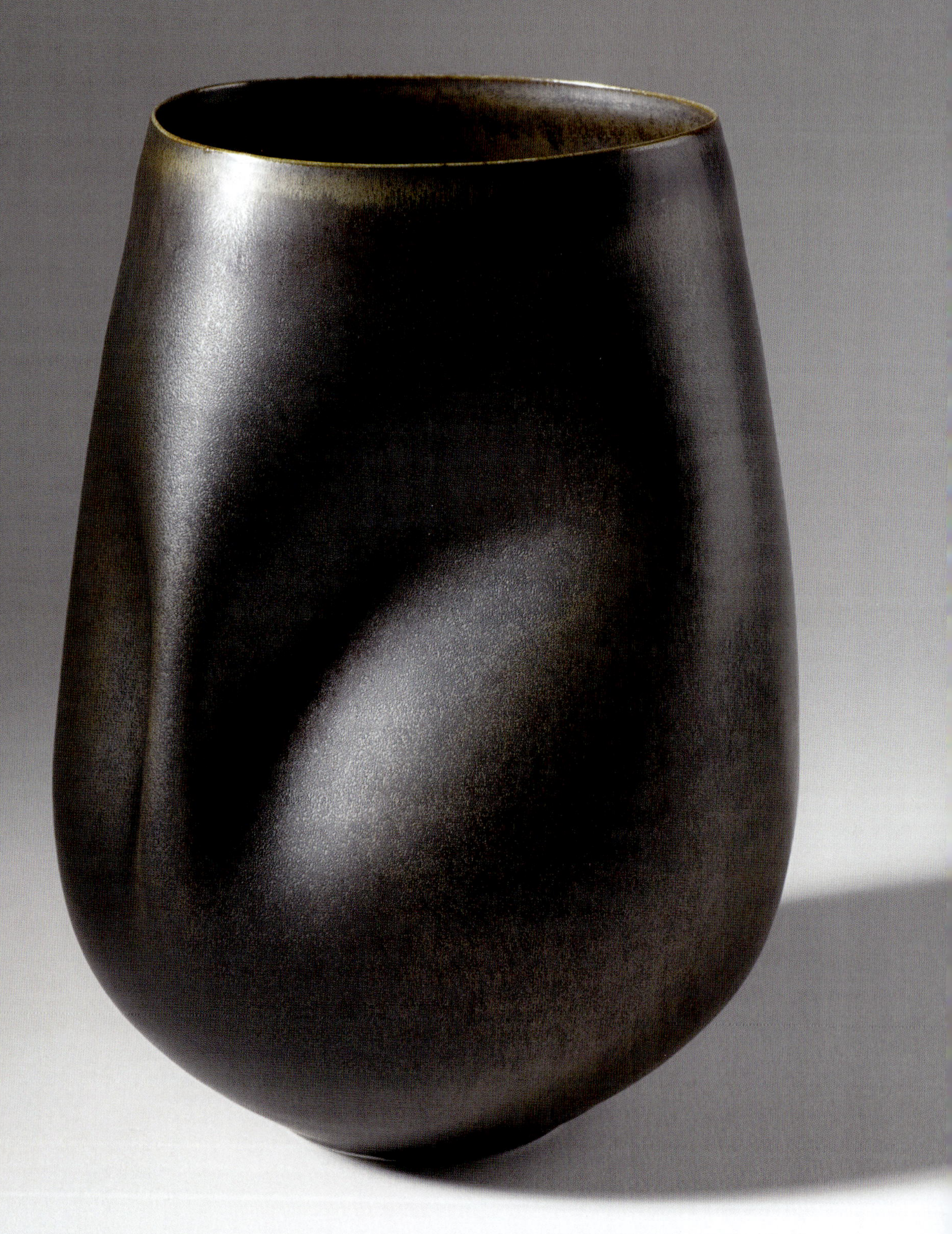

7

Applying glazes

LEFT: *Soft Spine Vessel*, Sara Flynn, thrown porcelain, sprayed glaze with 25% manganese dioxide, reduction-fired, 2008. *Photo: Roland Paschhoff.*

Glazes are usually applied to biscuit-fired ware, which has been fired to around 1000°C (1832°F) to make the ware stronger and easier to handle. Applying glazes to unfired ware is called raw glazing. Glazes for application to leather-hard pots should contain a high proportion (20–30%) of ball clay, to allow shrinkage with the pot. Glazes can be applied to bone-dry pots, but great care should be taken not to over-wet the pot, particularly at joints and handles. Glazes should contain a proportion of clay, which prevents them from becoming powdery when dry. Low-alumina glazes may need the addition of a few per cent bentonite, a highly plastic clay which aids suspension of the glaze and increases raw strength.

Glazes can be applied by pouring, dipping or brushing. Dipping is the simplest way to get an even coating, but a large quantity of glaze is required. The glaze should be stirred thoroughly, and the pot dipped in and held for a few seconds. The pot walls absorb the glaze, and large, thick pots soak up more glaze than thin-walled pots. Very thin porcelain should be glazed separately on the inside and outside, leaving time for the pot to dry in-between. Glaze can be poured into pots and swilled around to glaze the inside. If the pot is very large, glaze can be poured over the outside. The pot is held over a bucket or placed on a wheel, and glaze is poured over while it is slowly rotated. Glaze must be scraped and sponged from the base or foot-ring of stoneware and porcelain pots. Earthenware can be glazed all over and placed on three-point stilts in the kiln.

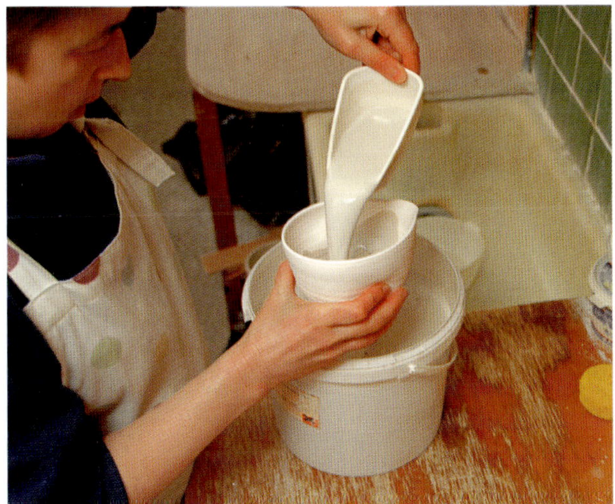

Pouring glaze into a jug.

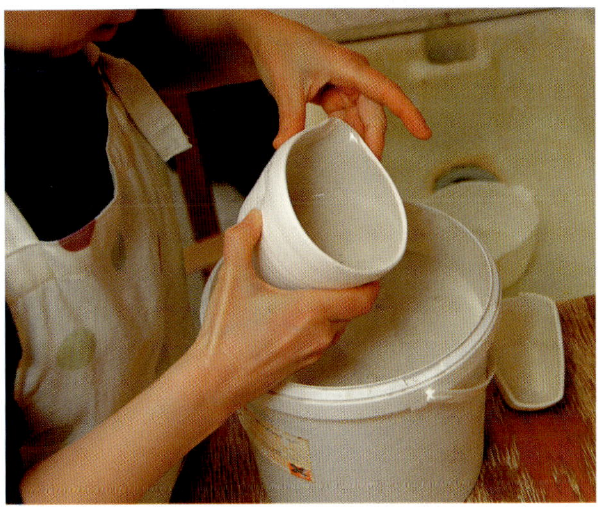

Swilling glaze around the inside.

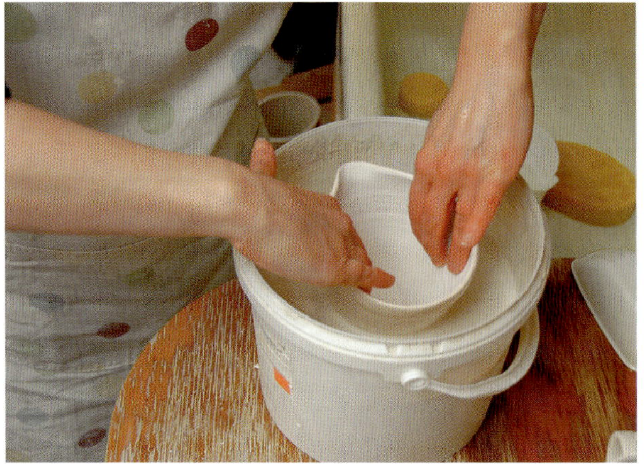

Dipping the outside of a jug.

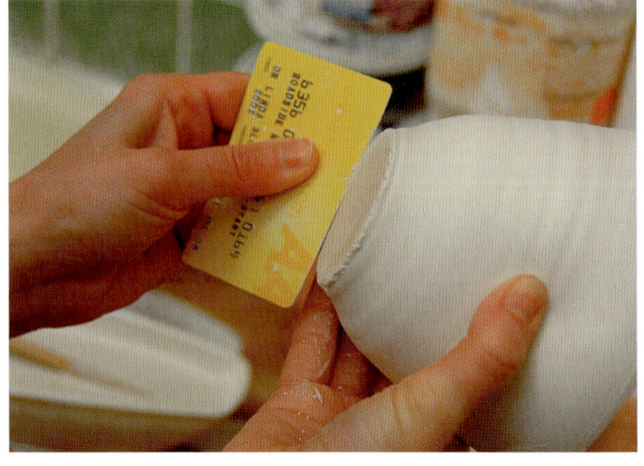

Scraping glaze off the base.

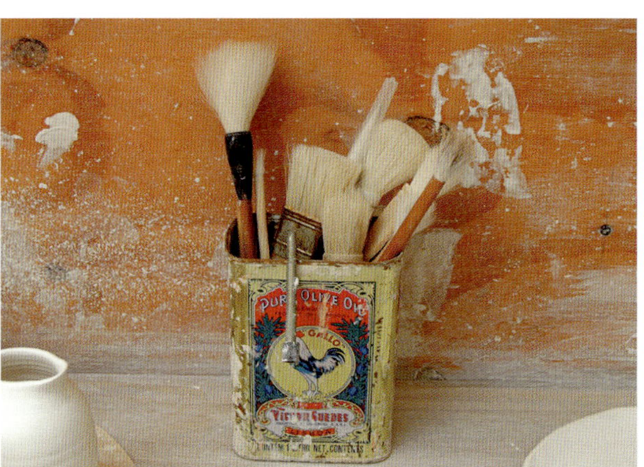

A selection of brushes used for glazing.

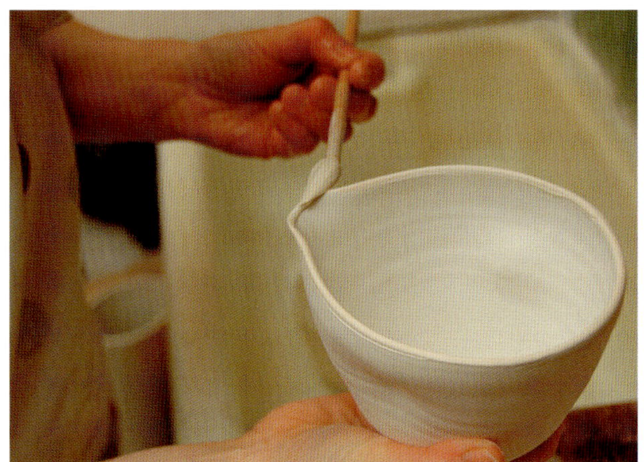

Brushing glaze onto the rim of a pot.

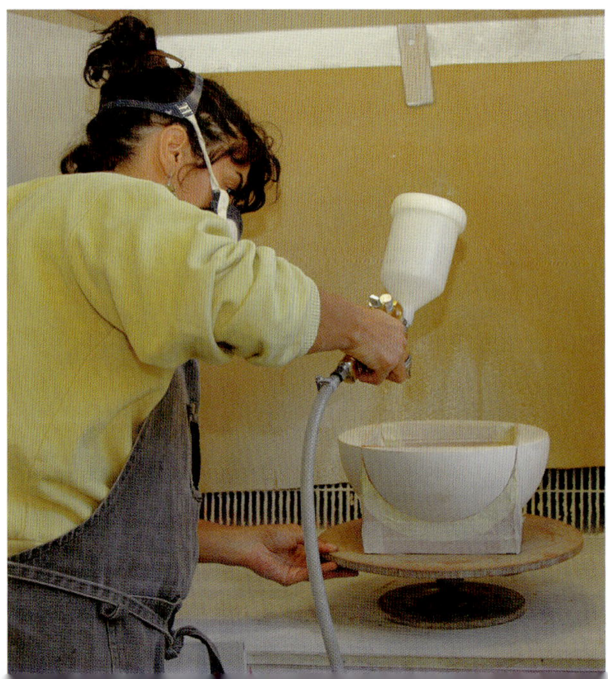

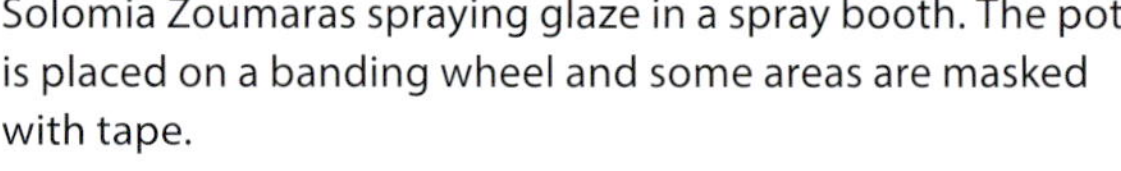

Solomia Zoumaras spraying glaze in a spray booth. The pot is placed on a banding wheel and some areas are masked with tape.

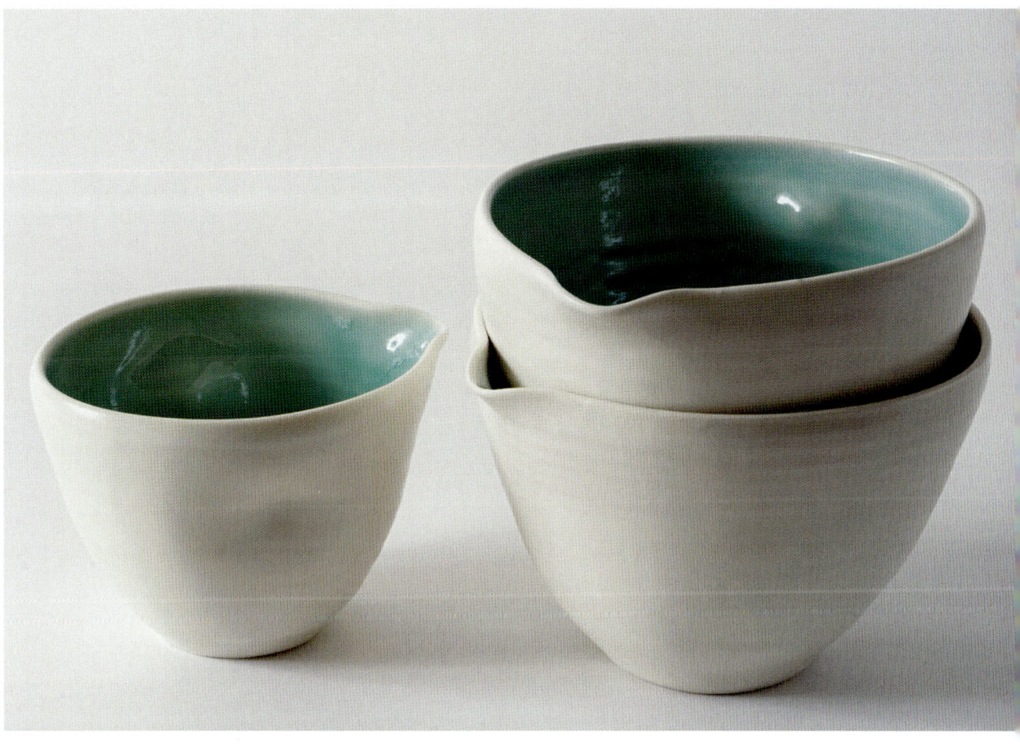

RIGHT: *Pouring bowls*, Linda Bloomfield, 2010. Thrown porcelain, copper turquoise glaze on inside, satin matt on outside. *Photo: courtesy of Jacqui Hurst*.

Glazes and oxides can be applied with a brush. Chinese brushes, wide hake brushes or glaze mops are often used by potters. Gum arabic can be added for smooth application, particularly when re-glazing a pot that has already been fired. Glazes can be sprayed, but a spray booth and compressor are required. Glaze for spraying should be sieved through a 120s-mesh sieve to avoid clogging the spray gun.

Potters can brighten colours by using adjacent bands of complementary colours (see p.132), or applying a line of contrasting colour to a rim or foot.

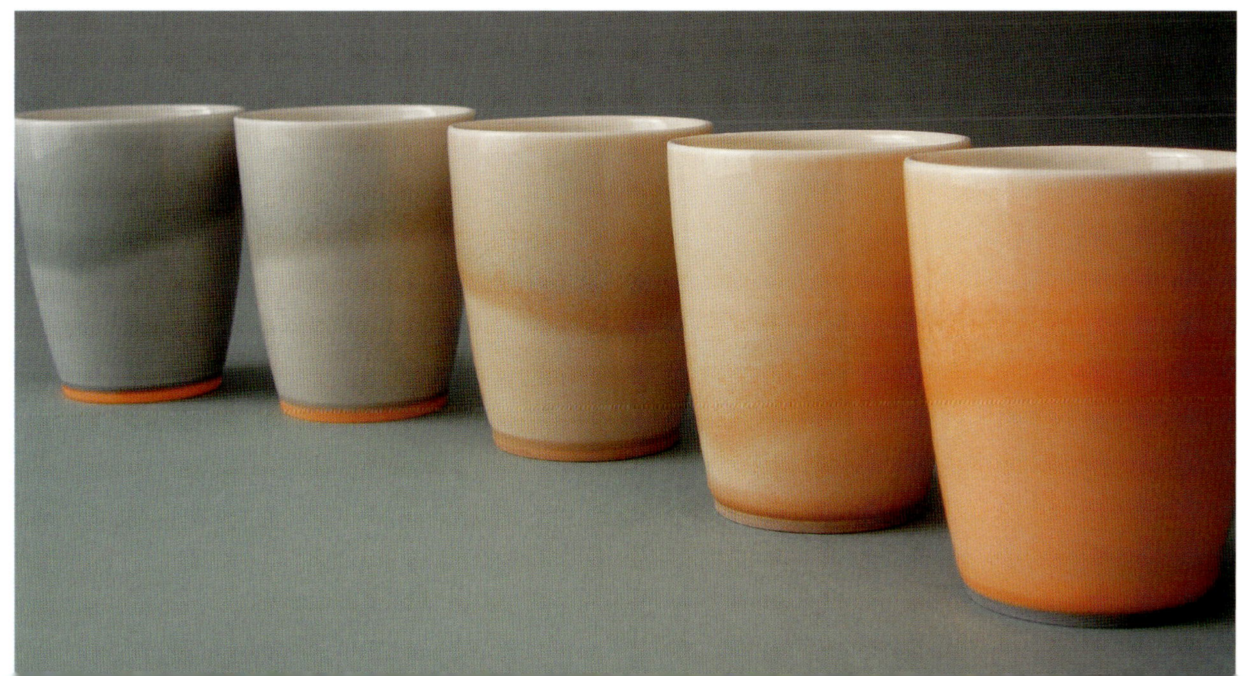

BELOW: *Beaker lineblend*, James and Tilla Waters, 2009. Orange to grey glazes with contrasting slips, porcelain, ht: 8cm (3¼in). *Photo: James and Tilla Waters*.

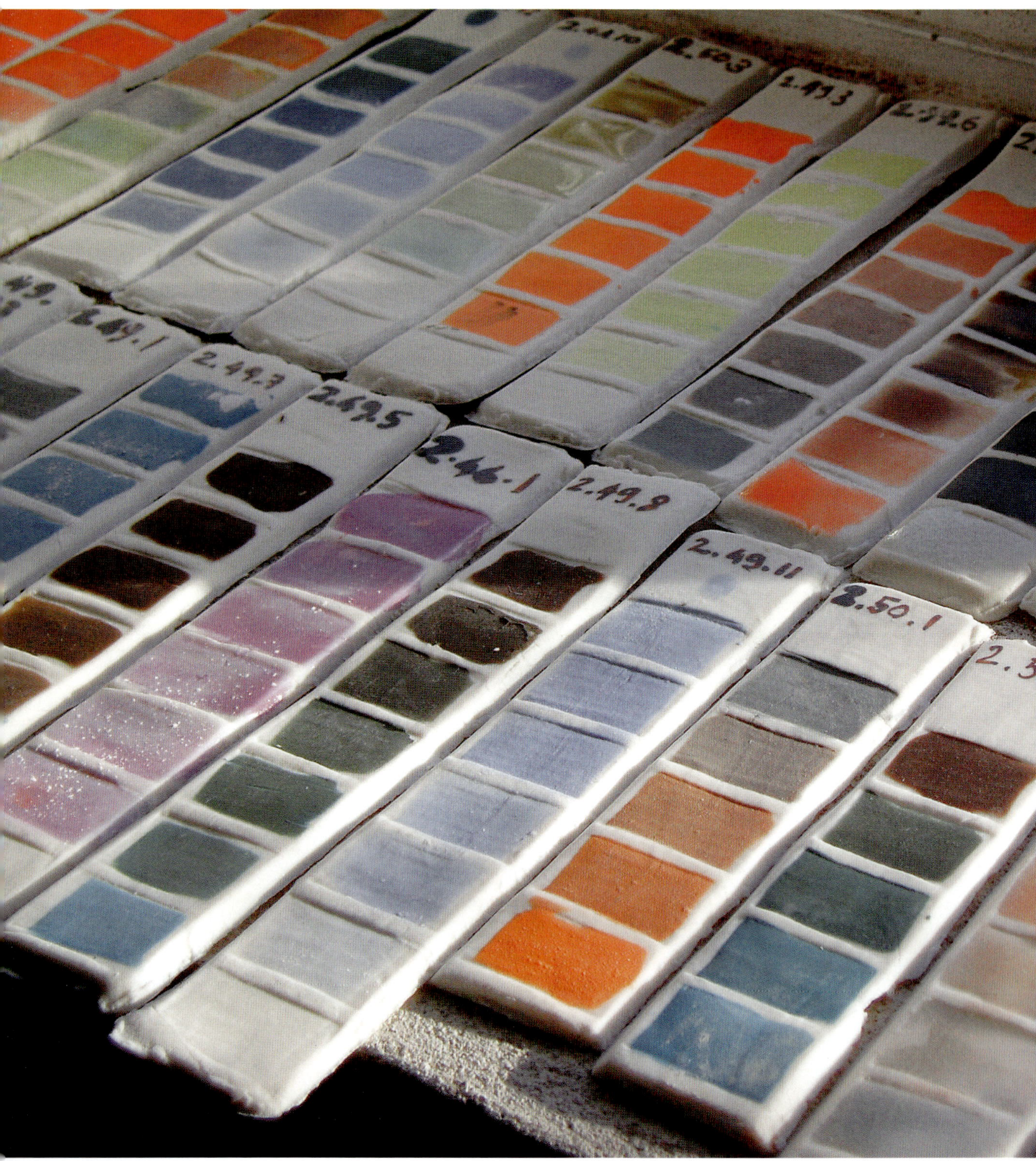
2.49.1
2.49.5
2.46.1
2.49.8
2.49.11
2.50.1

8

Testing glazes

Test tiles and line blends

New glazes should always be tested on a tile and fired before glazing a whole batch of pots. The outcome may not be as expected and will depend on the clay used, the glaze thickness and the kiln temperature and atmosphere. A small batch of glaze can be made (about 100g/3.5oz is enough) and tested on a tile. The test tile should be half dipped again to get a thicker application and labelled with underglaze pencil or a mixture of iron and manganese oxides on the back before firing. Colouring oxides can be added incrementally in a line blend, adding, for example 0.5, 1, 1.5 and 2% oxide. Two colouring oxides can be varied in a cross blend. A cross blend is a series of tests using two colouring oxides, where one oxide increases as the other decreases, for example:

Copper oxide	0.5	1	1.5	2	2.5%
Rutile	10	8	6	4	2%

Colouring oxides sometimes react together, forming an unexpected result, for example, cobalt and chromium form an opaque teal blue-green. A long strip of clay can be used for a series of test tiles, with each glaze in the line blend brushed or poured on separately. Test tiles can be cut from a slab, extrusion or a section of a thrown cylinder, which can be placed vertically in the kiln to check the fluidity of a glaze. A colour blend is a method of testing a base glaze with additions of different colouring oxides, for example, cobalt, copper, chromium, iron and manganese oxides. A large batch of base glaze (such as 500g dry weight) is weighed out and mixed with water,

LEFT: Tilla Waters, line blends and cross blends, glazes and slips with stains and oxides. *Photo: Tilla Waters.*

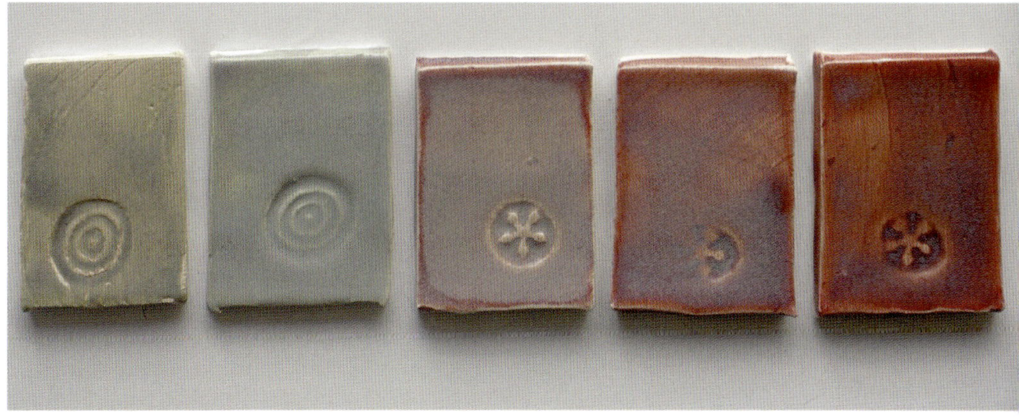

RIGHT: Line blend, whiting in a chrome-tin pink earthenware glaze fired at 1100°C (2012°F). Calcium borate frit 39, soda feldspar 27, quartz 23, China clay 6, tin 5, chromium oxide 0.1, whiting 5%, 10%, 15%, 20%, 25%. Chrome-tin pink develops when there is more than 15% whiting. Adding more whiting increases the firing temperature and makes the glaze matt.

then separated into five cups, each with a different colouring oxide. These are each sieved separately. Each different-coloured glaze is then wet blended in equal amounts (50:50) with every other coloured glaze as shown in the diagram, using a tablespoon or plastic syringe. Test tiles are dipped in each colour blend and fired.

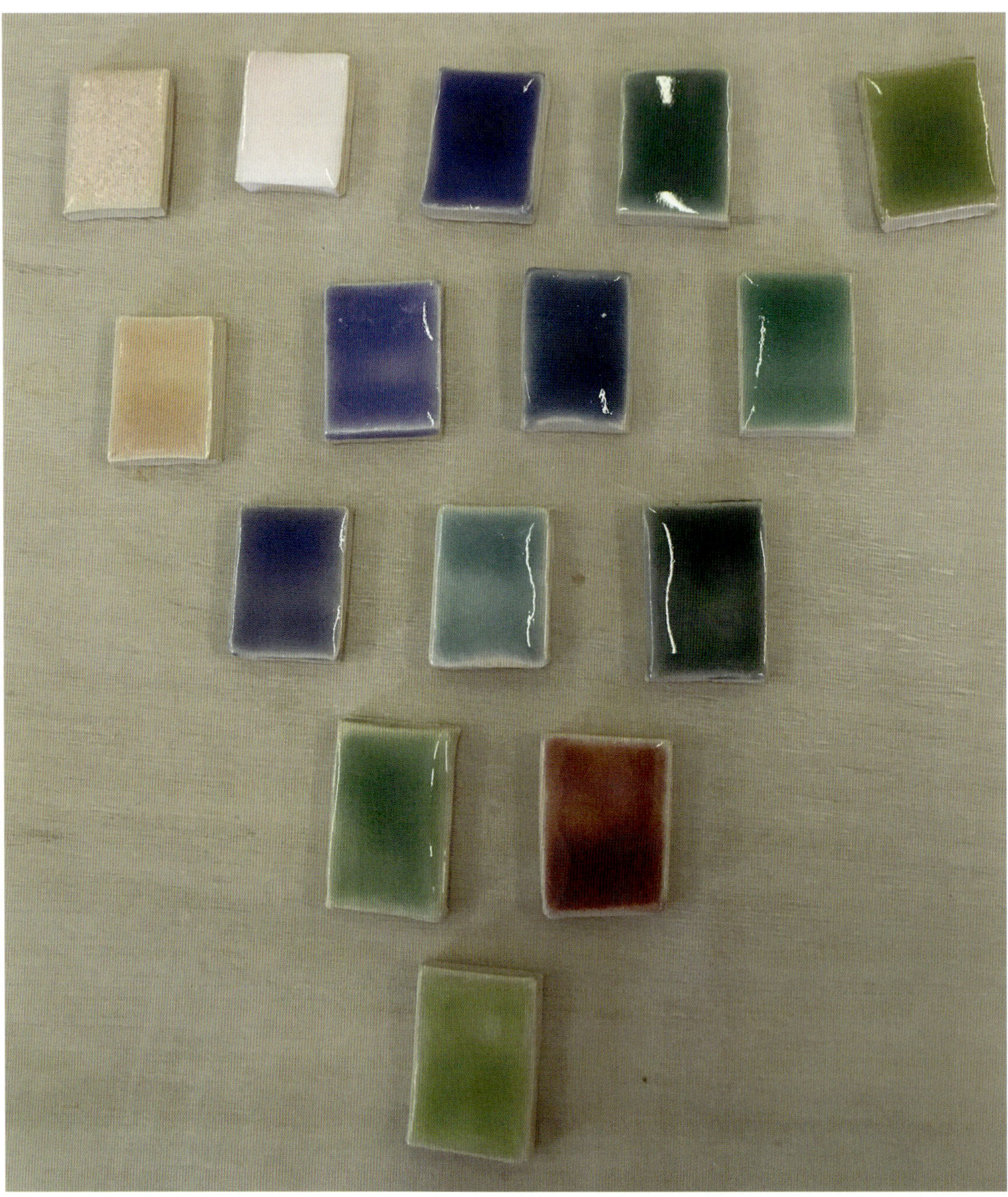

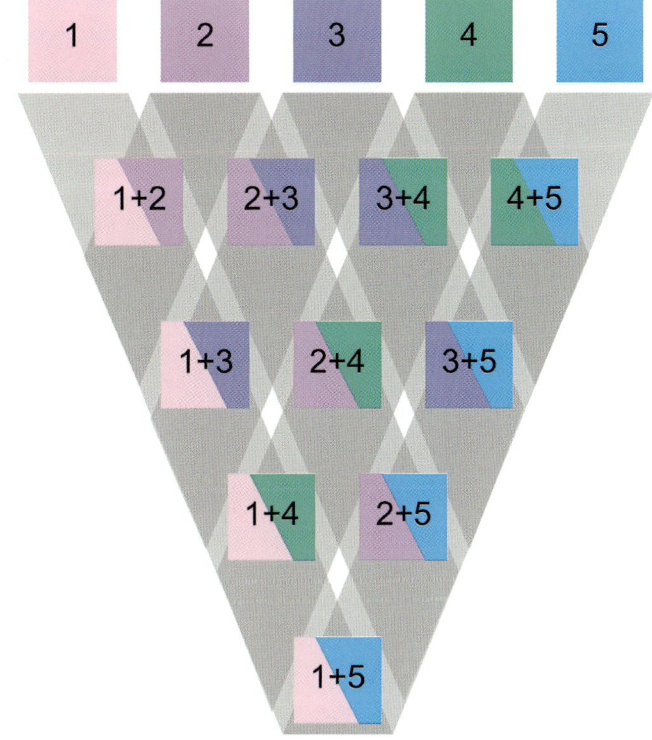

LEFT: Colour blend using transparent glaze recipe on p.19 with, top row; 5% rutile, 4% tin oxide, 0.2% cobalt oxide, 2% copper carbonate and 0.2% chromium oxide.

Below the top row, each test tile is a 50:50 blend of two of the glazes above.

RIGHT Schematic diagram of a colour blend.

Grids

When testing glazes, it is simplest to vary one thing at a time, either changing one material, or using a different firing temperature. To pinpoint an elusive glaze, such as cobalt titanium green or cobalt pink, a biaxial grid can be useful (see p.131). In a biaxial grid, the alumina and silica are varied in a 7 x 5 grid of 35 test tiles, so that (in the example shown) the glazes near the bottom left-hand corner are very runny and those near the top right-hand corner are very stiff. This means it is less important to get the firing temperature exactly right. The fluxes and colouring oxides are constant, and only the alumina and silica vary. Each of the four corner glazes can be added in different proportions and mixed to create the 35 glazes. This is most easily done by wet blending, measuring wet glaze by volume using a syringe.

The behaviour of the colouring oxide will be affected by the alumina, silica and flux in the glaze. For example, cobalt-titanium green occurs only in high-alumina glazes or slips used for salt glaze. Cobalt-pink crystals form when there is low silica in magnesia glazes. The crystals are pyroxene, calcium magnesium silicate ($CaMgSi_2O_6$), which grow with slow cooling of the kiln, causing the glaze to become matt. The pink crystals often grow in a matrix of blue glaze.[4]

[4] Cobalt is blue in four-fold co-ordination with oxygen atoms, which occurs in cobalt silicate, and pink in six-fold co-ordination, which occurs in pyroxene crystals.

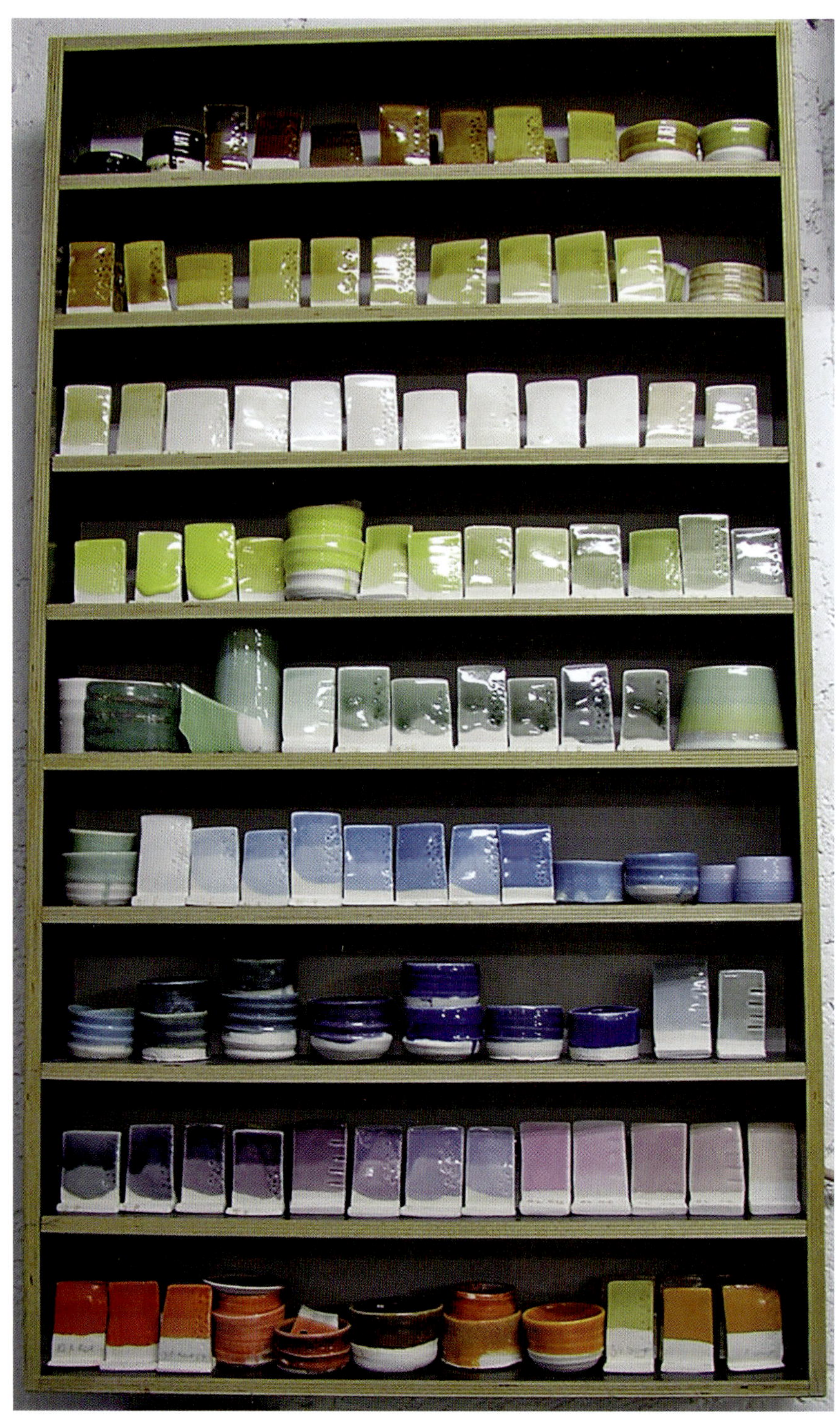

LEFT: Louisa Taylor, glaze research board, stain and oxide blends, Cockpit Arts, London.

RIGHT: Biaxial grid with cobalt oxide in a magnesium glaze with increasing clay (vertical 'y' axis) and silica (horizontal 'x' axis), fired to 1260°C (2300°F) on porcelain. Cobalt-pink crystalline matt (second column from left, central row:) soda feldspar 41, dolomite 22, whiting 3, zinc oxide 5, china clay 18, quartz 11 + 0.75% cobalt oxide. (See p.52.)

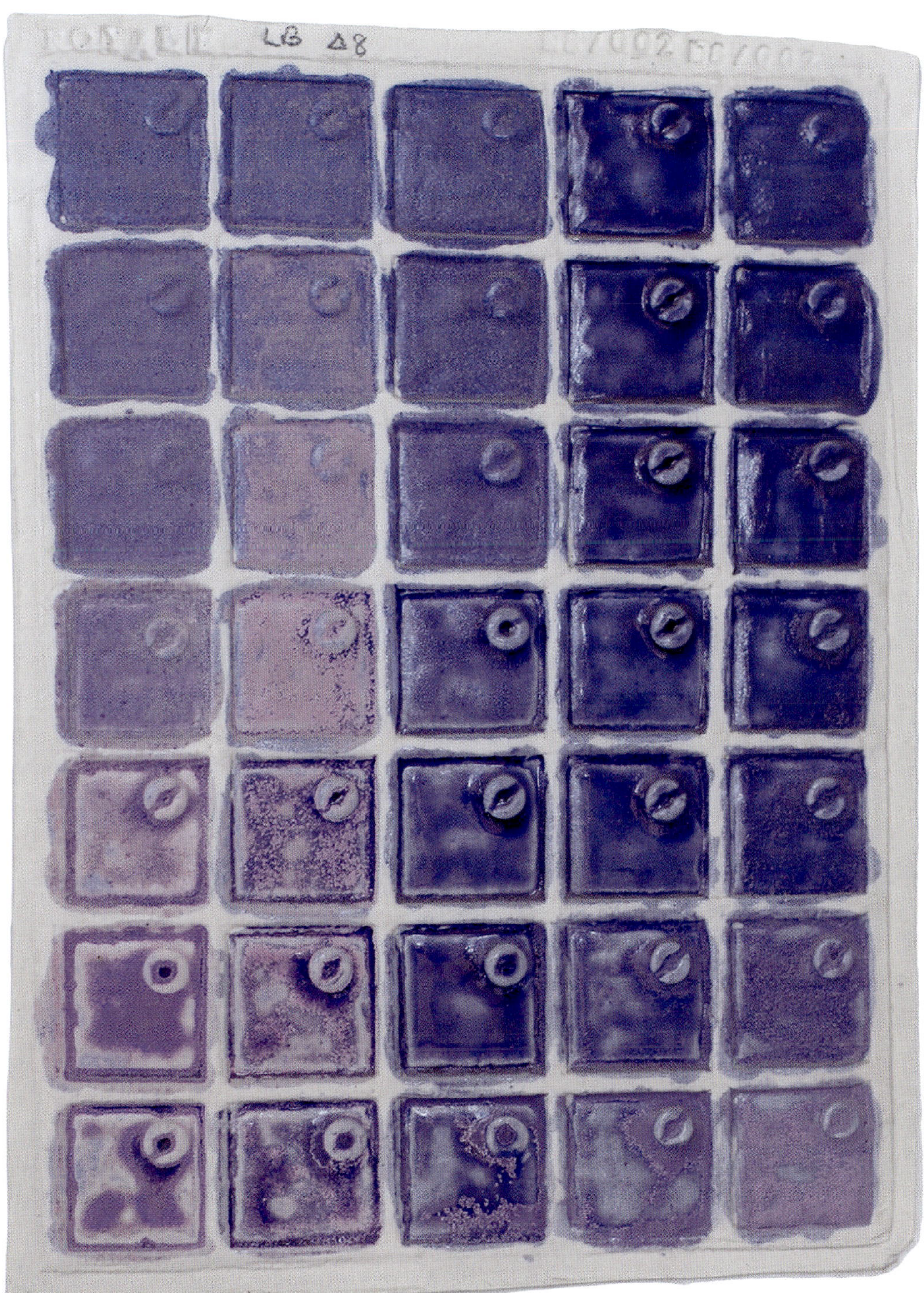

CLAY 0–40%

SILICA 0–50%

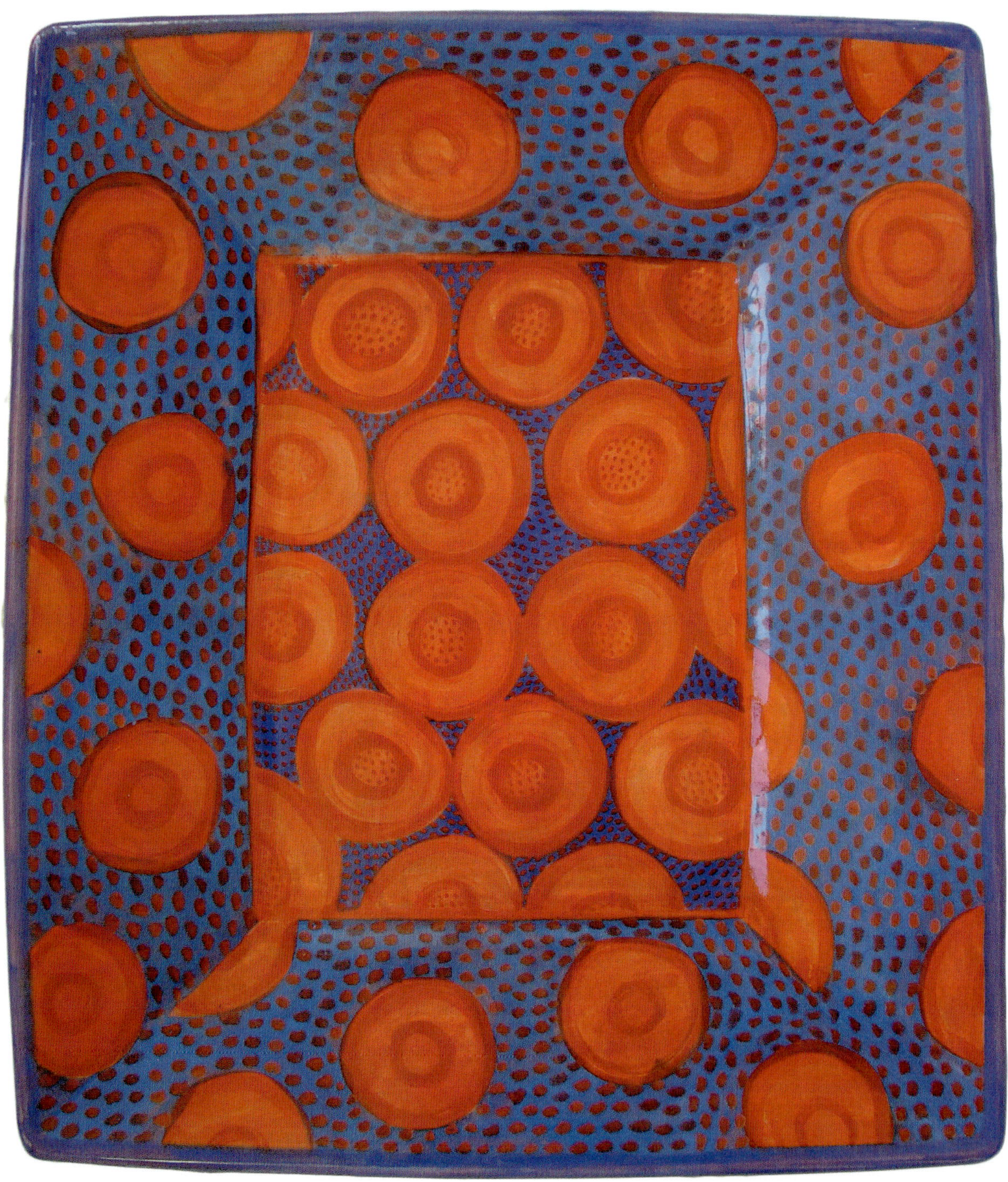

9

Firing

Pots are usually fired twice. The first firing is called the biscuit firing, and is usually around 1000°C/1832°F. It strengthens the pots and reduces the risk of damage during handling and glazing. The glaze-firing temperature is between 1200°C and 1300°C/2192°F and 2372°F for stoneware and porcelain. In the case of earthenware, the biscuit firing is often to a higher temperature than the glaze firing, the method used in industry. This ensures that the ware is strong, but still enables the use of bright earthenware glazes. Typical firing temperatures for earthenware are 1060°C–1100°C/1940°F–2012°F. Some potters fire only once, raw-glazing the unfired pots at the leather-hard or bone-dry stage.

Glazed pots must be packed carefully in the kiln, with at least 5mm (¼in) between pots, or more for large pieces. In earthenware firings, the pots can be glazed all over and placed on three-point stilts. In stoneware and porcelain firings, the base or foot-ring must be cleaned of all traces of glaze. The kiln shelves can be painted with several coats of batt wash (a mixture of two parts alumina hydrate to one part China clay) to prevent pots from sticking to the shelves. Kiln shelves are placed on three or four equidistant props, each lined up with the ones on the shelf below.

Temperature inside kilns is measured with a pyrometer connected to a thermocouple, encased in a ceramic sheath inside the kiln. Pyrometric cones can also be placed behind spy holes to check the temperature at the end of firing. Three cones are usually used,

LEFT: *Small earthenware plate*, Pauline Zelinski, 2007. Red and blue underglaze stains, lead borosilicate glaze. The blue background makes the red appear brighter. *Photo: Pauline Zelinski.*

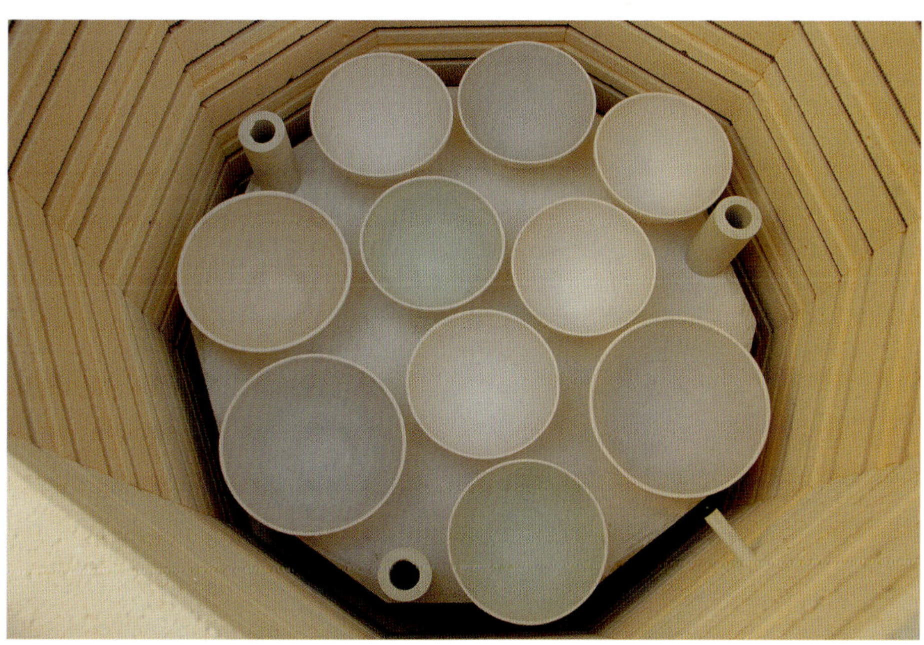

RIGHT: Glazed bowls placed inside an electric top-loader kiln.

one lower than the firing temperature and one higher (the centre cone is the target temperature) . The cones bend over so that the tip is pointing downwards when the top temperature is reached. The deformation of cones depends on both the temperature and the time, with a slower heating rate causing cones to bend at a lower temperature.

Firing should proceed slowly, to ensure that all the water has evaporated from the clay and glazes. Above 100°C/212°F, the firing rate can increase, but care should be taken until the quartz inversion point at 573°C/1063°F is reached. At this point, the quartz in the clay body changes structure and undergoes a sudden increase in volume, which can cause cracking. Around 600°C/1112°F, the chemically combined water in clay is driven off, and any carbonates decompose to oxides. The clay body changes colour and becomes stronger. At this stage kiln vents can be closed. Pots are usually biscuit fired to 900°C–1000°C/1652°F–1832°F. This makes them easier to handle and able to absorb and hold the glaze well on the surface of the work, without it disintegrating, before being glaze fired.

Above 900°C/1652°F, fluxes such as sodium, potassium and boron start to act, and the glaze starts to melt. As the temperature rises, more fluxes (calcium, zinc and barium) come into action and a body-glaze layer starts to form, which strengthens the glaze. This layer is composed of needle-shaped crystals of mullite, aluminium silicate, which grow above 1050°C/1922°F. At the maturing temperature, the glaze is fully melted and crystals such as wollastonite (calcium silicate) and pyroxene (calcium magnesium silicate) can begin to form. A soak for 10–30 minutes can help to mature the glaze throughout the kiln. If the kiln is cooled quickly, no more crystals will form, and the liquid glaze will be frozen in a glassy state. However, if it is cooled very slowly, more crystals can devitrify from the melt, and a matt surface may form. Kiln controllers are available which can control the soak and cooling, which is particularly useful when firing crystalline glazes. During cooling, there are two silica inversion points at 573°C/1064°F and 226°C/439°F, where the different forms of crystalline silica (quartz and cristobalite) in the clay body undergo a sudden contraction. Care must be taken not to allow draughts into the kiln at these temperatures or dunting may occur. The kiln can be opened when it has cooled to below 100°C/212°F.

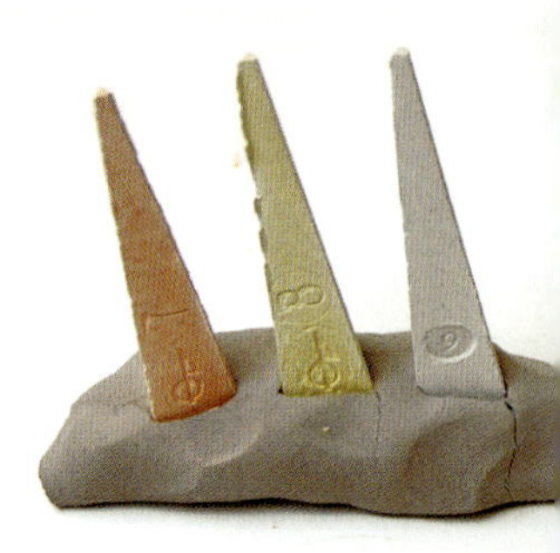

Orton cones before firing.

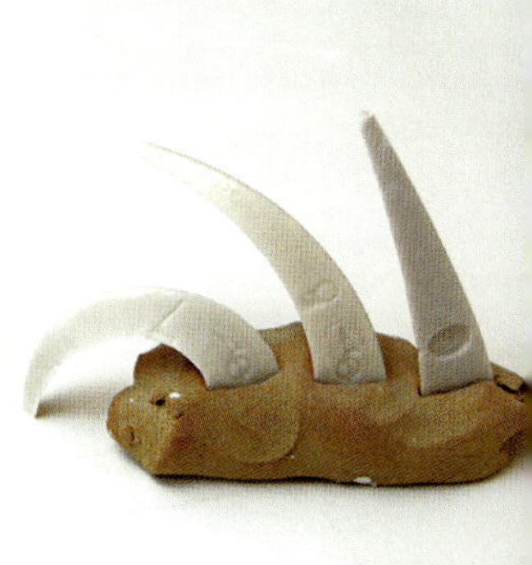

Orton cones after firing. In this photo the left hand cone is fired to maturity. You will get to know the degree of melt you require, indicated by the cones.

RIGHT: Salt glaze tests, Mirka Golden-Hann, 2008. Salt-glazed stoneware and porcelain. Columns from left: erbium, cerium, neodymium, praseodymium, white slip. Rows from front: raw Shino, barium matt, gloss transparent, gloss opaque, magnesium satin matt glazes with 2%, 5%, 10% and 15% oxide fired to 1280°C (2336°F) in a reduction atmosphere. *Photo: Mirka Golden-Hann.*

Oxidation

In oxidation, there is sufficient oxygen available and any iron oxide in the clay body turns tan-yellow (or red-brown in the case of red earthenware). Porcelain is creamy white and stoneware is tan or buff when fired in oxidation. Glaze colours are bright and most industrial pottery is fired in oxidation.

Reduction

In fuel-burning kilns a reduction state can be developed by restricting the air supply, so that there is insufficient oxygen for combustion, and oxygen is drawn instead from the clay and glazes. Iron oxide in the clay body is reduced to black iron oxide (FeO), which acts as a flux. Porcelain turns grey-blue and stoneware grey, with orange flashing where it comes into contact with sodium in the glaze or kiln atmosphere. Celadons, tenmoku, ash glazes and copper reds should be fired in reduction to achieve their characteristic colours (copper is usually green in oxidation), for the best results. Because reduction causes any iron in the clay body to turn grey, colours tend to become muted, unless porcelain is used.

Some lustres require reduction firing, particularly those involving copper. Metal salts are mixed with clay and brushed onto the fired glaze surface. They are fired to a low temperature, around 750°C (1382°F) in reduction. Copper oxide, tin oxide and silver nitrate are often used in post-reduction raku firing (see p.138). Resin-based gold and silver lustres are available that can be fired in oxidation.

Wood and salt

Wood firing is often used for the effects of volatile gases and fly ash. These react with the clay to produce a toasted orange colour and molten rivulets of ash glaze. In sodium-vapour glazing, salt or sodium bicarbonate is introduced into the kiln at a high temperature. The sodium is volatile and flows through the kiln, reacting with silica in the clay surface to form a glaze. Colour can be introduced using oxides, slips and glazes. Brown and orange come from iron and titanium in the clay body or slip, blue and green from cobalt and titanium or copper. Other colouring oxides can be used with salt glaze, such as the rare earths, which give pinks, purples and yellow-greens.

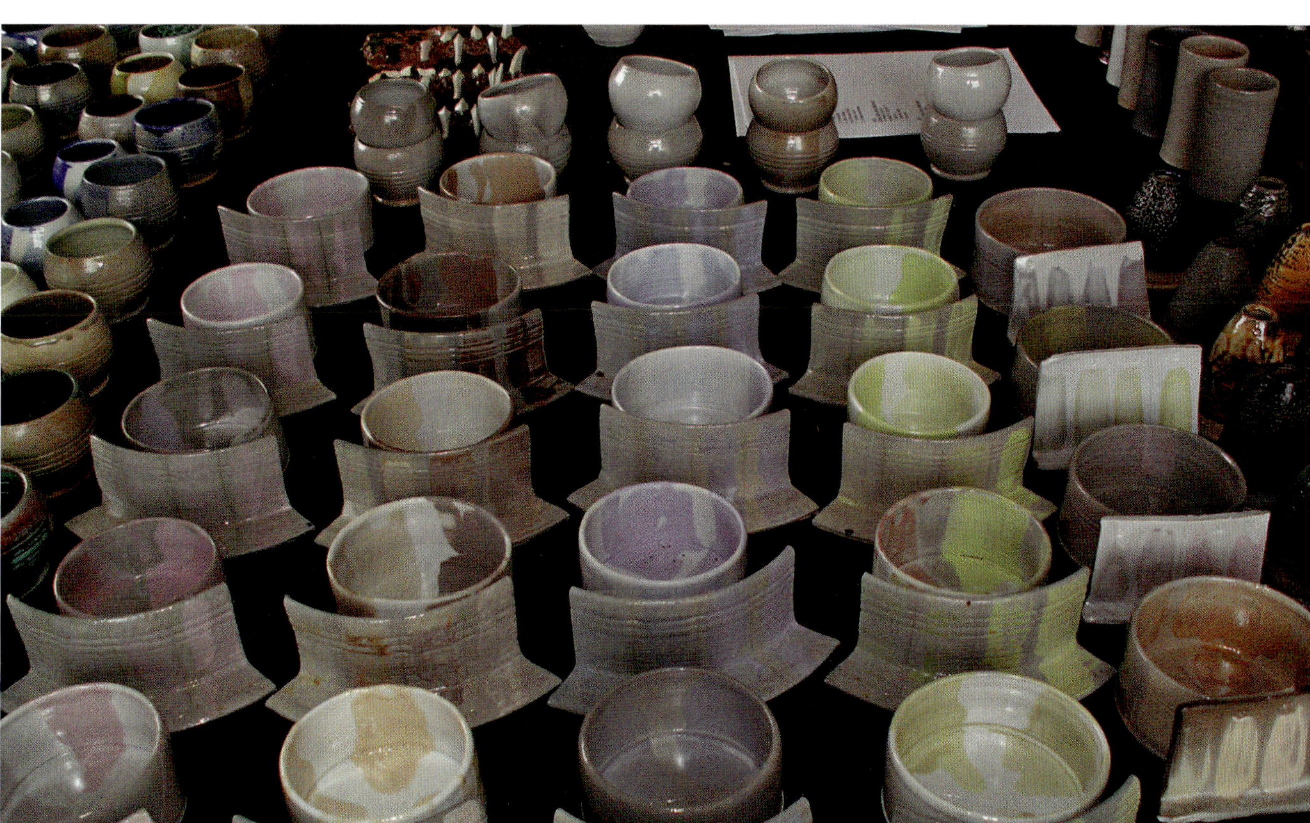

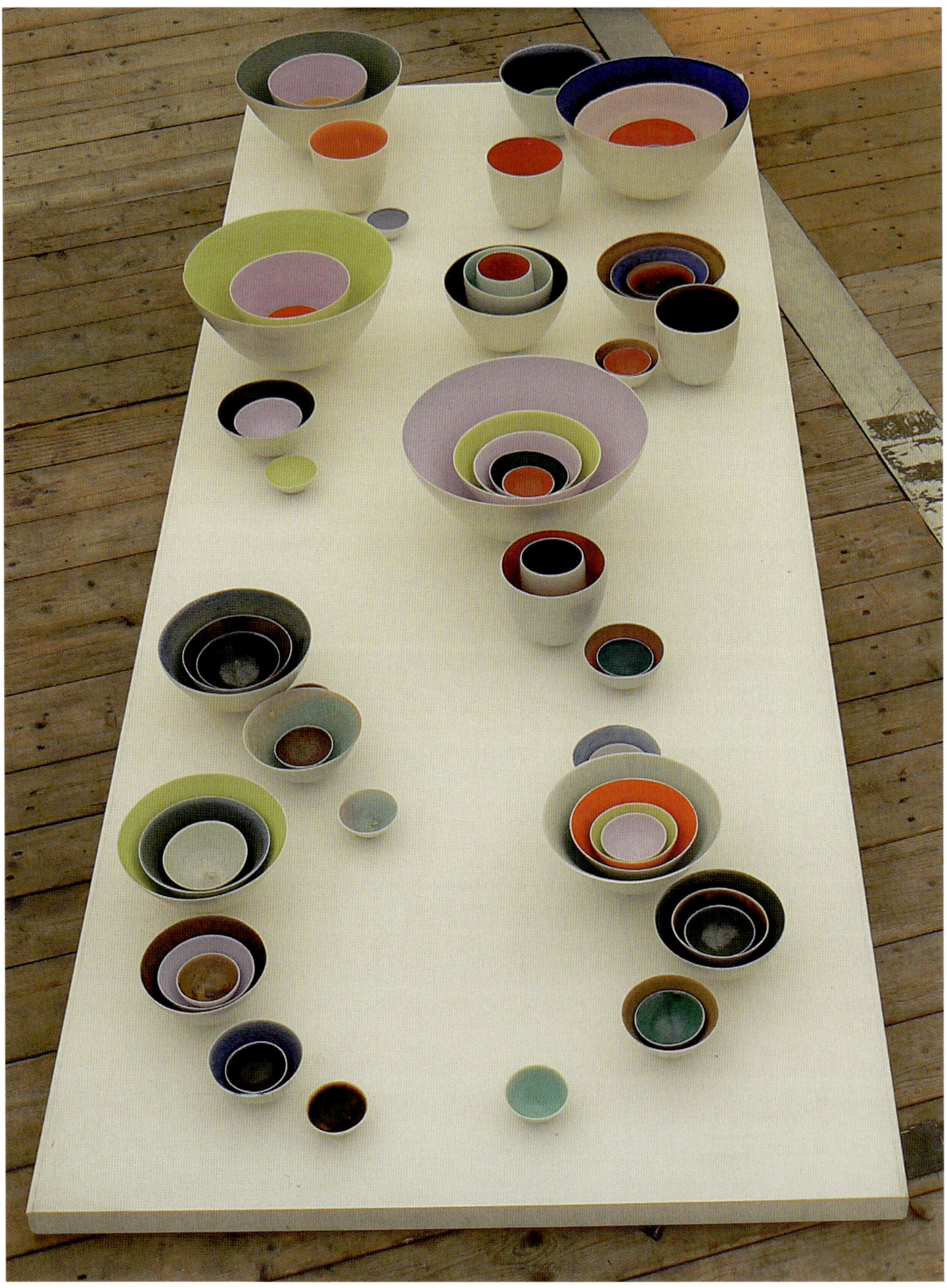

Salt glaze colour tests by Mirka Golden-Hann

Slips and glazes for salt glaze, 1280°C/2336°F

White slip

China clay	30
Ball clay Hyplas 71	40
Flint	15
Nepheline syenite	15

Shino raw glaze

Potash feldspar	33
Cornish stone	33
Ball clay Hyplas 71	33

Barium matt

Soda feldspar	40
Barium carbonate	31
Dolomite	12
China clay	9
Flint	9

Transparent gloss

Potash feldspar	20
Cornish stone	50
Flint	5
China clay	10

Opaque gloss (apply thickly)

Potash feldspar	42
Flint	21
Whiting	16
China clay	9
Zinc oxide	2
Nepheline syenite	8

Magnesium satin matt

Talc	23
Potash feldspar	26
China clay	22
Whiting	13
Flint	22

Adjusting glazes to fire at different temperatures

Many potters fire in the mid-temperature range of 1180°C–1250°C/2156°F–2282°F, between stoneware and earthenware temperatures. This saves energy and lengthens the life of electric kiln elements. High-fire 1280°C/2336°F glazes can be adjusted by adding low-temperature fluxes such as borax frit or zinc oxide. However, zinc oxide adversely affects some colouring oxides such as chromium, which it turns brown. Cornish stone and potash feldspar can be replaced by soda feldspar, nepheline syenite or lithium feldspar. Lithium carbonate is also a useful flux, although it is slightly soluble and should only be used in small quantities, up to 10%, or shivering may occur. As well as lowering the firing temperature, sodium and lithium will brighten colours, producing turquoise from copper and lime green from chromium. The alumina and silica in the glaze can also be reduced, provided they remain within the limits for stable glazes (see Appendix 3, p.148). Glazes for earthenware temperatures 950°C–1150°C/1742°F–2102°F should contain a high proportion (up to 80%) of alkaline or borax frit, or a mixture of frit and feldspar, together with some clay and silica. Traditional earthenware glazes are made from lead-silicate frits, but these are now often replaced by alkaline and borosilicate frits. The colour response from oxides in glazes containing sodium or boron is cooler than in lead glazes; for example, copper oxide gives turquoise in sodium and boron glazes and green in lead glazes. If the boron content is too high, chrome-tin pinks will not develop.

LEFT: *Installation*, Mirka Golden-Hann, 2010. Stains, oxides, rare earths, salt glaze, fired to cone 9. *Photo: Mirka Golden-Hann.*

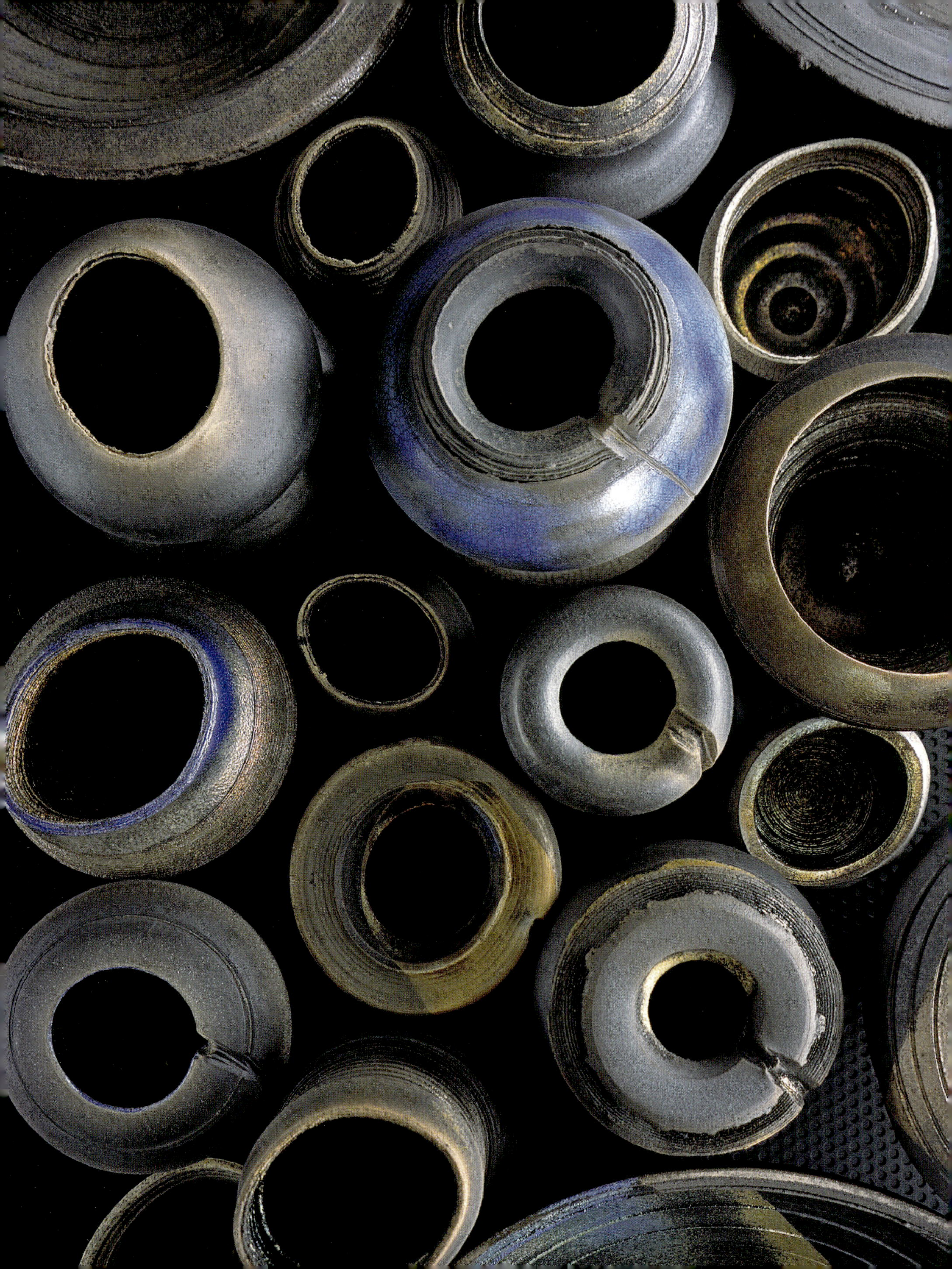

10 Correcting glaze faults

Some glaze faults, such as crazing or crawling, are used as decorative features. However, they make the glaze less suitable for use on functional ware, and should be eliminated if the ceramic will be used for a purpose other than for decoration.

Crazing

Crazing occurs when the glaze contracts more than the clay body on cooling, which is common in alkaline glazes containing high sodium and potassium. This results in a network of fine cracks, called crackle when used as a decorative effect. Crazing reduces the strength of the pot, and also makes the glaze less hygienic for functional use. On earthenware, crazing allows water to leak out through the porous clay walls. To correct crazing, silica and clay can be added to the glaze in the ratio 5:4 (test batches with additions of 2.5% silica and 2% clay or 5% silica and 4% clay). Low-expansion fluxes such as calcium borate frit or talc can be used to replace some of the feldspar or alkaline frit, which can cause these problems. Lithium carbonate or a lithium feldspar can be used instead of sodium or potassium feldspar.

Shivering

Shivering is the opposite of crazing, and it occurs when the glaze is too big for the clay body. When this happens, there is stress at the rim and on the edges of handles, where glaze chips off in thin, sharp flakes. The stress can even cause the pot to crack, particularly if the pot is thin-walled. Adding feldspar or reducing the silica can eliminate shivering, by increasing the coefficient of expansion of the glaze.

Crawling

Crawling is a glaze fault in which the glaze surface tension is too high, and the glaze forms beads with bare clay in between. Materials with high surface tension on melting include alumina, zirconium and tin, and these should be reduced if crawling becomes a problem. Crawling can also occur in thick glazes with high shrinkage, which crack on drying. Materials that cause the glaze to shrink on drying include clay, zinc and light magnesium carbonate. Calcined china clay (molochite) can be used instead, to reduce shrinkage. Biscuit ware should also be free of dust and grease (if dusty, wash first and dry overnight before glazing, and try latex gloves to avoid grease marks), and glazed

LEFT: David Jones, raku-fired vessels with cobalt and silver lustre. *Photo: Rod Dorling.*

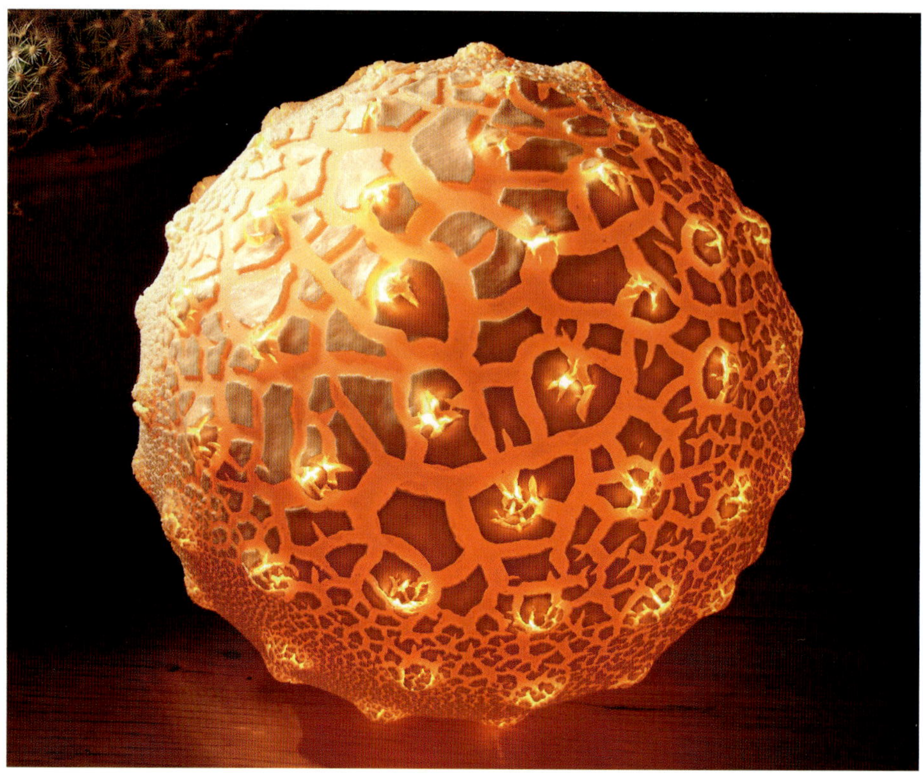

Pollen, Amy Cooper, 2006. Slip-cast porcelain, shrink and crawl glaze containing light magnesium carbonate. *Photo: Amy Cooper.*

pots should be left to dry thoroughly before firing; otherwise, steam escaping from the pot may cause the glaze to lift off.

Pinholes and blisters

Gases escaping from the glaze can cause pinholes and blisters. Glaze materials such as whiting (calcium carbonate) have spherical particles which trap air during glaze application, forming bubbles in the glaze. Whiting can be replaced with wollastonite (calcium silicate), which has needle-like particles, at the same time reducing the amount of quartz in the glaze. Zinc oxide can cause pinholes owing to local reduction and evaporation of the zinc (even in an electric kiln). Surface pits left by grog in the clay body can also cause pinholes when covered with a viscous glaze. Glaze application on to over-fired biscuit ware or damp biscuit ware can also cause pinholes. In viscous glazes, the craters may not have had time to heal over, resulting in pinholes. Soaking for 15 to 30 minutes at the top temperature can help to smooth out the glaze.

Blisters form when glazes are overfired and some fluxes start to become volatile, giving off large amounts of gas. Bone ash can cause blistering and is often calcined before adding to the glaze. Underfiring the biscuit can cause bloating and pinholing, where carbon in the clay body is released as carbon dioxide and becomes trapped under the maturing glaze layer. Poorly prepared clay may bloat if there are any air bubbles left in it. Glaze faults are increasingly being used as special effects by studio potters, particularly crackled, crawled and volcanic glazes. These effects can give interest and character to the work and have long been admired in Japanese pottery.

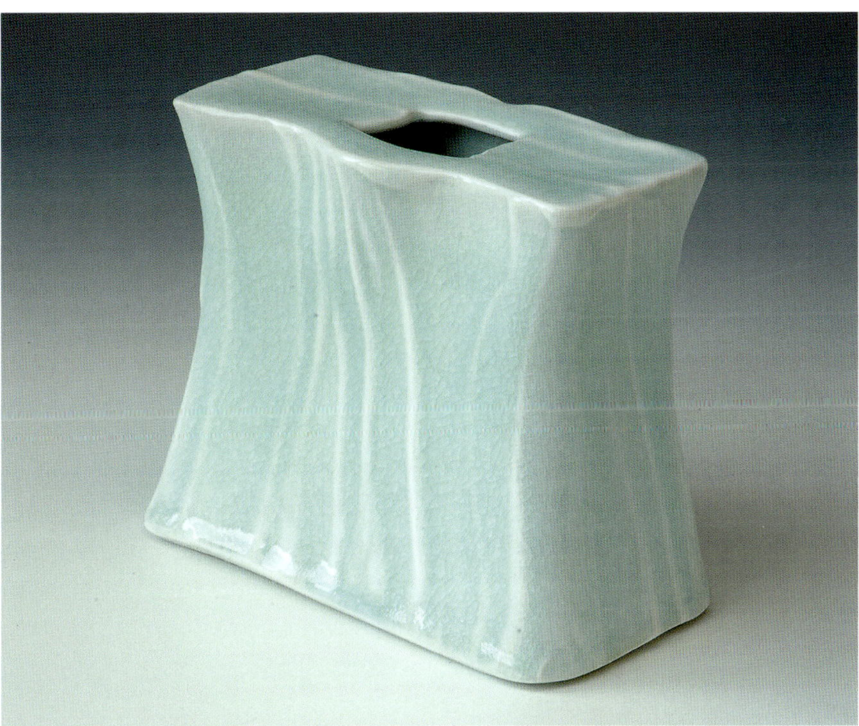

Box vase, Joanna Howells, 2007. Porcelain, celadon crackle glaze. *Photo: Joanna Howells.*

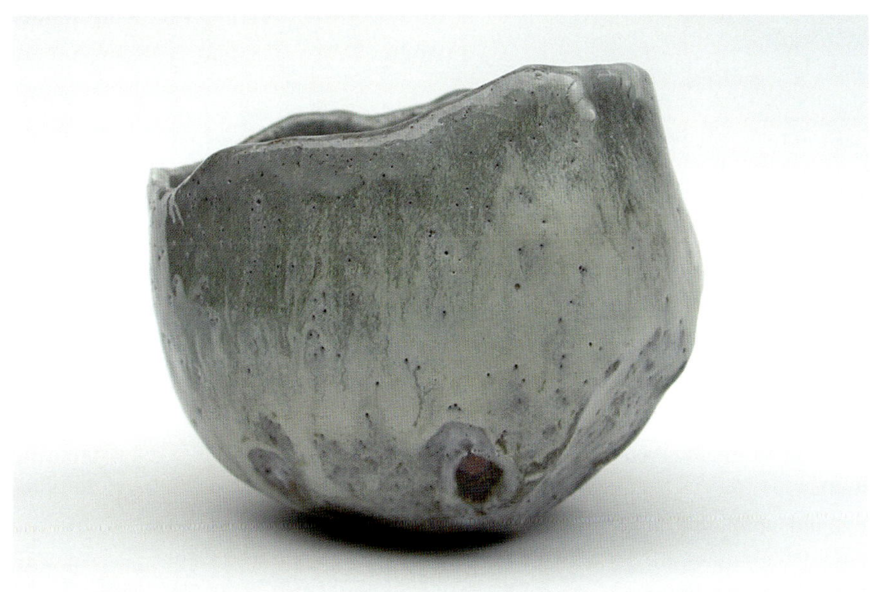

Stoneware tea bowl, Akiko Hirai, 2007. Pin-holed glaze, reduction-fired. *Photo: Toshiko Hirai.*

Glossary

alkali metals metals in the first column of the periodic table: lithium, sodium and potassium.

alkaline earths metals in the second column of the periodic table: magnesium, calcium, strontium and barium.

alkaline frit a frit containing sodium, potassium and silica.

alkaline glaze glaze which is high in sodium, lithium or barium.

amphoteric exhibiting both acidic and alkaline properties.

ball clay fine-grained, plastic secondary clay.

ball mill a rotating drum containing ceramic pebbles for grinding colouring oxides in glazes.

banding wheel a turntable rotated by hand.

base glaze a glaze to which colouring oxides are added.

batt wash a mixture of alumina hydrate and China clay, which prevents glaze from sticking to the kiln shelf.

bentonite a very plastic clay, used to suspend glazes.

biscuit firing a first firing, usually to around 1000°C (1832°F), done before applying a glaze.

blistering blisters in a fired glaze, caused by gas escaping during firing.

bloating blisters in the clay body, caused by trapped bubbles of gas.

body stain a stain for colouring clay or slip.

borax frit a frit containing sodium, calcium, boron and silica.

calcine to heat materials in a kiln to drive off volatile compounds.

celadon a type of pale, grey-green or blue-green glaze containing iron oxide.

China clay kaolin, pure white clay.

Chun a pale blue, opalescent glaze.

close-packed crystal structure in which the atoms are packed as densely as possible.

CMC carboxymethyl cellulose gum, used as a binder and to suspend glaze ingredients in water.

cone a small, slender pyramid of glaze material, set in the kiln, which bends over when fired to the correct temperature.

Cornish stone a feldspar found in Cornwall.

crawling a defect where glaze pulls away from the body, leaving bare patches.

crazing a network of fine cracks caused by a higher coefficient of expansion in the glaze than in the clay body.

cristobalite a crystalline form of silica, which forms in the clay body above 1100°C/2012°F and contracts suddenly on cooling at 226°C/439°F.

crystalline a glaze in which crystals have grown during cooling.

devitrify the growth of crystals from the molten glaze, which is then no longer in the glassy state.

Dispex deflocculant made from a sodium-based polymer used to increase the fluidity of slips and glazes.

Dunting cracking caused by cold air entering the kiln during cooling.

earthenware fired to a low temperature, below 1150°C/2102°F, where the clay body remains porous.

enamel low-temperature, coloured glaze fired at 800°C/1472°F for painting onto fired glaze.

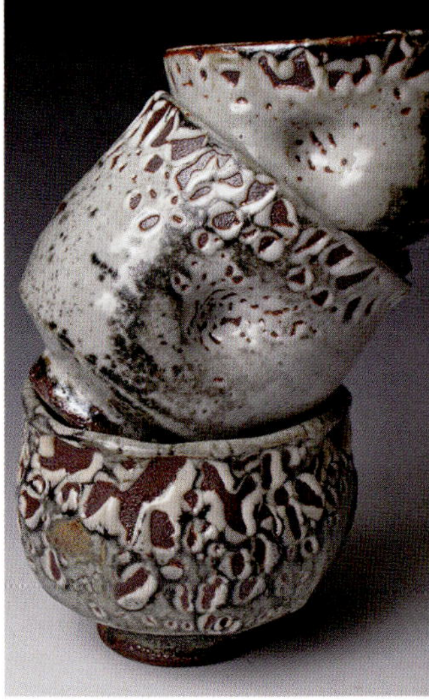

Hollis Engley, Hatchville Pottery, 2010. Crawled carbon trap shino bowls, reduction-fired stoneware. *Photo: Hollis Engley.*

engobe vitreous slip containing flux, for use on biscuit ware.

eutectic the lowest melting combination of two materials.

feldspar a mineral derived from granite containing potassium, sodium and alumino-silicate, it can also contain lithium or calcium.

flashing colour resulting from volatile compounds released during firing.

flux a material that lowers the melting temperature of a glaze.

foot-ring an unglazed ring of clay on the base of a pot.

frit glaze fluxes melted with silica and ground to a powder.

glost term used in industry for glaze firing, where the glaze-firing temperature is lower than that of the biscuit firing.

greenware unfired pots.

kaki a red-brown, high-iron glaze. Kaki is the Japanese word for persimmon.

lustre metallic decoration obtained by reducing precious metal salts.

Maiolica decorated, tin-glazed earthenware.

molochite finely ground, calcined China clay.

Nuka a Japanese glaze made from rice-hull ash.

opacifier a material that does not dissolve in a glaze, causing it to become opaque.

oxidation firing in the presence of sufficient oxygen, usually in an electric kiln.

pinholes small holes in a glaze, caused by burst bubbles that have not healed over during firing.

porcelain a white clay fired to 1250°C–1400°C/2282°F–2552°F becoming translucent and vitrified.

pyrometer a device used to measure the temperature inside a kiln.

reduction the act of limiting the air available during firing, so that oxygen is drawn from the clay and glaze.

refractory able to withstand high temperatures.

salt firing introducing salt into the kiln at high temperature, to combine with silica in the clay and produce a glaze on the surface.

Shino a white Japanese glaze made from feldspar and clay.

shivering glaze flaking off at rims and edges of handles, caused by poor glaze fit, with the glaze contracting less than the clay body.

silica silicon dioxide, found in quartz, flint or sand.

slake to add water to dry glaze materials to soak until completely wetted.

slip clay mixed with water.

soak to maintain the top firing temperature to mature the glaze evenly throughout the kiln.

soda firing introducing soda (sodium carbonate) into the kiln at high temperature to combine with silica in the clay to produce a glaze on the surface.

spinel stable, close-packed cubic structure with the formula $MgAl_2O_4$, used for ceramic stains. The magnesium and aluminium in the formula can be replaced with colouring oxides such as iron, cobalt and chromium.

stain industrially-produced ceramic pigment containing colouring oxides and opacifiers.

stoneware fired to a high temperature, above 1200°C/2192°F, so that the clay body is vitrified and non-porous.

tenmoku a brown-black, high-iron glaze.

underglaze a colouring oxide or stain that is applied under a transparent glaze.

vitrify to fire to a glassy state.

Appendices

APPENDIX 1 Ceramic materials list

Ceramic materials, chemical formulae and molecular or equivalent* weights (containing one molecule). Atomic weights are given in the periodic table.

Material	Formula	Molecular weight
Alumina	Al_2O_3	102
Alumina hydrate	$Al(OH)_3$	78*
Barium carbonate	$BaCO_3$	197.3
Bentonite	$Al_2O_3.4SiO_2.H_2O$	360.3
Bone ash (calcium phosphate)	$Ca_3(PO_4)_2$	103*
Borax	$Na_2O.B_2O_3.10\ H_2O$	381.4
Boric oxide	B_2O_3	69.6
Calcium borate	$Ca(BO_2)_2$	125.7
Cerium oxide	CeO_2	172.1
China clay	$Al_2O_3.2SiO_2.2H_2O$	258.2
Chromium oxide	Cr_2O_3	152
Cobalt oxide	CoO	74.9
Colemanite	$2Ca_O.3B_2O_3.5H_2O$	206*
Copper oxide	CuO	79.5
Cornwall stone	$K_2O.Al_2O_3.8SiO_2$	676.8
Cryolite	Na_3AlF_6	210
Dolomite	$CaCO_3.MgCO_3$	184.4
Erbium oxide	Er_2O_3	382.5
Feldspar lime (anorthite)	$CaO.Al_2O_3.2SiO_2$	278.2
Feldspar potash (orthoclase)	$K_2O.Al_2O_3.6SiO_2$	556.4
Feldspar soda (albite)	$Na_2O.Al_2O_3.6SiO_2$	524.4
Fluorspar	CaF2	78.1
Ilmenite	$FeO.TiO_2$	151.7
Iron (ferric) oxide (red)	Fe_2O_3	159.7
Iron (ferrous) oxide (black)	FeO	71.8
Kaolin	$Al_2O_3.2SiO_2.2H_2O$	258.2
Kyanite	$Al_2O_3.SiO_2$	162
Lead bisilicate	$PbO.2SiO_2$	343.4
Lead oxide (litharge)	PbO	223.2
Lead sesquisilicate	$2PbO.3SiO_2$	313.3*
Lead sulphide (galena)	PbS	239.2
Lepidolite	$LiFKF.Al_2O_3.3SiO_2$	366.3
Lithium carbonate	Li_2CO_3	73.9
Magnesia	MgO	40.3
Magnesium carbonate	Mg_2CO_3	84.3
Manganese dioxide	MnO_2	87
Mullite	$3Al_2O_3.2SiO_2$	426.1
Neodymium oxide	Nd_2O_3	336.5
Nepheline syenite	$K_2O.3Na_2O.4Al_2O_3.8SiO_2$	389.6*

Material	Formula	Molecular weight
Nickel oxide	NiO	74.7
Petalite	$Li_2O.Al_2O_3.8SiO_2$	612.5
Praseodymium oxide	Pr_2O_3	329.8
Quartz	SiO_2	60.1
Rutile	TiO_2	79.9
Silica	SiO_2	60.1
Silicon carbide	SiC	40.1
Spinel	$MgAl_2O_4$	142.3
Spodumene	$Li_2O.Al_2O_3.4SiO_2$	372.2
Strontium carbonate	$SrCO_3$	147.6
Talc (magnesium silicate)	$3MgO.4SiO_2.H_2O$	126.4*
Tin oxide	SnO_2	150.7
Titanium oxide (anatase)	TiO_2	79.9
Vanadium pentoxide	V_2O_5	181.9
Whiting (calcium carbonate)	$CaCO_3$	100.1
Wollastonite (calcium silicate)	$CaSiO_3$	116.2
Zinc oxide	ZnO	81.4
Zirconium silicate	$ZrSiO_4$	183.3

*Equivalent weights (containing one molecule) are sometimes given where the chemical formula contains a multiple number of molecules. For example, talc contains three molecules of magnesia, so the total molecular weight is divided by three to give the equivalent weight of talc containing one molecule of magnesia.

APPENDIX 2 Periodic table

The periodic table was worked out by Mendeleev in the 19th century, before all the elements had been discovered. In the periodic table, the elements are arranged in ascending atomic number (the number of protons in the nucleus). The elements in vertical columns have similar properties, with the alkali metals and alkaline earths on the left and the halogens and noble gases on the far right. Most of the elements are metals, but the few non-metals are grouped in the upper right-hand corner, above a diagonal line joining boron, silicon, arsenic, etc. The transition metals are in the central block including the lanthanides and actinides. These metals include the colouring oxides, and many have several oxidation states.

Uranium is the heaviest stable element. The super-heavy elements beyond this on the bottom row of the periodic table are unstable, and are not found naturally but are synthesised in particle accelerators.

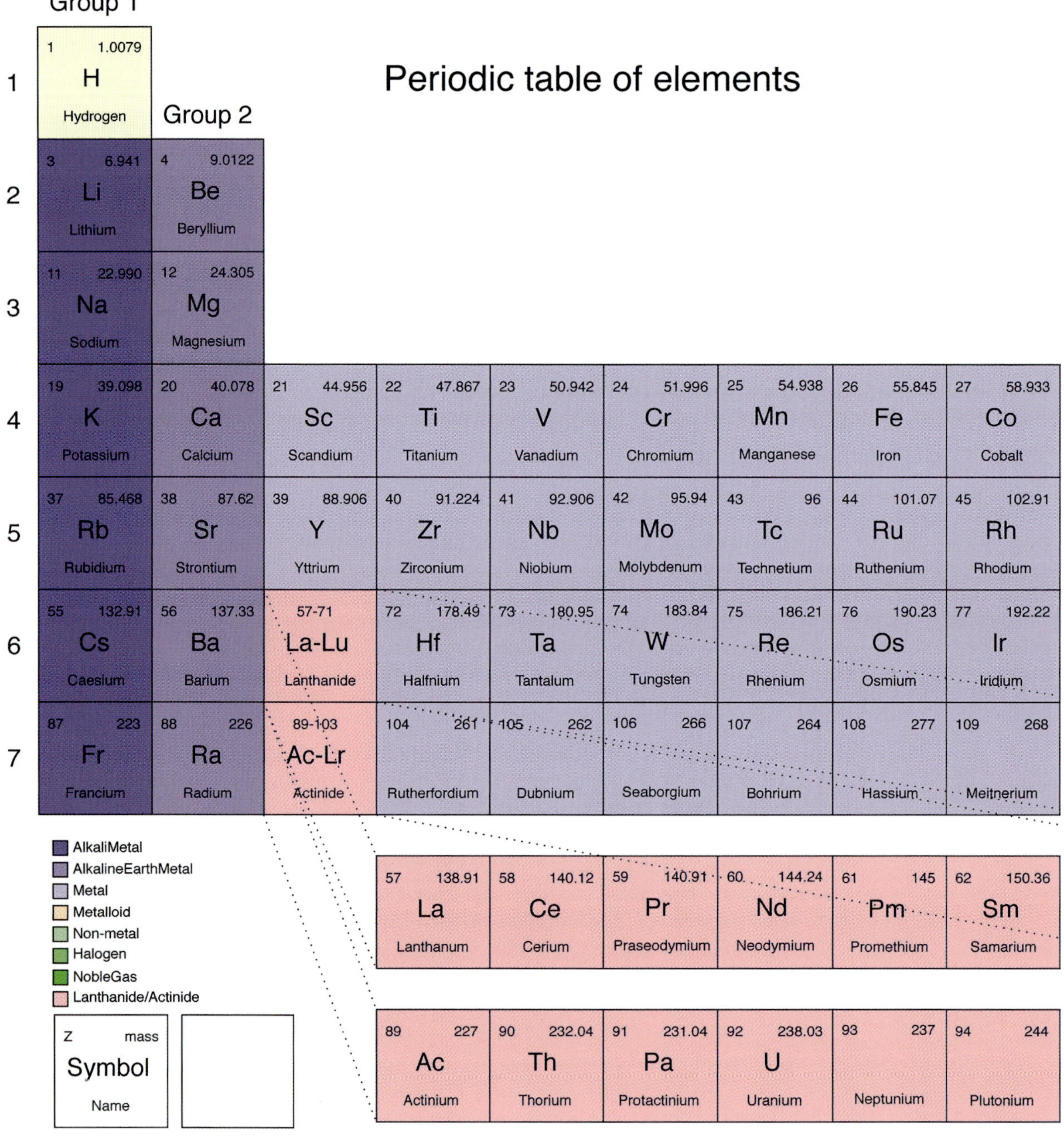
Periodic table of elements
Group 1
Group 2
1
2
3
4
5
6
7
1 1.0079 H Hydrogen
3 6.941 Li Lithium
4 9.0122 Be Beryllium
11 22.990 Na Sodium
12 24.305 Mg Magnesium
19 39.098 K Potassium
20 40.078 Ca Calcium
21 44.956 Sc Scandium
22 47.867 Ti Titanium
23 50.942 V Vanadium
24 51.996 Cr Chromium
25 54.938 Mn Manganese
26 55.845 Fe Iron
27 58.933 Co Cobalt
37 85.468 Rb Rubidium
38 87.62 Sr Strontium
39 88.906 Y Yttrium
40 91.224 Zr Zirconium
41 92.906 Nb Niobium
42 95.94 Mo Molybdenum
43 96 Tc Technetium
44 101.07 Ru Ruthenium
45 102.91 Rh Rhodium
55 132.91 Cs Caesium
56 137.33 Ba Barium
57-71 La-Lu Lanthanide
72 178.49 Hf Halfnium
73 180.95 Ta Tantalum
74 183.84 W Tungsten
75 186.21 Re Rhenium
76 190.23 Os Osmium
77 192.22 Ir Iridium
87 223 Fr Francium
88 226 Ra Radium
89-103 Ac-Lr Actinide
104 261 Rutherfordium
105 262 Dubnium
106 266 Seaborgium
107 264 Bohrium
108 277 Hassium
109 268 Meitnerium
57 138.91 La Lanthanum
58 140.12 Ce Cerium
59 140.91 Pr Praseodymium
60 144.24 Nd Neodymium
61 145 Pm Promethium
62 150.36 Sm Samarium
89 227 Ac Actinium
90 232.04 Th Thorium
91 231.04 Pa Protactinium
92 238.03 U Uranium
93 237 Neptunium
94 244 Plutonium
AlkaliMetal
AlkalineEarthMetal
Metal
Metalloid
Non-metal
Halogen
NobleGas
Lanthanide/Actinide
Z mass
Symbol
Name

			Group 3	Group 4	Group 5	Group 6	Group 7	Group 8
								2 4.0025 He Helium
			5 10.811 B Boron	6 12.011 C Carbon	7 14.007 N Nitrogen	8 15.999 O Oxygen	9 18.998 F Flourine	10 20.180 Ne Neon
			13 26.982 Al Aluminium	14 28.086 Si Silicon	15 30.974 P Phosphorus	16 32.065 S Sulphur	17 35.453 Cl Chlorine	18 39.948 Ar Argon
28 58.693 Ni Nickel	29 63.546 Cu Copper	30 65.39 Zn Zinc	31 69.723 Ga Gallium	32 72.64 Ge Germanium	33 74.922 As Arsenic	34 78.96 Se Selenium	35 79.904 Br Bromine	36 83.8 Kr Krypton
46 106.42 Pd Palladium	47 107.87 Ag Silver	48 112.41 Cd Cadmium	49 114.82 In Indium	50 118.71 Sn Tin	51 121.76 Sb Antimony	52 127.6 Te Tellurium	53 126.9 I Iodine	54 131.29 Xe Xenon
78 195.08 Pt Platinum	79 196.97 Au Gold	80 200.59 Hg Mercury	81 204.38 Tl Thallium	82 207.2 Pb Lead	83 208.98 Bi Bismuth	84 209 Po Polonium	85 210 At Astatine	86 222 Rn Radon
110 281 Darmstadtium	111 280 Roentgenium	112 285 Copernicum	113 284 Nihonium	114 289 Flerovium	115 288 Moscovium	116 293 Livermorium	117 292 Tennessine	118 294 Oganesson

63 151.96 Eu Europium	64 157.25 Gd Gadolinium	65 158.93 Tb Terbium	66 162.50 Dy Dysprosium	67 164.93 Ho Holmium	68 167.26 Er Erbium	69 168.93 Tm Thulium	70 173.04 Yb Ytterbium	71 174.97 Lu Lutetium
95 243 Americium	96 247 Curium	97 247 Berkelium	98 251 Californium	99 252 Einsteinium	100 257 Fermium	101 258 Mendelevium	102 259 Nobelium	103 262 Lawrencium

APPENDIX 3 Glaze formula calculation

Example: Recipe to formula

Glaze recipe for alkaline glaze, fired to 1240–1260°C/2264–2300°F (cone 6–8)

Soda feldspar	47
Calcium borate frit	16
Whiting	14
Quartz	18
China clay	5

To calculate a glaze formula from a recipe, the weight of each material is divided by its molecular weight. This gives a number that represents the relative number of molecules of each material in the glaze. Using the chemical formula for each material, the number of molecules of each oxide present in the glaze is calculated. For example, China clay has the formula $Al_2O_3.2SiO_2.2H_2O$, so it contributes one molecule of alumina and two of silica, as well as water, which is driven off during firing. If frits are used, the analysis from the manufacturer will be required. The oxides are arranged in three columns: alkaline, amphoteric and acidic, and the totals of each type of oxide are calculated. In this example, the fluxes are sodium, potassium and calcium from the soda feldspar, calcium borate frit and whiting. Boric oxide is also a flux, but it is included as an amphoteric. Dividing by the total number of basic (alkaline) fluxes gives the unity formula.

Basic		*Amphoteric*		*Acidic*	
Na_2O	0.19	Al_2O_3	0.38	SiO_2	3.10
K_2O	0.06	B_2O_3	0.38		
CaO	0.75				
Total	1.00				

Averaging the cone 6 and cone 10 limits for stable glazes opposite, this glaze is near the lower limits for alumina and silica, but enables bright colours such as turquoise from copper and lime green from chromium oxide. The high boron content prevents crazing, and the high calcium makes the glaze suitable for obtaining chrome-tin pinks.

The digitalfire.com website has a useful ceramic materials database, as well as glaze calculation software (Insight by Tony Hansen). Glaze calculation software is also available from HyperGlaze by Richard Burkett (hyperglaze.com), Glaze Master by Hesselberth and Roy (masteringglazes.com) and Matrix by Lawrence Ewing (matrix2000.co.nz). Free glaze calculation programs are available to use online at glazy.org and glazesimulator.com.

Limits for stable glazes

Stable glazes (those that are dishwasher safe and food safe) will generally have a ratio of alkali metal (potassium, sodium) to alkaline earth (calcium, magnesium) oxides of around 0.3:0.7 (±0.1). The amounts of silica and alumina will increase with firing temperature. For glazes fired below cone 9 1280°C/2336°F, enough boron is needed to fully melt the glaze (0.1 B_2O_3 for cone 8 glazes to 0.5 B_2O_3 for cone 04 earthenware glazes).

The pink area shows the alumina and silica limits for glazes fired to cone 5–8.

These are guidelines for producing stable, durable glazes. Many interesting colour responses are found outside these limits.

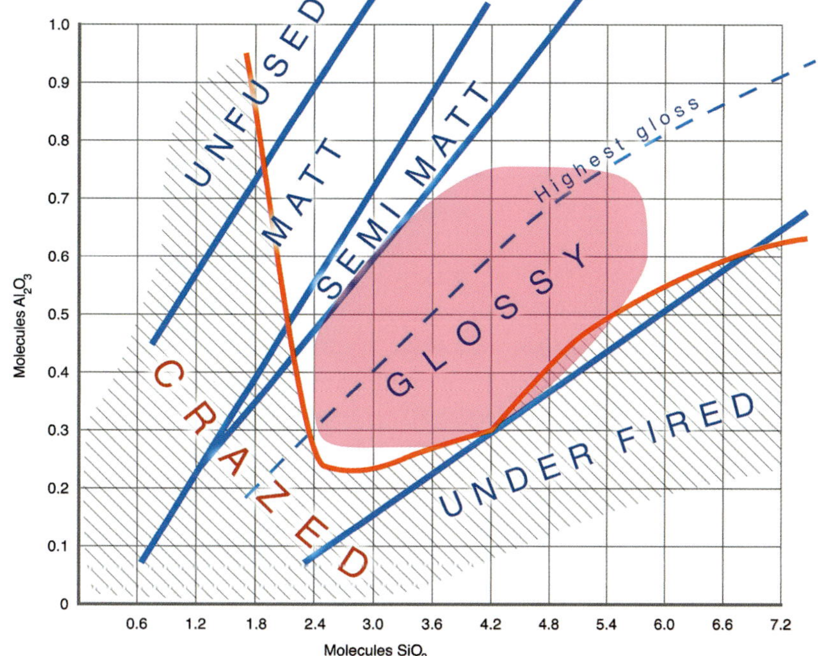

Graph of alumina against silica in porcelain glazes fired to cone 11 with constant flux 0.3 K_2O and 0.7 CaO. The ratio of 1:5 alumina to silica gives a semi-matt glaze, while 1:8 gives a shiny glaze. The straight lines on the chart represent alumina:silica ratios of 1:4 (matt) 1:5 (semi-matt) and 1:12 (glossy, crazed glaze). The dashed line is 1:8 Al_2O_3:SiO_2 (highest gloss glaze). The hatched area shows crazed glazes on porcelain. Data from R.T. Stull 1912.

Alumina and silica limits (Cooper and Royle, 1984)
Cone number and temperature. Number of molecules in unity formula.

Cone 04	1060°C/1940°F	Al_2O_3	0.1-0.45	SiO_2	1.375-3.15
Cone 5	1200°C/2192°F	Al_2O_3	0.275-0.65	SiO_2	2.4-4.7
Cone 6	1225°C/2237°F	Al_2O_3	0.325-0.70	SiO_2	2.6-5.15
Cone 8	1250°C/2282°F	Al_2O_3	0.375-0.75	SiO_2	3.0-5.75
Cone 9	1275°C/2327°F	Al_2O_3	0.45-0.825	SiO_2	3.5-6.4
Cone 10	1300°C/2372°F	Al_2O_3	0.50-0.90	SiO_2	4.0-7.2

Recommended maximum flux in glaze unity formula (Cooper and Royle, 1984)

Cone	Temp °C	MgO	BaO	ZnO	CaO	B_2O_3	K+Na
5	1200	0.325	0.40	0.30	0.55	0.35	0.375
6	1225	0.330	0.425	0.32	0.60	0.30	0.35
8	1250	0.335	0.45	0.34	0.65	0.25	0.325
9	1275	0.340	0.475	0.36	0.70	0.225	0.30
10	1300	0.345	0.50	0.38	0.75	0.21	0.275

Alumina and silica limits for increasing cone number and temperature shown in the table on the previous page.

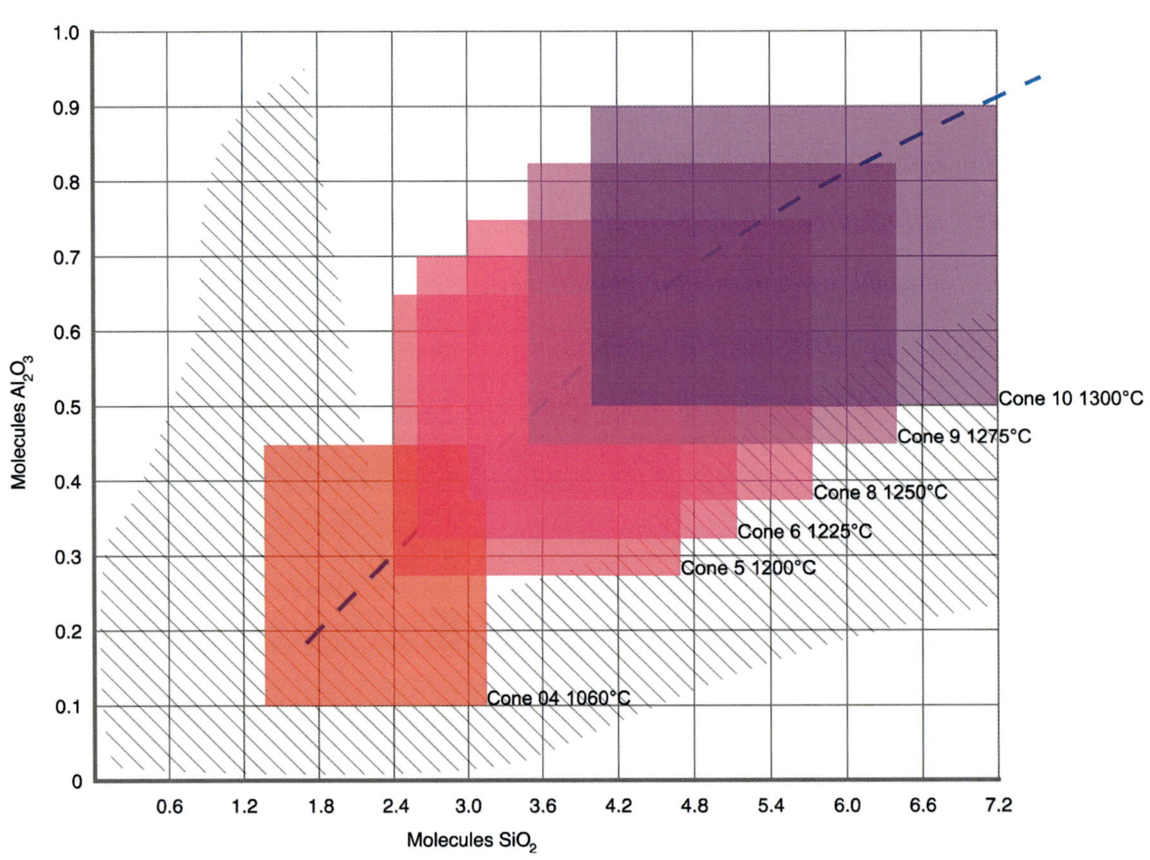

APPENDIX 4 Materials analysis for UK frits, clays and feldspars

Frits, unity formula analysis (Bath Potters Supplies, Michael Bailey)

	K_2O	Na_2O	Li_2O	BaO	CaO	MgO	ZnO	Al_2O_3	B_2O_3	SiO_2	Mol. wt.
Calcium borate frit	0.01				0.99	0.01		0.1	1.5	0.62	209
Standard borax frit	0.04	0.35			0.61	0.01		0.18	0.62	1.98	240
High-alkaline frit	0.21	0.59	0.01	0.09	0.1			0.1	0.1	1.71	196
Low-expansion frit	0.03	0.2			0.76	0.01		0.55	1.02	3.39	390

Clays and feldspars, percentage composition (LOI = loss on ignition)

	SiO_2	TiO_2	Al_2O_3	Fe_2O_3	P_2O_5	CaO	MgO	K_2O	Na_2O	LOI
China clay	48.8	0.1	35.4	0.8				1.6	1.5	11.8
AT Ball clay	54	1.1	29	2.4		0.3	0.4	3	0.5	9.3
HP71 Ball clay	70	1.6	19	0.8		0.2	0.4	2	0.5	5.5
HVAR Ball clay	60.3	1.5	26.7	0.9		0.2	0.3	2.6	0.4	7.1
Cornish stone	73.2	0.06	15.3	0.13	0.47	1.47	0.13	4.45	3.44	1.35
Nepheline syenite	60.5		23	0.1		1		5	10.2	0.2
Potash feldspar	65.8		18.5	0.1		0.38		12	2.89	0.33
Soda feldspar	67.9		19	0.11		1.88		2.8	7.5	0.81
FFF feldspar	67.7		18.9	0.16		0.72		7.62	4.85	0.05

APPENDIX 5 Materials analysis for US frits, clays and feldspars

Frits, unity formula analysis (Michael Bailey)

	K_2O	Na_2O	Li_2O	BaO	CaO	MgO	ZnO	Al_2O_3	B_2O_3	SiO_2	Mol. wt.
Ferro 3110	.060	.650			.290			.095	.097	3.029	260
Ferro 3124	.021	.282			.698			.269	.519	2.554	275
Ferro 3134		.317			.683				.633	1.890	191
Ferro 3195		.336			.654	.01		.392	1.136	2.656	337
Ferro 3249					.171	.829		.357	1.137	1.919	274

Clays and feldspars, percentage composition (LOI = loss on ignition)

	SiO_2	TiO_2	Al_2O_3	Fe_2O_3	P_2O_5	CaO	MgO	K_2O	Na_2O	LOI
EPK	45.91	.34	38.71	0.42		0.09	.12	.22	.04	14.15
Georgia kaolin	45.20	1.95	38.02	0.49		0.26	.30	.04	.02	13.72
OM-4 Ball clay	55.20	1.20	29.70	1.10		0.30	.40	1.00	.30	12.60
Tennessee no.5 Ball clay	53.30	1.40	31.10	1.00		0.30	.20	1.50	0.80	10.40
Custer feldspar	68.50		17.50	0.08		0.30	.01	10.40	3.00	0.21
G-200 feldspar	65.76		19.28	0.06		0.98	.01	10.36	3.20	0.35
Kona F-4 feldspar	66.77		19.59	0.04		1.70	.01	4.50	7.00	0.39
NC-4 feldspar	68.81		18.74	0.07		1.60	.01	3.76	6.89	0.12
Minspar 200	68.80		18.20	0.07		1.50		4.10	6.50	0.30

APPENDIX 6 UK and US materials conversion chart

Some materials have no direct equivalent but can be substituted with a combination of several other materials.

UK	USA
Ballclay HVAR	Tennessee Ballclay
Ballclay Hymod AT	Kentucky OM-4 ballclay
Ballclay Hyplas 71	Kentucky Stone
Bentonite	Bentonite, Macaloid, Veegum
Borax frit	Ferro 3124, Pemco P-54, Gerstley borate
Calcium borate frit	Ferro 3134, Ferro 3195, Colemanite
China clay	EPK (Edgar plastic kaolin), Tile 6 kaolin, Georgia kaolin
Cornish stone	Cornwall stone
Feldspar FFF	Custer feldspar plus Minspar or nepheline syenite
Feldspar potash	Custer feldspar, G-200, Mahavir feldspar
Feldspar soda	Kona F-4, NC 4, Minspar 200
Flint	Silica
Fremington red clay	Redart clay, Alberta slip
High-alkaline frit	Ferro 3110, Pemco P-25
Low-expansion frit	Ferro 3249
Quartz	Silica
Zirconium silicate	Zircopax, Superpax or Ultrox

APPENDIX 7 Stains and alternative oxides (for oxidation)

Stain	Mason stains	Potterycrafts	Contem	Alternative oxide
Dark blue CoSi	Mason 6388	P4132	GS6	Cobalt oxide, iron and manganese
Bright blue CoZnAl	Mason 6339	–	GS20	Cobalt carbonate
Blue green CoCr	Mason 6371	P4137	GS4	Cobalt oxide and chromium oxide
Green Cr	Mason 6209	P4143	GS3	Chromium oxide or copper oxide
Yellow green ZrVSn	Mason 6211	P4138	GS32	Chromium oxide in alkaline glaze
Turquoise ZrVSi	Mason 6315	P4129	GS5	Copper oxide in alkaline glaze
Pink CrSn	Mason 6001	P4186	–	Rutile and tin oxide
Maroon CrSn	Mason 6006	P4131	GS10	Chromium oxide and tin oxide
Purple CoCrSn	Mason 6317	P4182	GS8	Cobalt, chromium and tin oxide
Dark brown FeZnCrMn	Mason 6190	–	GS13	Iron oxide and manganese dioxide
Red brown FeZnCr	Mason 6113	P4133	GS12	Iron oxide and tin oxide
Yellow brown FeZnCrAl	Mason 6121	P4134	GS11	Iron oxide or ilmenite in calcium glaze
Yellow ZrPrSi	Mason 6450	P4140	GS1	Iron oxide and titanium or rutile
Bright yellow ZrSiCdS	Mason 6479	P4189	GS16	No alternative
Bright orange ZrSiCdSe	Mason 6028	P4188	GS17	Yellow and red stain
Rust red ZrFeSi	Mason 6032	P4135	GS9	Iron oxide and bone ash
Bright red ZrSiCdSe	Mason 6021	P4187	GS18	No alternative
Black CoCrNiFe	Mason 6600	P4130	GS14	Cobalt, iron, manganese and chromium
Grey CoNiSn	Mason 6591	P4139	GS37	Cobalt oxide and nickel oxide
White ZrSi	Mason 6700	–	–	Tin oxide or zirconium silicate

APPENDIX 8 Orton pyrometric cone temperatures, large regular cones

Pyrometric cones measure heat work and so depend on the heating rate. A slower temperature rise will cause the cone to bend at a lower temperature.

Cone no.	60°C/hour	108°F/hour	150°C/hour	270°F/hour
09	917	1683	928	1702
08	942	1728	954	1749
07	973	1783	985	1805
06	995	1823	1011	1852
05	1030	1886	1046	1915
04	1060	1940	1070	1958
03	1086	1987	1101	2014
02	1101	2014	1120	2048
01	1117	2043	1137	2079
1	1136	2077	1154	2109
2	1142	2088	1162	2124
3	1152	2106	1168	2134
4	1160	2120	1181	2158
5	1184	2163	1205	2201
6	1220	2228	1241	2266
7	1237	2259	1255	2291
8	1247	2277	1269	2316
9	1257	2295	1278	2332
10	1282	2340	1303	2377
11	1293	2359	1312	2394
12	1304	2379	1324	2415
13	1321	2410	1346	2455
14	1388	2530	1366	2491

Suppliers

UK

Bath Potters' Supplies
Unit 18, Fourth Avenue,
Westfield Trading Estate,
Radstock, Nr Bath BA3 4XE
Tel: 01761 411077
www.bathpotters.co.uk

Ceramatech
16-17 Frontier Works,
33 Queen Street,
London N17 8JA
Tel: 0208 885 4492
www.ceramatech.co.uk

CTM Potters Supplies
Unit 10A, Mill Park Industrial Estate,
White Cross Road,
Woodbury Salterton,
Exeter EX5 1EL
Tel: 01395 233077
www.ctmpotterssupplies.co.uk

Potterycrafts
Campbell Road,
Stoke-on-Trent,
Staffordshire ST4 4ET
Tel: 01782 745000
www.potterycraft.co.uk

Scarva Pottery Supplies
Unit 20, Scarva Road
Industrial Estate,
Banbridge, County Down,
Northern Ireland, BT32 3QD
Tel: 028 406 69699
www.scarvapottery.com

Top Pot Supplies
Oak Barton,
Barlaston,
Stoke-onTrent,
ST12 9AF
Tel: 01782 399990
www.toppotsupplies.co.uk

USA

Amaco Brent
6060 Guion Road,
Indianapolis
IN 46254-1222
Tel: 317 244 6871
www.amaco.com

Bailey Ceramic Supplies
62–68 Tenbroeck Avenue,
Kingston, New York 12401
Tel: 845-339-3721
www.baileypottery.com

Bracker's Good Earth Clays
1831 E. 1450 Road
Lawrence, KS 66044
Tel: 785 841 4750
www.brackers.com

Clay Planet
1775 Russell Avenue,
Santa Clara, CA 95054
Tel: 800-443-2529
www.clay-planet.com

Columbus Clay Co.
1080 Chambers Road,
Columbus, OH 43212
Tel: 866-410-2529
www.columbusclay.com

Georgie's Ceramic & Clay Co
756 NE Lombard
Portland OR 97211
Tel: 503 283 1353
www.georgies.com

Hammill & Gillespie
420 Clermont Terrace
Unit D,
Union,
NJ 07083
Tel: 973 822 8000
www.hamgil.com

Laguna Clay Co.
14400 Lomitas Avenue,
City of Industry, CA 91746
Tel: 800-452-4862
www.lagunaclay.com

Minnesota Clay Co.
2960 Niagara Lane
Plymouth
MN 55447
Tel: 763 432 0875
www.mnclay.com

US pigments
815 Schneider Drive
South Elgin
IL 60177
Tel: 630 893 9217
uspigment.com

CANADA

Plainsman Clays
702 Wood Street SE,
Medicine Hat,
Alberta,
Canada,
T1A 1E9
Tel: 403-527-8535
plainsmanclays.com

AUSTRALIA

Pottery Supplies Brisbane
51 Castlemaine Street
Milton
Queensland 4064
Tel: 07 3368 2877
www.potterysupplies.com.au

Walker Ceramics
5 McLellan Street
Bayswater
Victoria 3153
Tel: 03 8761 6322
www.walkerceramics.com.au

Laboratories for leach testing of glazes

Lucideon
Queens Road, Penkhull,
Stoke-on-Trent, ST4 7LQ UK
Tel: 01782 764428
www.lucideon.co.uk

Brandywine Science Center
204 Line Road,
Kennet Square,
PA 19348 USA
Tel: 610-444-9850
www.bsclab.com

Northern Testhouse,
Scraptoft Business Centre
Main Street,
Scraptoft,
Leicester LE7 9TD
Tel: 01162418811
www.nthleicester.co.uk

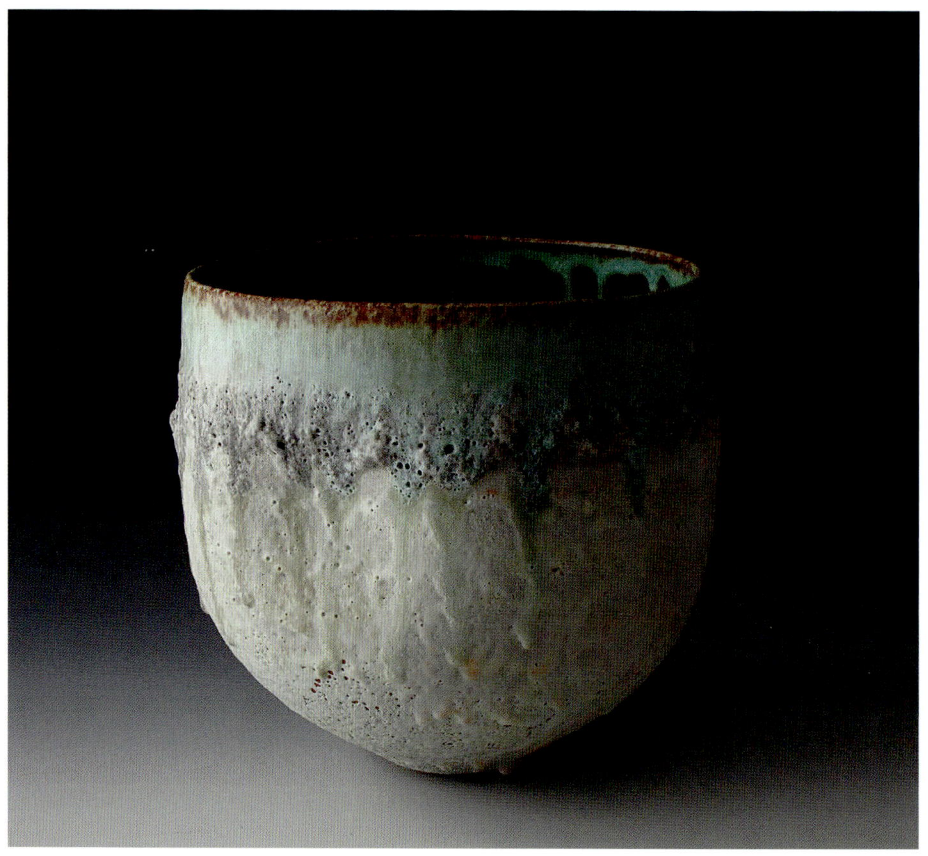

LEFT: *Volcanic glazed bowl* Katrina Pechal, thrown stoneware with silicon carbide slip and barium glazes. *Photo courtesy of the artist.*

Linda Bloomfield porcelain tableware, coloured glazes using copper, praseodymium, cobalt and nickel oxides. *Photo by Emma Lee.*

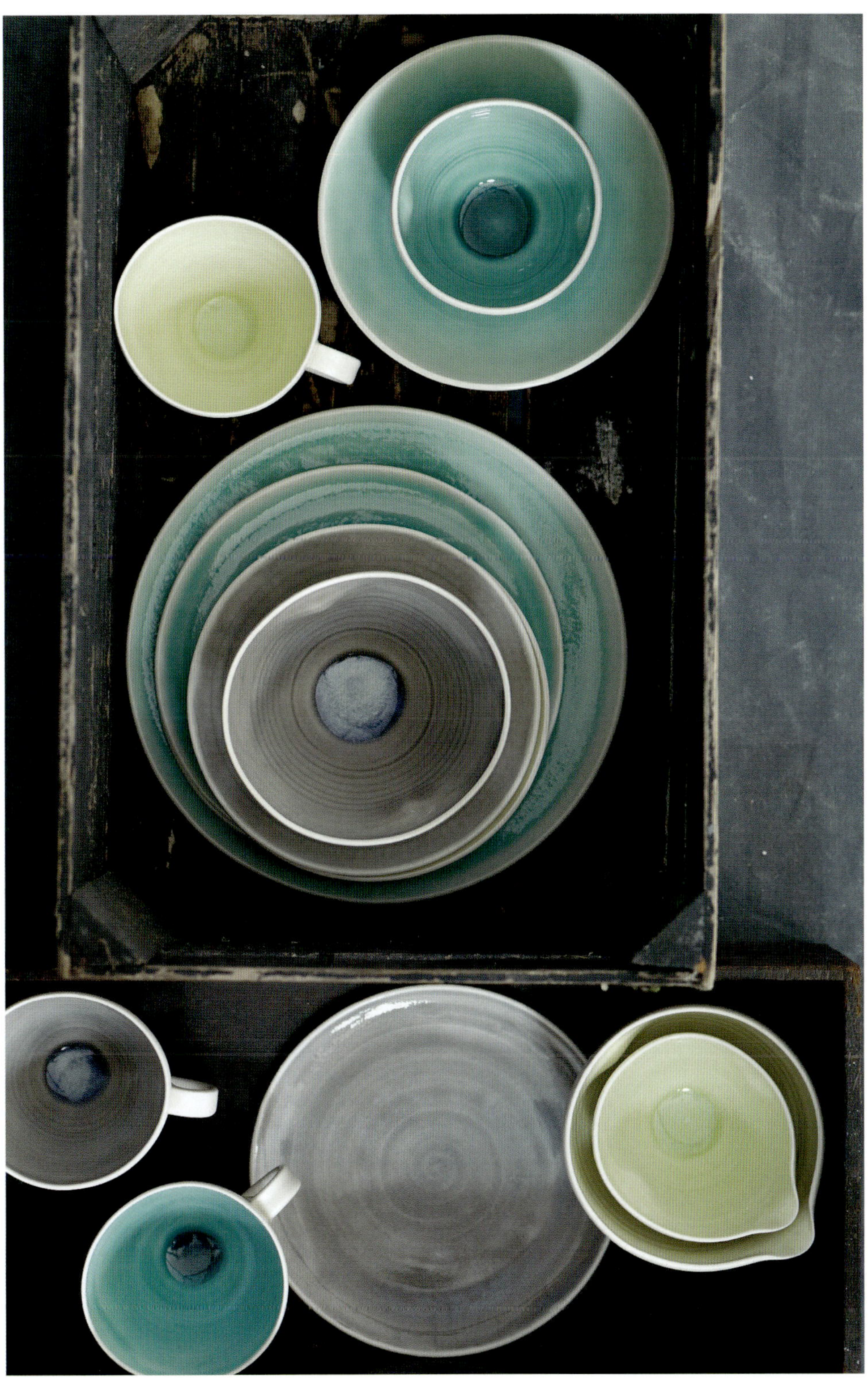

Bibliography

Bailey, Michael. *Glazes Cone 6 1240°C*, A&C Black, 2001

Bloomfield, Linda. *The Handbook of Glaze Recipes*, Bloomsbury 2014

Bloomfield, Linda. *Science for Potters, 2018*, American Ceramic Society, 2017

Britt, John. *The Complete Guide to High-fire Glazes: Glazing & Firing at Cone 10*, Lark Books, 2004

Constant, Christine and Ogden, Steve. *The Potter's Palette*, Quarto, 1996

Cooper, Emmanuel. *Cooper's Book of Glaze Recipes*, Batsford, 1987

Cooper, Emmanuel. *The Complete Potter: Glazes*, Batsford, 1992

Cooper, Emmanuel and Royle, Derek. *Glazes for the Studio Potter*, Batsford, 1984

Currie, Ian. *Revealing Glazes using the Grid Method*, Bootstrap Press, 2000

Eppler, R.A. and Eppler, D.R. *Glazes and Glass Coatings*, American Ceramic Society, 2000

Fraser, Harry. *Glazes for the Craft Potter*, A&C Black, 1973

Green, D. *Pottery Glazing Basics*, Coles Publishing Company, 1980

Hamer, F & J. *The Potter's Dictionary of Materials and Techniques*, Fourth edition, A&C Black, 1997

Hesselberth, John and Roy, Ron. *Mastering Cone 6 Glazes: Improving Durability, Fit and Aesthetics*, Glaze Master Press, 2002

Hopper, Robin. *The Ceramic Spectrum: A simplified approach to glaze and colour development*, Krause publications, 1984

Murfitt, Stephen. *The Glaze Book*, Thames and Hudson, 2002

Parmelee, C.W. *Ceramic Glazes*, revised by C.G. Harman, Third edition, Cahners publishing company, 1973

Recipes for Enamel, Underglaze and Majolica Colours and Lustres; also for Relief Colours, Bodies and Glazes for China and Earthenware, Smith, Greenwood and Co, Publishers of the *Pottery Gazette*, London, 1880s

Rhodes, Daniel. *Clay and Glazes for the Potter*, Krause publications, 1973

Taylor, J.R. and Bull, A.C. *Ceramics Glaze Technology*, Pergamon Press, 1986

Index

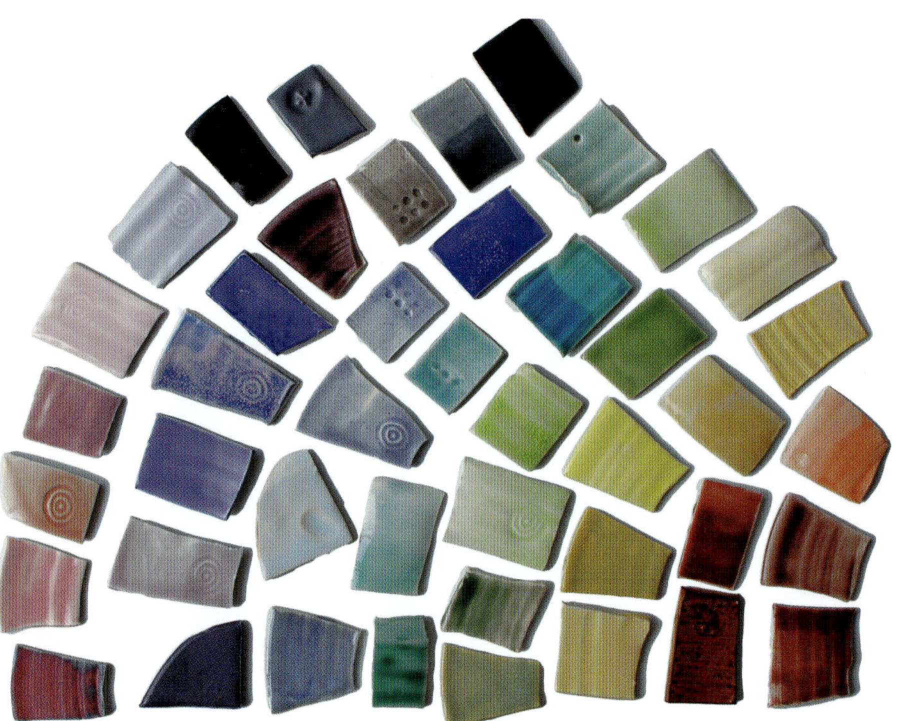

Porcelain test tiles.